How Stories Change Us

ALSO BY ELAINE REESE

Tell Me a Story: Sharing Stories to Enrich Your Child's World
(translated into Romanian as Spune-Mi o Poveste, Te Rooog!)

Contemporary Debates in Childhood Education and Development
(co-edited with Sebastian Suggate)

For other articles and blogs on the role of stories in
child development, please visit
www.elainereese.org

How Stories Change Us
A Developmental Science of Stories from Fiction and Real Life

Elaine Reese

OXFORD
UNIVERSITY PRESS

OXFORD
UNIVERSITY PRESS

Oxford University Press is a department of the University of Oxford. It furthers
the University's objective of excellence in research, scholarship, and education
by publishing worldwide. Oxford is a registered trade mark of Oxford University
Press in the UK and certain other countries.

Published in the United States of America by Oxford University Press
198 Madison Avenue, New York, NY 10016, United States of America.

© Oxford University Press 2024

All rights reserved. No part of this publication may be reproduced, stored in
a retrieval system, or transmitted, in any form or by any means, without the
prior permission in writing of Oxford University Press, or as expressly permitted
by law, by license, or under terms agreed with the appropriate reproduction
rights organization. Inquiries concerning reproduction outside the scope of the
above should be sent to the Rights Department, Oxford University Press, at the
address above.

You must not circulate this work in any other form
and you must impose this same condition on any acquirer.

CIP data is on file at the Library of Congress

ISBN 978–0–19–774790–2

DOI: 10.1093/oso/9780197747902.001.0001

Printed by Marquis Book Printing, Canada

For my mother, Mary Nell Taylor Reese
December 2, 1934–March 13, 2023

CONTENTS

Copyright Credits   ix
Preface   xi

1. The Bright Side of Stories   *1*
   Fiction Readers Rule   *2*
   Can We Benefit From Visual Fiction, Too?   *9*
   The Upside of Real-Life Stories   *11*
   Your Brain on Stories   *16*
2. The Gender Gap in Stories   *18*
   Women Love Book Clubs, Too   *20*
   Visualizing Worlds Through Words   *23*
   Men Prefer Visual Stories   *24*
   Visualizing Stories in Our Minds   *26*
   Do These Gender Differences Really Matter?   *29*
3. How Children Grow to Love Stories   *33*
   The Nature and Nurture of Stories   *33*
   Real-Life Stories Arrive on the Stage   *38*
   Girls Gain Ground Early   *40*
   Quality Matters, Too   *42*
   What About Stories From TV and Movies?   *46*
   The Gender Gap Widens   *48*
   How Parents, Teachers, and Librarians Can Help   *49*
4. Growing Teens Who Use Stories Wisely   *51*
   Benefits of Books for Tweens and Teens   *52*
   The Gender Gap in Reading Continues to Grow   *57*
   What Are Teens Doing Instead?   *58*
   How Parents, Teachers, and Librarians Can Help   *59*
   Teens Are Doing Real Life (Sort of)   *62*
   The Teenage Brain on Stories   *62*
   Teens *Do* Listen to Family Stories   *64*
   What About Writing?   *67*

(viii)   Contents

5. The Dangers of Fictional Stories   *69*
  The Pitfalls of Stories From Books   *70*
  The Dark Side of Visual Stories From Screens   *73*
  Action Stories: The Most Dangerous of All?   *80*
  Too Many Stories?   *84*
6. The Dangers of Real-Life Stories   *88*
  The Science of Memory for Real-Life Events   *88*
  The Contaminated Stories We Tell About Our Own Lives   *93*
  The Dangers of Family Stories   *98*
  Telling It Like It Isn't: Stories of Ourselves and Others
    on Social Media   *99*
7. The Thin Line Between Reality and Fantasy in Stories   *106*
  The Functions of Fantasy   *107*
  The Stirrings of Story Play   *107*
  Friendships, Real and Imagined   *108*
  I'll Make Up My Own Friends   *109*
  Secret Countries   *111*
  Even Adults Have Pretend Friends   *114*
  The Dark Side of Imagination   *117*
  Riffing on Reality   *119*
  Imagining What Could Have Been   *121*
8. The Story Delivery System   *125*
  Is the Medium *Really* the Message?   *125*
  Experimenting With Story Delivery Systems   *127*
  The Magic of Audiobooks   *130*
  Double-Duty Stories   *132*
  High-Tech Stories   *136*
  Is Mental Imagery the Key?   *137*
  The Final Word on Story Delivery Systems: Watch This Space   *140*
Epilogue: The Stories in Our Future   *143*
  The Future of Stories   *144*
  The End of Our Stories   *145*

Acknowledgments   *147*
Recommended Stories   *151*
Notes   *157*
Index   *215*

COPYRIGHT CREDITS

Chapter 1: Excerpt(s) from THE LITTLE PARIS BOOKSHOP: A NOVEL by Nina George, translated by Simon Pare, translation copyright © 2015 by Simon Pare. Used by permission of Crown Books, an imprint of the Crown Publishing Group, a division of Penguin Random House LLC. All rights reserved

Chapter 2: From The Living by Annie Dillard. Copyright (c) 1992 by Annie Dillard. Used by permission of HarperCollins Publishers.

Chapter 5: Quotation by Daniel Anderson used with permission.

Chapter 6: Excerpt(s) from THE BURGESS BOYS: A NOVEL by Catherine Crawford, Text copyright © 2013 by Catherine Crawford. Used by permission of Random House, an imprint and division of Penguin Random House LLC. All rights reserved.

Chapter 7: *The Voyage of the Dawn Treader* by CS Lewis © copyright 1952 CS Lewis Pte Ltd. Extract used with permission.

Chapter 8: Excerpt(s) from THE LIVING SEA OF WAKING DREAMS: A NOVEL by Richard Flanagan, copyright (c) 2020 by Richard Flanagan. Used by permission of Alfred A. Knopf, an imprint of the Knopf Doubleday Publishing Group, a division of Penguin Random House LLC. All rights reserved.

All other epigraphs are in the public domain.

PREFACE

Fiction is like a spider's web, attached ever so lightly perhaps, but still attached to life at all four corners.

—Virginia Woolf, *A Room of One's Own*

I have loved fiction for as long as I can remember, in all its guises. One of my earliest memories is of cuddling against my mother as she read me a picture book—which one I cannot recall. The soothing sound of her voice, the feel of her bare arm nestled against my cheek, the fragrance of coffee on her breath all combine to create a sheer coziness that must be what the Danish call *hygge*, but for which in English we do not have a word. At times I think that my love of fiction—some would say my obsession—is an attempt to return to the complete encircling security of those early experiences with books, indelibly attached to the people I love most in the world.

Movies, too, were emotionally charged beyond their storyline. As a child in the early 1970s, movies were a special experience that occurred only outside the home. On weekend nights, my dad would take the whole family to the local drive-in movie theatre. I can still feel the metallic chill of the station wagon's rooftop where my brother and sister and I were allowed to lie on top of an old quilt to watch Charlton Heston's 1970 version of *Julius Caesar*. (My dad despised Disney movies.) Eventually we became so tired and uncomfortable that we crawled into the back seat to sleep. And on Saturday afternoons, my mother dropped us all off at the only theatre in town to watch more appropriate fare (my favorite was *Escape to Witch Mountain*), fueled by Sugar Babies, Junior Mints, and Mike 'n Ikes.

Even after I could read on my own, my experience with fiction was still largely social. My sister, Jen, and I avidly read the *Little House on the Prairie* and *All of a Kind Family* series of books repeatedly, to the point that we could recreate whole scenes and dialogue with each other and with our more compliant neighborhood friends. Undoubtedly influenced by Jo March's family plays from *Little Women*, I "wrote" and directed an outdoor summer play that was an unabashed mashup of *The Sound of Music* meets *Little House on the Prairie*. Growing up in west Texas, we were particularly fascinated with the idea of deep snow. My brother Andrew's role in the play was up on the patio roof engineering precipitation (aka Dreft soapflakes) to drift upon us at critical moments of crossing the mountains or plains.

In my teens, reading for pleasure became a more solitary pursuit, but my high school friends Diane and Amy and I would discuss heatedly whatever book or play we were assigned to read in English—*A Tale of Two Cities*, *The Scarlet Letter, Hamlet*—and these stories crept into our everyday lives. I named my first car Beatrice in honor of a character in *Much Ado About Nothing*, and we took turns doing send-ups of the malevolent Madame DeFarge, who occasionally morphed into our English teacher.

The advent of the VCR in the early 1980s changed everything. For the first time, we could watch a movie of our choice in our own living room whenever we wanted. Yet even though we could now more easily watch movies solo, my memory is that this rarely happened. Most often, I would watch movies with my family or friends. The ritual of choosing the movie together beforehand at the video store was almost as important a part of the evening as actually watching the movie. Which movies had all of us not yet seen? Who was in it? What had we heard about it beforehand from others who *had* seen it? Pre-Internet, we consulted the video store's thumbed-over copy of Leonard Maltin's *Movie Guide* to help us decide. And afterward, if we were all still awake, would come the fevered discussion of whether it was a "good" movie or not, and why.

Flash forward to 2023.

I now live in New Zealand, about as far away from the desert of west Texas as I could get. The external landscape has changed, but my internal landscape feels much the same. I still love fiction fiercely and always have a novel (or three) waiting on my nightstand. Occasionally I go to the movie theatre for special big-screen events with friends and family, usually to watch a local film that I wouldn't be able to see any other way. More often I consume my visual fiction at home via streaming, alone or with my partner, Lou. In an unexpected twist, my experience of books is now more social than my TV or movie watching. I've joined a book club, and the discussions we have every month about our latest assignment are just as passionate and fun as the ones I used to have with my high school friends. After reading Kathryn Stockett's *The Help*, fellow book club member Megan made a version of Minny's chocolate pie and dared us to eat it. (For those of you who haven't read the book or seen the movie, let's just say that Minny put a secret ingredient into her chocolate custard pie after being fired for using the White folks' toilet.) These lively discussions about books are almost always with other women, just as they were in high school. My discussions of fiction with men are usually about movies or TV.

WHAT ABOUT REAL LIFE?

Stories in books and movies may seem to have little to do with the stories of our everyday lives. After all, fiction is—well, fiction—whereas our lives are actually happening. As the aphorism goes, "Life is just one damned thing after another." Yes, there's a definite beginning to the story of our lives, and a very long and in turns tedious/joyous/devastating middle. None of us gets to tell the ending of our story. The narrative arc is at best bumpy, full of turning points and denouement, and then yet another episode begins before the last one has properly finished. If an unedited story of the details of even one person's life were encapsulated in a book, it would be a *Through the Looking Glass* sort of tale, muddled and nonsensical, not at all the polished version of biography or biopic. One of my favorite writers, Elizabeth Strout, refers to our life stories as "feeble words dropped earnestly and haphazardly over the large stretched-out fabric of a life with all its knots and bumps."[1]

Life stories are based on real events, not fiction. But the way we remember and tell them, both to ourselves in private moments and in journals, and in conversations with others or online, reflects and shapes who we are. As Michelle Obama claims in her autobiography *Becoming*, "Even when it's not pretty or perfect. Even when it's more real than you want it to be. Your story is what you have, what you will always have. It is something to own."[2]

Real-life stories thus have far more in common with fiction than most of us wish to believe. Like a fiction writer, we are highly selective in the details of our lives that we remember and that we choose to tell to others. If certain events don't fit easily into our current version of our story, we find ways to relegate them to the backwaters of memory by not thinking or talking about them with others. The bits we like—often misfortunes that we've turned to triumphs—we showcase at every opportunity, strengthening our memories of these events in the process. We *work* on these stories until they are burnished to a high sheen. If we had put as much effort into our literary essays in high school, we all would have earned A's and made some underpaid, overworked English teachers very happy.

(xiv) Preface

Like many young people who love to read fiction, I wanted to major in English literature when I started at Trinity University in San Antonio. For that first year, I continued to read obsessively and attempted to learn the principles and techniques of literary theory. I loved the reading part. I probably never would have read Italo Calvino's *If On a Winter's Night a Traveler* or Milan Kundera's *The Unbearable Lightness of Being* outside of a class. But the close analysis of structure and themes and literary devices seemed to deaden, not nourish, my passion for books. Then I discovered psychology. I tried to integrate my two passions by studying undergraduates' memory for Flannery O'Connor's *Good Country People* for my honors thesis with supervisor Paula Hertel. Our findings were murky at best; this study will forever remain unpublished. But the epiphany I had during the process was worth it. I realized that what I really loved about fiction was meeting the characters and trying to understand why they acted as they did. I am curious about *people*, whether they are people in books or in real life.

Ever since, I have been trying to unite my addiction to fiction with my study of real-life stories.

It's no coincidence that I chose a graduate program with an interdisciplinary focus—Emory University's Cognition and Development program, just at the start of Ulric Neisser's (the father of cognitive psychology) 5-year interdisciplinary symposia on the self. My PhD advisor Robyn Fivush introduced me to longitudinal studies of child development, which became my life's work. As a developmental scientist, I follow characters over time—real live people—to understand the forces that shape their personalities and predilections over a life. Longitudinal studies are inherently interdisciplinary because to understand development over time, one must understand all aspects of a person. Nearly every research study I have done since then has turned into a longitudinal one, even if it didn't start out that way. I can't seem to help myself from asking "What will happen next? What kind of people will these children become?" It's the scientific equivalent of reading a book series that just keeps going. The difference is that I am able to observe the unfolding of real lives in real time, not fictional ones molded by an author's will.

I call my longest-running longitudinal study *Origins of Memory*, because my goal was to track the beginnings of children's autobiographical memory. I began *Origins* back in the mid-1990s in Dunedin, a small seaside city in New Zealand. With the help of funding from the Royal Society of New Zealand and the University of Otago, my students and I have followed over 150 families to watch their children grow from toddlers into young adults.

Our focus in *Origins* has always been on real-life stories. When do children start to tell those first fledgling stories of their own experiences? How

PREFACE (xv)

do those baby stories evolve into the searching stories of adolescence, and eventually into the insightful (or not) stories of young adulthood? What part do personality traits, cognitive proclivities, and personal circumstances play in young people's developing life stories? As a society, we intuitively believe that family stories are good for us and for our children. In indigenous cultures, such as Māori culture in New Zealand, these oral stories may carry even more weight.[3] But do family stories that parents tell about their own childhood always contribute to their adolescents' well-being?

Although *Origins* started as a study of autobiographical memory, it evolved into a study of all sorts of stories. Alongside the children's real-life stories, we also collected data on the books they read as adolescents and young adults. We asked them, too, about the movies they watched, the video games they played, and the social media platforms they used. Altogether, we have amassed a wealth of information on how children grow into readers and tellers and consumers of stories in young adulthood.

I would now like to share this story of the science of stories with you, with the help of three very important participants from *Origins*. I introduced readers to Anna, Charlie, and Tia in my first book, *Tell Me a Story: Sharing Stories to Enrich Your Child's World*. All three persona are based on participants from *Origins*, but with identifying details changed or borrowed from other participants. I selected them from the larger sample because they were all thriving, in different ways, as teenagers. At the end of that book, I left studious and artistic Anna, athletic and fun-loving Charlie, talented and effervescent Tia as happy and healthy 16-year-olds. I will now be able to reveal how they have grown into young adults. The patterns of their lives illustrate what we have come to learn about the science of stories.

The story does not stop there. Knowing the origins of story for Anna, Charlie, and Tia can help us all to understand our own story preferences in adulthood. For instance, the science of stories illuminates why it is that I and so many other women love to read fiction and talk about fiction with others in book clubs. Fewer boys grow into men who love reading fiction— why? And does it have to be that way in the next generation?

Because of this disparity, gender is an important theme in this book. My view, and the current stance in psychological science, is that gender is a diverse construct, not a binary.[4] Each one of us varies in the degree to which we endorse and enact both masculine and feminine aspects of ourselves; the difference between two women on any trait or behavior can be a much greater gulf than the difference between a woman and a man. Other gender identities reject the male-female continuum, such as *bissu* among Bugis of Indonesia, who are "a powerful combination of both."[5] Yet most existing psychological research has coded gender as a male-female binary, so I will often need to refer to gender as such.[6] Fortunately, a new generation of researchers is treating gender in more sophisticated and nuanced ways.[7]

The human need for stories appears to be universal, as Jonathan Gottschall argued convincingly in his book, *The Storytelling Animal*.[8] People in all cultures studied throughout history engage in oral storytelling. And stories from books, TV, movies, and video games are quickly becoming cultural universals on the order of oral stories.[9] Most of the existing psychological research on stories, however, is still based on English speakers from WEIRD societies (Western, educated, industrialized, rich, and democratic).[10] I will supplement that focus whenever possible with research and stories from less WEIRD samples.

A ROAD MAP

This book is about the science behind stories of all types: fictional stories from books, movies, TV shows, and video games, as well as real-life stories, both oral and written. In Chapter 1, I reveal how cutting-edge research shows that stories from fiction and real life can act as a force for human connection, understanding, identity, and even as a healing balm. Chapter 2 addresses the gender gap in stories, with women in contemporary Western societies far more likely than men to read fiction and to talk about fiction through book clubs; women also recall more vivid and detailed real-life stories than men. In Chapter 3, I trace the developmental origins of this gender gap in stories, which culminates in girls around the world becoming better readers, on average, than boys. Chapter 4 follows children into their teenage years to explore the ways that early reading preferences and skills compound over time to affect academic achievements and aspirations, and ultimately young people's well-being. Family stories also play a vital role for children of all ages and across cultures to foster identity and connections to others. Chapters 5 and 6 tackle the dark side of stories, both from fictional sources, such as video games, and real life—including social media. Chapter 7 blurs the boundaries between fact and fiction with a consideration of the role of the imagination in our lives from near birth to death, including disorders of imagination, such as schizophrenia. Chapter 8 returns to the beginning to explicitly compare the benefits and dangers of all of these stories from different sources, and to introduce two promising story delivery forms to track in future research: audiobooks and virtual reality. Which stories are best, and why? Finally, in the Epilogue I consider the role of stories in all of our futures, young and old, as we face the world's current challenges.

PREFACE (*xvii*)

Throughout the book, I address the fundamental role of the brain in the way we receive and tell stories. Neuroscience research has boomed in the past 15 years to deepen our understanding of stories. Neuroscientists tell us that imagining the future and remembering a real-life event are experienced in similar ways in the brain, with startling implications for the line between reality and fantasy.[11] When we remember real-life events, we are constantly and unconsciously filling in bits of the memory from our general knowledge base—what we know or think to be true—alongside what we actually remember. And when we imagine the future, we draw upon our memories of real-life experiences to combine them in new and creative ways. What is going on in our brains when we read a book, watch a movie, or play a video game? Do these same forces of memory and imagination come into play?

This book is also about the human stories behind the science of stories.[12] Alongside Anna's, Charlie's, and Tia's stories, I share with you my own twists and turns in my quest for knowledge about the impact of stories across the lifespan. My hope is that these human stories will render the science more memorable, and ultimately more useful, in your everyday lives.

THE PRACTICAL SIDE OF STORIES

As a developmental scientist, I have devoted my career to discovering how the stories we read to our children, let them watch, and encourage them to tell shape their development. If you are a parent, you may believe intuitively that stories of all kinds are good for you and your children. But are they always so? Do stories from books grant us something special that cannot be gleaned in other ways? What are the downsides to stories? Are stories from video games as dangerous for our teens as many would have us believe? Can stories from real life, including real-life stories on social media, be equally or even more dangerous? As adults, why do we often feel sad and empty when we've finished a book or a favorite TV series, as if we've lost our best friend? Are audiobooks a poor substitute for reading?

In these pages, I will seek to answer these practical questions as I take you through the latest scientific research on the role that stories play in all of our lives every day. Understanding the way stories come to shape us all will inform the study of narratives across a wide range of disciplines: humanities, social sciences, the arts, and health sciences. Perhaps a developmental science of stories will even lead to new interdisciplinary programs in which students from all these areas come together to learn the different ways that humans create and are shaped by stories. Professionals from education, communication, social work, library science, and healthcare fields can also draw on the developmental science of stories to enhance their work with students, clients, patrons, and patients.

Ultimately, I hope that this knowledge about the science of stories will enrich your own experiences with stories of all kinds, and that it will help you to choose your own and your family's stories thoughtfully. If you're intrigued by any of the books, TV shows, movies, and video games I mention, please see my recommended reading/viewing/gaming list at the end.

This book is not about the history of stories or the art of storytelling. It is a book about how we live with stories in our everyday lives—how and why we seek out the stories that we do, and the effects they have on us— sometimes for worse, but mostly for better.

CHAPTER 1

⌒⌣

The Bright Side of Stories

Books are more than doctors, of course. Some novels are loving, lifelong companions; some give you a clip around the ear; others are friends who wrap you in warm towels when you've got those autumn blues. And some . . . well, some are pink candy floss that tingles in your brain for three seconds and leaves a blissful void. Like a short, torrid love affair.
—Nina George, *The Little Paris Bookshop*

For millennia, humans have loved stories. Stories apparently began in our hunter-gatherer past as gossip, a way of telling who was trustworthy and who wasn't.[1] These real-life stories helped to keep rule breakers in line and to promote rule followers to positions of prominence. Those fabled tales around the campfire every evening? They helped to connect tribe members to each other and to their ancestors, and to pass down vital information across generations.[2] Modern anthropologists have deduced that tribes with more skilled storytellers per capita were more likely to cooperate with each other, which meant not only surviving but thriving.[3]

We all still love a good story, one that is packed with heroes and foes, fears and desires, thwarted or fulfilled. Are stories still good for us in this millennium?

Throughout my career of researching stories, I have often wondered whether my own obsession with stories, from both fiction and real life, was a healthy one. This professional curiosity hit home hard when I was recovering from breast cancer surgery in 2016. Exhausted and sore, I was couch-bound most of each day for several months. Although I had a generous stack of books on the coffee table beside me, reading was difficult.

How Stories Change Us. Elaine Reese, Oxford University Press. © Oxford University Press 2024.
DOI: 10.1093/oso/9780197747902.003.0001

My fictional therapy came instead in the form of *Orange Is the New Black*—the TV series *and* the book—and progressively gorier Scandi-noir crime series such as *The Killing* and *The Bridge*. I had to ration myself to a few hours of viewing a day. I seemed to need series in which characters were undergoing complex ordeals—but not the same as my own. For instance, I tried but failed to watch *The Big C*, in which suburbanite Cathy Jamison discovers she has cancer, even though I loved Laura Linney in all her other work.

Understand that before my illness, I did not typically watch crime dramas, and that now, 8 years later and healthy, I am unable to watch the goriest ones. I've run back from *The Bridge* to *Broadchurch*. Why did I need the dark stuff at such a dark time of my life? Was it for the transporting effect of fiction to another world? Yes, but not just to escape. I needed a different darkness from my own, but with a touch of (black) comedy. I needed a safe place to experience others' intense emotions of fear and grief and anger, because I couldn't bear to experience them to that same degree in my own life. But were these stories damaging for me instead of healing?

Fortunately, new evidence shows that stories from fiction *and* real life have powerful benefits for our minds, our emotions and attitudes, our behavior—even our body's ability to heal itself.

FICTION READERS RULE

This story starts in 2006, when psychologists Raymond Mar and Keith Oatley published a paper with the intriguing title of "Bookworms Versus Nerds" to establish whether a predilection for reading fiction predicted better social skills, compared to reading nonfiction.[4] Mar and Oatley first asked undergraduates to report on their reading habits using a clever method originally developed by reading expert Keith Stanovich and colleagues.[5] On the Author Recognition test, participants select real book authors from a list that also contains fake book authors. Then participants completed several tests of empathy (experiencing another person's feelings) and theory of mind (understanding what others might be thinking or feeling).[6] The most popular of these tests for adults is called the "Reading the Mind in the Eyes" test.[7] Psychologist Simon Baron-Cohen (yes, he is Sacha's cousin) developed this test as a measure of individual differences in understanding others' emotions. The test is also good at discriminating neurotypical adults from those with high-functioning autism, a disorder characterized by difficulties inferring others' mental states. Each of us differs dramatically in our ability to read emotions in this way. Try it out for yourself at http://socialintelligence.labinthewild.org/mite/.

THE BRIGHT SIDE OF STORIES *(3)*

Young adults in Mar and Oatley's study who recognized more real authors of fiction were indeed better at theory of mind on this test. The results were specific to reading fiction, not to reading other genres. In fact, young adults who recognized more nonfiction authors were actually worse at reading others' emotions. Mar and Oatley concluded that bookworms (aka fiction readers) were in fact more socially skilled than the stereotype implies, and that only the nerds (aka nonfiction readers) were socially impaired. Of course, some of us read a vast number of fiction *and* nonfiction books. I'll say more about these nerdy bookworms in Chapter 2.

This single study spawned a tidal wave of research in the next decade on whether fiction reading actually benefits one's empathy and theory of mind, or if those who are drawn to reading fiction simply start out more socially attuned. One obvious question is whether the personalities of fiction readers differ in fundamental ways from those who prefer nonfiction. Although most of us would wager that fiction reading is more common among introverts, introversion turns out to be a poor predictor of a preference for reading fiction. Instead, the distinguishing trait of fiction readers is openness to experience—our willingness to expand our minds and our worlds.[8]

For instance, Anna from my longitudinal *Origins of Memory* study (whom I first introduced in my book *Tell Me a Story*) is continuing to pursue both her academic and artistic pursuits at university with a double-major in social work and music. Despite her heavy workload, Anna is still an avid fiction reader at age 20. Fellow *Origins* participant Tia is now putting her acting and singing abilities to use by training to become a preschool teacher. At age 20, like Anna, Tia reports still reading often for pleasure. Although the two young women differ in their personalities, with Anna more introverted and Tia more extraverted, they are both high on the distinguishing trait of openness. Yet even when Mar and Oatley controlled for openness to experience, fiction readers still scored higher on the Mind in the Eyes test. So the benefits of reading fiction can't be reduced merely to personality differences among fiction readers.

Another obvious question is whether all types of fiction are equally linked to social attunement. To put it bluntly: No. When people's reading habits were categorized into different types of fiction—romance, domestic/literary, suspense/thriller, and science fiction/fantasy—it was the romance lovers who had the best theory-of-mind skills, with literary fiction and suspense fans close behind.[9] A science-fiction/fantasy bent was not linked to better theory of mind. In contrast, the romance and theory-of-mind link stayed strong even after controlling for personality traits and nonfiction reading. But what if romance readers simply start out with better theory-of-mind skills? So far, these studies were all correlational, which means that the association between reading fiction and theory of mind might be explained by other factors. Experimental research—in which participants are randomly assigned to read different passages, and then tested for differences in their theory of mind—was needed to resolve the controversy.

In 2013, a landmark paper published in the journal *Science* did just that in a series of five experiments testing the effects of reading fiction on adults' theory of mind.[10] One group read a passage of literary fiction (prize-winning short stories such as "The Runner" by Don DeLillo and "Chameleon" by Chekhov), a second group read a piece of popular fiction ("Space Jockey" by Robert Heinlein and *Gone Girl* by Gillian Flynn), and a third group read a nonfiction story from the *Smithsonian* magazine ("How the Potato Changed the World" by Charles C. Mann). In experiment after experiment, literary fiction boosted scores on the Mind in the Eyes task over both popular fiction and nonfiction. The authors proposed that literary fiction is especially good at helping us to understand the nuanced emotions of others.

The popular media loved these results, especially the more literary outlets such as *The New York Times* and *The Atlantic Monthly*: "Does Reading Fiction Make You Better?" and "Now We Have Proof Reading Literary Fiction Makes You a Better Person." Soon bloggers were advising folks to read a short passage of literary fiction before going out on a date or to an important business meeting.

Does fiction really have these almost magical powers of connection?

Over the next few years, teams of researchers across the world set out to replicate these astounding findings with thousands of readers. This is about as suspenseful as it gets in the field of psychology.

What was the result of this massive replication effort? A 2018 megastudy of 14 experimental studies, called a meta-analysis, showed that reading fiction really does promote theory of mind and empathy.[11] Most of the passages in these experiments were drawn from literary fiction, many with dark themes. For instance, in Don DeLillo's "The Runner," a jogger observes a child being kidnapped from a park. Although a few individual studies failed to show the effect, the overall finding was that reading a short passage of fiction (compared to reading nonfiction or no reading) creates a small boost in the reader's social understanding skills.[12]

A few studies even show that reading fiction can decrease prejudice toward minority ethnic groups, such as Muslim women, and increase prosocial behavior, such as helping out an experimenter by completing a follow-up survey for only 5 cents.[13] The overall effect is not whopping—instead, it's what psychologists like to call "small but real." It would be odd if reading a single passage of fiction, or even a single book, could dramatically change one's ability to connect with other people. Yet the idea is that these benefits accrue steadily over a lifetime as a result of the extra practice readers of fiction get simulating others' experiences and emotions.[14] And that is exactly what another meta-analysis of 30 correlational studies found: People's fiction reading over a lifetime is the best predictor of having better theory-of-mind skills, and slightly better empathy skills, compared to their nonfiction reading habits.[15]

Bookworms, pat yourselves on the back. People who read a lot of fiction really *are* more socially attuned.

But are these effects restricted to literary fiction, with its greater use of stylistic features and more nuanced depictions of characters' mental states?[16] The meta-analyses were not able to fully test the differences between literary and popular fiction because most of the studies have used only a few excerpts of each. It's fair to question the distinction between literary and popular fiction altogether, and between fiction and nonfiction. I am not a literary theorist, but I hear from those who are that the line between these genres in modern writing can be blurry. Some contemporary popular works of fiction, such as Ann Patchett's *The Dutch House*, could also be classified as literary. Even purported works of nonfiction, especially biographies and memoir, contain many elements of fictional storytelling. History books in particular vary dramatically in their narrative qualities, with nonnarrative accounts of names and dates at one extreme, and historical fiction at the other.

Yet Lisa Zunshine, who *is* a literary theorist, argues that the line between fiction and nonfiction is real and is adaptive.[17] Zunshine believes that knowing the genre of a book at the outset as mostly imaginary versus mostly real enables us to more easily enter its world and to process the events accordingly *as it actually happened* or *as-if it had happened*. Neuroscientist Ulrike Altmann and colleagues supported this split by showing that people responded differently at a neural level to the same short passage about a crime or accident when labeled as "fact" versus "fiction."[18] Reading in either frame of mind promotes brain activation associated with imagination, but in different ways. When we read a story as fact, we imagine what happened as if we were observing the events in real time, which activates the brain regions associated with processing actions in the real world. When we read the same story as fiction, we are trying harder to understand the characters and feel their emotions in order to better understand their intentions. Reading as fiction activates brain regions associated with inferential thinking, empathy, and theory of mind.

Specifically, reading a passage as fiction activates the "default network" in the brain, which goes to work whenever we're not intensely focused on something out in the world, allowing our minds to wander. The default network connects a number of regions from the front to the back of the brain, including those involved in empathy, theory of mind, autobiographical memory, imagination, and spatial processing.[19] Reading a passage as fiction prompted participants to consider what *might have* happened, what *could* happen, and *why* it happened, rather than simply *what* happened.

The line between literary and popular fiction, however, may be much fuzzier. Take one of my favorite authors, for example: Alexander McCall Smith, of *The No. 1 Ladies' Detective Agency* and *44 Scotland Street* series. He is one of the most popular writers in the world today with over 100 books published in 47 languages. His books are both highly readable and addictive. If left to my own devices (if I didn't belong to a book club), I would probably read nothing but Alexander McCall Smith books. Although English professors would not consider his books to be literary fiction, they contain complex sentence structures, rare and sometimes arcane words (in English and in Scots), and, most importantly for the present dilemma, a rich consideration of the characters' thoughts and emotions. In her fascinating book *Why We Read Fiction*, Lisa Zunshine talks about the mental workout we undergo when we read a work of literary fiction. As an example, she analyzes this "random" passage from Virginia Woolf's *Mrs. Dalloway*, in which Mrs. Dalloway's husband, Richard, and his friend Hugh go to Lady Millicent Bruton's house to help her compose a letter to the newspaper that could change the future of Great Britain:

> And Miss Brush [Lady Bruton's secretary] went out, came back; laid papers on the table; and Hugh produced his fountain pen; his silver fountain pen, which had done twenty years' service, he said, unscrewing the cap. It was still in perfect order; he had shown it to the makers; there was no reason, they said, why it should ever wear out; which was somehow to Hugh's credit, and to the credit of the sentiments which his pen expressed (so Richard Dalloway felt) as Hugh began carefully writing capital letters with rings round them in the margin, and thus marvellously reduced Lady Bruton's tangles to sense, to grammar such as the editor of the Times, Lady Bruton felt, watching the marvellous transformation, must respect.
>
> —Virginia Woolf, *Mrs. Dalloway*

To truly understand this passage, Zunshine argues that the reader must employ complex theory-of-mind skills. Zunshine claims that "Woolf intends us to recognise [by inserting a parenthetical observation, 'so

Richard Dalloway felt'] that Richard is aware that Hugh wants Lady Bruton and Richard to think that because the makers of the pen believe that it will never wear out, the editor of the *Times* will respect and publish the ideas recorded by this pen."[20]

I read *Mrs. Dalloway* in my mid-20s for fun, not for an English class, and I'm sure I didn't even begin to grasp this complexity. According to Zunshine, this passage from *Mrs. Dalloway* entails sixth-order theory of mind, a mental workout equivalent to a marathon. To backtrack, first-order theory of mind is simply understanding that others can have different thoughts and feelings from our own, as in "Mary doesn't know there will be a surprise party." Second-order theory of mind entails thinking about thoughts and feelings, as in "John hopes that Mary doesn't know about the surprise party." Both first-order and second-order theory of mind are mastered in childhood.[21] Third- and fourth-order theory of mind are much more difficult,[22] and even highly skilled adults flounder when confronted with fifth-order theory of mind, as in "Tom imagines that Alice believes that Bob thinks that John hopes that Mary doesn't know that there will be a surprise party." Sixth-order theory of mind is probably restricted to literary theorists and graduate students of literature, not to other, mere mortal, readers like the rest of us.

In contrast, take a random passage from my favorite McCall Smith series featuring philosopher Isabel Dalhousie:

> While Isabel paged through the book, Tom said, "That's a beautiful song. Really beautiful." He was sitting next to Angie on the sofa near the fire and now, as Isabel played the first bars of the introduction, he took Angie's hand in his. Isabel, half watching, half attending to the printed music, thought it was possible that Tom knew exactly what Angie had in mind when she accepted his offer of marriage, but had decided that she might grow to love him because love can come if you believe in it and behave as if it exists. That was the case, too, with free will; perhaps, faith of any sort; and love was a sort of faith, was it not? But then she glanced at Angie, and she changed her mind again. "She would prefer him not to be around," she thought. "That is when she would love him. She would love him much more then."
>
> —Alexander McCall Smith, *The Right Attitude to Rain*

For popular fiction, this is a fairly dense passage involving complex sentence structures. Certainly both Virginia Woolf and Alexander McCall Smith are well-versed fans of the semicolon. Yet at most this passage entails third-order theory of mind (*Isabel thought that Tom knew what Angie had in mind*), a level that most adults can grasp readily. Both Woolf and

McCall Smith tell us at times what their characters are thinking and feeling. Yet in *Mrs. Dalloway* these direct declarations of mental states are deeply embedded in inferring others' thoughts and feelings ad infinitum, or at least to the sixth level. McCall Smith's writing integrates a satisfying combination of mental gymnastics with an ultimately transparent delivery of characters' thoughts and feelings. Simply put, McCall Smith's books are less demanding to read than hard-core literary fiction, but they are still more demanding of our social understanding skills than most other works of popular fiction. Perhaps that is one reason they are so beloved.

Although literary and popular fiction are distinct, there is much more of a continuum between the two than most psychology researchers acknowledge in their studies. An exception is psychologist and novelist Jennifer Lynn Barnes (of *The Inheritance Games* series for young adults) who argues that it is the *way* we read fiction that is important for our social skills, not the literary quality of the writing.[23] We can read popular fiction in a deep way that engages our emotions and our minds. For instance, every time you finish a book and then find yourself reflecting on what will happen next for the characters, imagining different scenarios, or relating the book to your own life, you're activating the default network of your brain. These lingering thoughts indicate that you have been reading deeply[24]—even if the book you just finished would never make it onto an English lit syllabus.

This ability to transport yourself into a story and to engage emotionally with the characters turns out to be the key for the benefits of fiction for theory of mind and empathy. Now the finding that reading romance novels predicts better theory of mind makes sense. Only readers who report being transported into the stories and feeling the emotions of the characters reap the benefits of fiction.[25] Science fiction, which can focus more on technology than people, does not have this same effect.[26] (It would be interesting, however, to test the effects of reading space opera sci-fi, with its greater psychological content, on social understanding.)[27] Across genres, it is the ability to be transported into the minds of the characters, not the literary quality of the story, that is important. In fact, the fictional story that so far has produced some of the strongest experimental effects on altruistic behavior was written by a middle school teacher.[28] Although emotionally evocative, this story is not literary:

> "See ya later, Eric," Brandon, my best friend, said with a shrug. "Yeah. Later," I replied as my heart sank with bitter disappointment. For the third time that week, my friends were all ditching me. . . . Last night's argument between my parents rang in my ears as I kicked a rock down the road. My legs carried me back to the bickering even as my brain tried to reason an excuse to stay away

for a few more hours. Each step brought back the stinging words my parents shouted at each other as they slammed their bedroom door. Yeah, I thought, like that will drown you out. Of course it had been about money, again. That was all anyone talked about in my house any more. Last night was no different. "How can you possibly spend $145 out with your friends when we supposedly can't even afford to spend half that on Eric's school supplies?" My mother had screamed from the other side of the bedroom door. Please, I had silently pleaded, leave me out of this.

To engage emotionally with a story, it must have social content—either people or other animals. Neuroimaging research shows that reading stories about people specifically engages the dorsomedial prefrontal cortex of the brain, which is implicated in theory-of-mind and empathy skills.[29] Stories with more abstract language, including descriptions of characters' mental states, also activate this region. In contrast, reading stories with vivid descriptions of physical scenes and actions engages the medial temporal and medial parietal cortex, critical for memory, visualizing scenes, and spatial skills. All of these regions are part of the default network. These different areas of brain activation for different types of stories are one possible reason why people who read romance, literary, or suspense novels have greater theory-of-mind and empathy skills compared to people who read mostly science fiction. When we read romance or literary novels, with their higher social or abstract content, we are activating brain regions associated with theory of mind and empathy.

CAN WE BENEFIT FROM VISUAL FICTION, TOO?

What about other forms of fiction than books, especially movies, TV shows, and video games? Are they as good as books for fostering our theory of mind and empathy?

Raymond Mar argues that regardless of medium, stories with accurate social content that encourage simulated social interactions will benefit the reader's, viewer's, or gamer's social understanding.[30] After all, when watching a TV show or movie, the viewer has to decode thoughts and feelings from the actors' facial expressions and actions. Essentially, watching a movie is like one long Mind in the Eyes test, but with lots of additional physical and verbal information to help us figure out what the characters are feeling and intending. Except in poorly scripted visual productions, however, films do not typically contain the direct declarations of thoughts and feelings that are present in novels. In his fascinating book

Flicker: Your Brain on Movies, neuroscientist Jeffrey Zacks discusses the differences between books and movies, and what makes a good (or poor) movie adaptation of a book.[31]

Jennifer Barnes and Jessica Black experimentally tested the benefits for theory of mind of watching award-winning "art" TV (*Mad Men, West Wing, The Good Wife*, or *Lost*) compared to watching an award-winning non-fictional documentary, or no viewing at all.[32] They found the same small benefits on the Mind in the Eyes test from watching art TV that others have found from reading fiction. Another study by anthropologist Robin Dunbar and colleagues showed that watching an emotionally arousing film about a disabled homeless man—*Stuart: A Life Backwards*—increased participants' sense of connectedness to the strangers with whom they watched the film, compared to those who watched a neutral documentary together.[33] Live theatre produces similar increases in empathy and prosocial attitudes, even charitable donations.[34]

Charlie from my *Origins* study is a good example of the power of visual fiction. Now 20 years old, Charlie is still a man of action; after high school he traveled overseas on a gap year to work as a hunting guide. At our interview, he was trying to figure out his next steps. Charlie is not as passionate a reader as Anna or Tia. Instead, he reports spending more time watching TV and movies and playing video games than reading. Yet his score on a popular test of empathy was nearly as high as Anna's and Tia's. Reading fiction is only one way of many to nourish social understanding.

Some video games can also boost social abilities. These video games—now called Empathy Games—all contain a storyline that encourages the player to delve deeply into the minds of the characters. Psychologists Daniel Boorman and Tobias Greitemeyer compared playing the video game *Gone Home*, an award-winning first-person "walking simulator" game with a strong character-driven storyline, to a first-person adventure video game called *Against the Wall* in which the player, well, climbs walls.[35] *Gone Home* produced immediate benefits on the Mind in the Eyes test compared to *Against the Wall*, which does not have a storyline. Boorman and Greitemeyer even contrasted two versions of *Gone Home* in which they instructed the players to focus on technical aspects of the game versus on the storyline. The storyline version of the same game was superior for theory of mind.

Watching fictional films can even be good for your health. A completely separate line of research from communication studies has explored the health benefits of watching short fictional films containing health messages.[36] A good example is the video *The Tamale Lesson* that communication researcher Sheila Murphy produced with professional filmmakers.[37] The film features the fictional Romero family preparing tamales for their teenage daughter Rosita's Quincieñara (15th birthday party). Older sister Connie overhears eldest sister, Lupita, telling her boyfriend that she tested positive for HPV in a PAP smear. Connie has never had a PAP smear and is afraid to get one. Lupita and Connie are joined by their mother, Blanca, and her friend Petra, who have also never had PAP smears. Lupita then demonstrates a PAP smear on a raw chicken to allay their fears. Watching this fictional portrayal of facts about cervical cancer and PAP smears led to greater growth in women's knowledge about cervical cancer and to more positive attitudes about PAP smears compared to watching a nonnarrative film containing the same information delivered by doctors. A full 6 months after watching the narrative film, those women who identified most with the less knowledgeable characters in the film (especially with the mother, Blanca) were more likely to have discussed PAP smears with their doctors. Nor was this effect restricted to women who were Mexican American; the strongest predictor of this behavior change was instead women's identification with the characters in the film, regardless of their own ethnicity.

Fictional stories from books, TV, films, theatre, and video games foster our social understanding, decrease prejudice, increase our prosocial actions—they can even persuade us to take steps to save our lives.

THE UPSIDE OF REAL-LIFE STORIES

The benefits of stories are not restricted to fictional tales. The stories we create about our own personal experiences can also boost our mental and physical health. We know about the benefits of real-life stories from two related threads of research on personal narratives: the Life Story approach and the Expressive Writing approach.

For the last three decades, psychologist Dan McAdams has been studying the stories that we tell about our lives and how they shape our identities. Although we share with many others our personality traits, such as a tendency toward introversion, or openness to new experiences, each one of our life stories is unique. No other person in the history of humankind has experienced your exact set of circumstances and life events. No other person has extracted from that set of events the exact same story. This is the story of *your* life. McAdams' books *The Stories We Live By: Personal Myths and the Making of Self* and *The Art and Science of Personality Development* are illuminating accounts of this field.

In McAdams' Life Story Interview (recently adapted by journalist Bruce Feiler in his inspiring book *Life Is in the Transitions*), people tell the stories of their lives in manageable chunks by narrating key events: their earliest memories, childhood and adolescent scenes, and the high points, low points, and turning points of their adult lives. Through fine-grained coding of the themes and shape of these stories, McAdams can discern those who have a more mature and positive appreciation of the events of their lives.[38]

An especially important aspect of these stories is the presence of redemption—taking the lemons in one's life and making lemonade. The presence of a redemption theme in one's life story is a harbinger of other good things to come. For instance, psychologists Will Dunlop and Jessica Tracy found that recovering alcoholics whose life stories contained redemption themes were more likely to stay sober over the next few months.[39] These benefits held regardless of their earlier dependence on alcohol, personality traits, or levels of depression. Here is one of their examples of a story with a redemption theme:

> I got uh, quite wasted, I was 7 months clean, and then that month I uh, I relapsed quite a few times, and uh, as a result I uh, slit my wrist, ended up in the psych ward at Vancouver General Hospital . . . I was feeling useless, unloved, lonely, depressed, ashamed, that I, you know, fell through on my recovery plan, and after losing 7 months you almost lose hope, right? But uh, I found my own strength again, through God, and through the NA and AA program, 11 days clean, I feel like the obsession has been lifted from me again, and I need to see everything I did wrong last time to make it better this time.

Are these positive portents of stories restricted to people experiencing great difficulty in their lives, such as recovering alcoholics? No. In a community sample of younger and older adults, redemption themes were once again linked to well-being—although only in stories of life's low points.[40] Our own dark tales, when reflected upon carefully, can play a positive role in our lives. Another consistent finding across different life stories, positive and negative, is that themes of personal growth, agency, and connection to others predict better psychological outcomes later in life.[41]

What do growth, agency, and connection look like in a life story? Here Charlotte, another 20-year-old member of my *Origins* study, tells us about a turning point in her life. After failing the first year of a challenging pre-med course, she went to a youth leadership event in Wellington to pull her life together:

> I was, like, "What are you doing with your life?" And so that was kind of when I decided to plan out, "Right, I'm going back down [to Dunedin], I'm going to like sort it out, I'm going to like take the year off and like, and like, get my life back together." It was a really good event, like um, we just hung out with, like,

other youth leaders around, like, just like worked on our leadership skills and stuff like that. And like, in that experience and like just chilling out for like a whole week with, like, people you don't know and, like, it was just so relaxing and like, well, for an extravert, and then, um, yeah just, I don't know, just put everything in perspective, and I was just like, "Wow!" So I took a gap year. And that was really good. And so now I'm at uni and I'm, like, actually enjoying it, so that's really good.

These positive spinoffs of life stories over months and years are compelling, but what if the folks with these positive themes in their life stories simply started out different in some unmeasured way, and that's why they were able to stay sober and happier for longer? As with the bookworm versus nerd problem, researchers have ruled out personality traits as an explanation—the effects remain even after controlling for other important predictors.[42] However, as psychologist Qi Wang compellingly argues in her book *The Autobiographical Self in Time and Culture*, cultures differ in the value placed on telling real-life stories, especially those told from an individual rather than a group perspective.[43] Adults from more collectivist cultures, as in Southeast Asia, who tell more detailed stories about their own lives actually report lower well-being, in contrast to the positive association demonstrated for European Americans.[44]

It has taken me years, but I've managed to craft redemptive, agentic, and connecting stories for some of the most difficult experiences of my life so far—the death of my father, divorce, and cancer. Right after the surgery, my fictional viewing therapy helped me to recognize and cope with all the dark emotions I was experiencing. Later, writing about these experiences has helped in a deeper way.

It turns out that the act of writing down even a small part of the most emotional events in our lives can boost our health.

Nearly four decades ago, psychologist James Pennebaker developed a technique he calls *Expressive Writing*. In the first of many experimental studies of expressive writing, Pennebaker and Sandra Beall asked one group of undergraduates to write privately about "your very deepest thoughts and feelings about an extremely important emotional issue that has affected you and your life" for 15 minutes a day over 4 consecutive days.[45] The students took the instructions seriously; two traumas they wrote about were a younger brother drowning in a sailing accident, and sexual abuse by a grandfather at age 12.

The students who engaged in this expressive writing exercise went on to make fewer visits to the student health center over the next 6 months compared to a control group of undergraduates who were instructed to write about trivial topics, such as the layout of their living room. These health benefits endured despite the fact that the undergraduates in the expressive writing group initially experienced a dip in their mood and an increase in their blood pressure immediately after the writing sessions. The students were confronting and actively processing these difficult, even traumatic, experiences.

This single small study sparked a tsunami of work across disciplines and around the world on the benefits of writing about one's difficult life experiences, with over 1,400 research studies of expressive writing at last count.[46] People who engage in expressive writing enjoy better physical and mental health over the ensuing weeks and months.[47] These benefits are for objectively measurable outcomes such as getting better grades, becoming employed, improving asthma symptoms, going to the doctor less often, and requiring fewer medications, as well as more subjective outcomes such as reporting lower levels of depression. Expressive writing even promotes faster wound healing.[48] All this comes from writing about a single diffi-cult experience for a grand total of 1 hour. See Pennebaker's how-to books on expressive writing if you're keen to try it for yourself: *Opening Up by Writing It Down* and *Expressive Writing: Words That Heal*.[49]

Similar to the effects of reading fiction on social understanding, ex-pressive writing seems like an elixir. How can writing so briefly about an upsetting experience produce such wide-ranging benefits? Pennebaker acknowledges that he still doesn't know exactly how expressive writing works its magic—he and health psychologist Joshua Smyth say that al-though we know the ingredients for the special sauce, we don't completely understand its essence.[50] However, we do have a few clues. Many of these clues have been discovered through detailed analysis of the stories them-selves using Pennebaker's word-counting software (Linguistic Inquiry and Word Count or LIWC, unintuitively pronounced "LUKE").[51] Try LIWC-ing your own writing sample at https://www.liwc.app/demo.

Pennebaker's fascinating book, *The Secret Life of Pronouns: What Our Words Say About Us*, offers an accessible overview of these detailed analyses.[52] The people who benefit the most from expressive writing are those who grow in their understanding of the event over the consecutive days of writing, as indicated by their increasing use of insight and causal words like *think*, *realize*, and *because*. These words indicate reflection on why the event was difficult and a change in processing the trauma over time. The gaps between writing sessions are most likely crucial for these insights to develop, but these gaps must be short—ideally between 1 and 3 days apart.[53] For some people who have experienced trauma, particu-larly those who have intrusive thoughts, it helps to adopt a third-person perspective.[54] Writing about these extremely difficult experiences as if you were a character in a book improves health even more than writing in the first person for these folks. Seeing a difficult event from an outsider's perspective is likely to help us to better understand the event.

Does all of this sound familiar? Perhaps expressive writing works because it sharpens our theory of mind—for understanding our own as well as others' past thoughts, feelings, and motivations. Through writing about our past experiences, we are able to see ourselves from different perspectives, to better understand the reasons behind our actions and reactions, to find some redemption in trauma.

Expressive writing can even help us to grant forgiveness to others. Psychologist Catherine Romero asked one group of undergraduates to write expressively about a time when someone transgressed against them, specifically focusing on empathizing with their offender and imagining the benefits of forgiveness.[55] Other undergraduates simply wrote about the facts of the offence or about mundane daily events. Three weeks later, those in the empathy group reported being less avoidant of their offender, and also scored higher on an empathy scale with items such as "I can understand why the offender acted that way" compared to those who wrote about daily events.

I'd love to know whether expressive writing also helps us to feel more empathy with ourselves, similar to a character in a book or a film. Do we forgive our past selves in addition to our transgressors as a result of expressive writing?[56]

Critically, the benefits of expressive writing have been found with *only* a few days of writing. In fact, Pennebaker cautions that continuing to write about a trauma may lead to rumination and negative effects on health.[57] The overall benefits of expressive writing may also mask large individual differences in its efficacy, including possible cultural differences.[58] For instance, Chinese American breast cancer survivors benefitted most from a modified version of expressive writing that first encouraged them to focus on the ways they had coped with cancer before pouring out their deepest feelings about having had cancer.[59]

I'm now teaming up with Dan McAdams and James Pennebaker, clinical psychologist Karen Salmon, and researchers Sean Marshall and Keren Segal to conduct randomized controlled trials—the gold standard of research designs—comparing expressive writing to turning-point narratives for their effects on young people's mental and physical health and well-being. My colleague Hitaua Arahanga-Doyle is also keen to test the best life story methods specifically for young Māori adults, whose mental health has declined disproportionately as a result of the pandemic.[60] Māori culture has a rich oral tradition, coupled with a sense of identity as bound up with one's social groups, so it will be important to trial the benefits of telling versus writing about shared group experiences as well as individual experiences.[61] Researchers are only beginning to untangle how we can tell the stories of our lives in ways that will help us the most.[62]

YOUR BRAIN ON STORIES

The COVID-19 pandemic has proved to be a catalyst for an increase in mental health difficulties, and many people around the globe today do not have access to high-quality mental healthcare.[63] Clearly no one would advocate reading books, watching movies, telling or writing life stories in the place of physical healthcare. I wouldn't have used expressive writing to cure my cancer. Yet expressive writing does help cancer survivors to manage their pain and to sleep better; it even helps to speed the healing rate for biopsy wounds.[64] Plus expressive writing is a free technique that anyone can use at any time, with minimal instruction. Pennebaker proposes that writing about difficult experiences could become a complementary form of therapy to trauma treatments such as cognitive behavioral therapy (CBT) or eye movement desensitization and reprocessing therapy (EMDR).[65]

What we don't know yet is how telling or writing real-life stories compares to reading or viewing fictional stories for improving our theory of mind, our empathy, our health. What we do know is that stories make a difference. Reading *and* watching *and* gaming *and* real-life storytelling are all associated with benefits for many people. In Chapter 8, I'll discuss the pros and cons of stories across these different platforms and new technologies, but so far the effects are similar.

These comparable effects for all kinds of stories are not surprising, given the latest neuroscience evidence showing that reading and listening to fiction, watching movies and TV, and remembering one's past and imagining one's future all recruit the default network in the brain.[66] The default network is vital for humans' abilities to have positive social interactions, to plan and solve problems, and to be creative. Although there are some slight differences in which subsystems of the default network are activated as a function of what kind of fiction we're reading or whether we're remembering or imagining, we're relying on the default network to generate the mental images associated with each. Across media, we're linking imagined events (from a book or movie or real life) with real events and general knowledge accumulated from our past. Video gaming, however, may not activate the default network to the same degree because of the external focus and body movements required while playing.[67] I'll say more about the neuroscience of video games in Chapter 5. So the next time you want to read a novel or watch your favorite TV series, just tell your family that you're exercising your default network.

My own life story has a happy ending, for now—I am healthier than ever, and I spend my time more thoughtfully than before I had cancer. I believe that my temporary immersion in dark story worlds helped. By empathizing with characters undergoing much direr experiences than my own, I was able to understand and accept my own dark emotions. It was only later that I was able to craft a redemptive story about my illness. Finally, knowing about the benefits of fiction means that I can indulge my reading and viewing habits—even for books and shows that are the equivalent of cotton candy—and justify going to book club every month without feeling guilty.

CHAPTER 2

✧

The Gender Gap in Stories

She read books as one would breathe air, to fill up and live.
—Annie Dillard, *The Living*

Stories of all types are good for us. Stories help us understand who we are and who we could be, and even help us heal. But are some of us getting more stories than are others?

As I delved into the research on the psychological benefits of reading fiction, I reflected on how most of the people I know who love to read fiction are women—my mother, my sister, my high school friends, my book club friends. There were a few notable exceptions of male fiction fanatics, such as my elder son, Ben; literary friends like writer/critic Ilan Stavans; and older men like my late colleague Jim Flynn, author of *The Torchlight List* of recommended reading through the ages.[1] Instead, most of the men I know who love to read books prefer nonfiction, including history and biography.

If you are a man reading this book, you may be one of the select few who regularly reads fiction. If you are a woman reading this book, you may be one of the fortunate few whose father, husband, partner, brother, or son reads fiction. But it is much more common for men who are voracious readers to read nonfiction, whereas women who love to read typically prefer fiction. In study after study, women correctly recognize more of the fiction authors on the Author Recognition Test than do men, indicating that they read fiction more often.[2]

Once again, Anna and Charlie from my *Origins* study exemplify this pattern. As a young adult, Anna reported reading widely across fictional

How Stories Change Us. Elaine Reese, Oxford University Press. © Oxford University Press 2024.
DOI: 10.1093/oso/9780197747902.003.0002

genres, including classics and romance, science fiction and fantasy, action and adventure, and comic novels. The last three books she read were Truman Capote's *Breakfast at Tiffany's*, literary/fantasy novel *The Night Circus* by Erin Morganstern, and J. K. Rowling's *Harry Potter and the Chamber of Secrets* (a reread). Anna told us, however, that she never reads any type of nonfiction for pleasure, even the crossover genre of memoir/biography. Charlie reported sometimes reading books for pleasure, but not as often as Anna. When he does read books, his tastes turn to nonfiction, especially sports biographies, with the occasional action/adventure, suspense, or comic novel. When we asked him about the last three books he'd read, he could come up with only two: rugby star Mark Ellis' *Good Fullas: A Guide to Kiwi Blokes* and popular thriller *The Girl With the Dragon Tattoo* by Stieg Larsson.

Anna and Charlie thus represent the typical—even stereotypical—female and male reader.[3] These differences in the average female and male reader, although robust, mask a whole world of complexity. Unlike Anna, Tia doesn't read widely among fictional genres; instead, she prefers to read nonfiction, with the occasional historical fiction book. The last three books she read were the memoir *Tuesdays With Morrie* by Mitch Albom, a history tome called *Pagan Symbology in Christianity*, and the historical fiction novel *Perfume: The Story of a Murderer* by Patrick Süskind. In contrast to Charlie, another *Origins* member, Joe, reported reading widely across fictional genres but no nonfiction at all. He even admitted to reading chick lit! Reading preferences differ widely among women and among men.

Yet Tia and Joe are exceptions to the rule. In survey after survey, women report reading more books than do men—an average of nine books per year compared to five—with an especially large divide for fiction reading.[4] A 2017 survey by the US National Endowment for the Arts (NEA) found that in the last year, 53% of women had read at least one work of fiction (novel or short story) versus only 36% of men.[5] In another 2017 survey, women read more books than men in every category except for history and fantasy.[6] This gender gap in fiction reading is so entrenched that researchers have to "control" for gender in their analyses linking fiction to theory of mind and empathy, lest the results simply reflect that women read more fiction than men.

Nor is this gap due solely to a preponderance of women writers churning out fiction that men do not want to read. Historically, of course, novelists were more likely to be men than women, and correspondingly, male novelists won more awards.[7] Although female novelists now dominate the literary prize lists—the Sally Rooney effect—that shift is very recent. Even into the 2010s, nearly all the literary prizes still went to male novelists, even though male and female writers had come to be roughly equally represented in the number of published novels.[8] Instead, the move toward women's dominance of the world of fiction may be because the people who most often read novels these days are women.

WOMEN LOVE BOOK CLUBS, TOO

Women also love to talk about what they read with others. In America, according to the same NEA survey, book club participation shot up from 2012 to 2017. Over 5 million American adults belong to an established book club, and that doesn't even count online groups. Most of those 5 million are women.

Nor is this solely an American phenomenon. Book clubs across the Western world—including the Tbilisi Wine, Women, and Wit Book Club, which I would love to visit someday—are dominated by women.[9] Occasionally you will come across a mixed-sex book club, usually made up of older and highly literate couples, and even more rarely you will come across an all-male book club. Barbara Brown, manager of New Zealand's Book Discussion Scheme, said that of their 1,300-plus book groups, a mere 13 are men's groups—a whopping 1%.[10]

My own book club experiences are a case in point. I have belonged to two book clubs in the past decade, with one still going strong. In this club, we are eight women, ranging in age from 30 to 59. Some of us have children; some do not. Some of us have husbands or partners; some do not. Some of us work outside the home; some do not. All of us love to read fiction.

Like Anna, we are catholic in our tastes—one month we will read a work of literary fiction, the next month a thriller. It seems that we are not alone in this eclecticism. Journalist Nathan Heller noted that "One New York club's reading list includes *Infinite Jest*, the *Hunger Games* series, the first *Dexter* novel, and *Don Quixote*. The lineup of another in Washington State includes a novel by Tracy Chevalier, a memoir by Ruth Reichl, and a biography of Cornelius Vanderbilt. Tossing darts across a Barnes & Noble could hardly produce a more scattershot list."[11]

In my book club, which is part of the New Zealand Book Discussion Scheme, we discuss the merits and demerits of each book with enthusiasm, reading aloud passages that are especially captivating or cringe-worthy. We argue about plot lines and character motivations and then defer to the reader who finished the book the night before. We eat cake and delicious cheeses. Then we talk about our jobs and our children and our partners and our pets and our houses. At the end of each year, we choose our favorite and least favorite books, and say why—loudly, with passion. I have as much fun in my book club as I did back in high school with my friends Diane and Amy arguing about the modern-day relevance of *The Scarlet Letter* and play-acting *A Tale of Two Cities*.

My other book club was different. It was *serious*. For starters, the person who led the discussion was a high school English teacher and a published fiction writer. Second, we read only literary fiction—esteemed novels that had won prizes—*The Luminaries* by Eleanor Catton and *The Goldfinch* by Donna Tartt. Third, this book club had a guy. One. He was a lawyer, married and with a young child, and he loved to read fiction. He put us all to shame. He was the one who read each book to the end first, in depth, and made the most incisive comments. He wasn't at all arrogant—he was simply an incredible reader of fiction. The rest of us, many of whom were mothers with demanding jobs, were doing well to make it through the assigned reading every month without falling asleep, never mind actually interpreting it. This book club disintegrated under its own erudite weight within a few months.

The first structured book clubs started back in the 1700s for upper-class English women who were deprived of a formal education. These women came to be known, derogatorily, as bluestockings, defined in *The New American Cyclopaedia* of 1863 as "pedantic or ridiculously literary ladies."[12] In the 20th century, however, book clubs became a way for women of all backgrounds to meet with other women to talk about something other than homemaking and child-rearing (although I'm guessing that these topics tended to come up alongside the book discussions).

This century, they divide into two camps: what Heller calls the "Oprah words-and-wine" variety versus the "stay-in-school club." My original (and longer-lasting) book club falls into the Oprah camp; my second short-lived one falls into the latter. Heller argues that "they're seeking the same thing: escape from the dullness of cultural extremes." In other words, women are looking for a safe place to air their views—and to hear others' views—on a wide range of topics that matter to them.

Most of the currently popular online book clubs are led by women and cater to women. Reese Witherspoon's Hello Sunshine, for instance, is unabashedly for women only and features only women writers (and producers) of stories of all types: print books, film and TV, and digital real-life story-telling. As the website states: "Hello Sunshine is on a mission to change the narrative for women."

Needless to say, Reese Witherspoon's book club falls more into the "words-and-wine" camp, with the website one month featuring a photo of her looking gorgeous, reading a work of serious fiction in her immaculately tended garden, while entertaining her young son. Her book list is similarly impeccable, with stunning novels such as my recent favorites, *Elinor Oliphant Is Completely Fine* by Gail Honeyman and *Where the Crawdads Sing* by Delia Owens. And I cannot count the great books I've read over the years at Oprah's suggestion, most recently the wonderful Elizabeth Strout novel *Olive, Again*.

For millennial book lovers, Emma Watson started Our Shared Shelf, a self-described "feminist ninja gang." I probably wouldn't have been inspired to reread *Little Women* recently—before seeing Greta Gerwig's movie adaptation—if it hadn't been for Emma Watson's Little Women Book Fairies project, in which she sponsored 2,000 free copies of *Little Women* hidden around the world, including in my town of Dunedin. Finally, Jenna Bush Hager's book club, Read with Jenna, is prominently featured on the *Today* show. Although Bush Hager is not restricting her selections to women writers, it's safe to say her choices, such as Kristin Hannah's *The Four Winds*, are primarily aimed at women readers.

It's harder to categorize all-male book clubs, given their scarcity. In *The New York Times* article entitled "Men Have Book Clubs, Too" journalist Jennifer Miller contrasts the New York City Gay Guys' Book Club with the International Ultra Manly Book Club. The vision of the latter is that "one day we could step out of the shadow of our mothers' book clubs and proclaim that yes, we too, are intellectuals." They've even banned books that are written by women or that were recommended by one of their mothers. Recent fare in the simply named Man Book Club includes *The Power of the Dog* by Thomas Savage and Henry Miller's *Tropic of Cancer*. Even the men who *do* read fiction often prefer a different sort of fiction than women. Would any all-female book club ever choose to read either of these two books? (Admittedly, Jane Campion's 2022 film of *The Power of the Dog* may make the 1967 novel more accessible.) Barbara Brown of the Book Discussion Scheme notes that the all-male groups also tend to select more nonfiction books than do the all-female groups.[13] Yet there appear to be common themes among all book clubs in their thirst for intellectual and social stimulation, accompanied by fitting beverages. One all-male New Zealand group calls itself the Beverage and Book Club to get straight to the main idea.

Why do so many women join book clubs? What do they do for us? Oprah Winfrey told Jenna Bush Hager that she started her book club to "help people know they are not alone."[14]

Communications researcher DeNel Sedo has conducted one of the few empirical studies of book club membership.[15] Her 250+ sample was recruited mainly through online book forums as a study focused on general reading habits. Of the 64% of respondents who said they belonged to a book club, nearly all were women (93%). From the reasons they offered, Sedo argued that women are seeking an intellectual space in book clubs that they may not be getting in other aspects of their lives. Perhaps book clubs offer women an opportunity that they can't get otherwise to talk about books, since so few of the men in their lives read fiction. Their reasons also differed for the face-to-face versus online clubs. People join face-to-face clubs to talk about books, of course, but also for companionship, and to broaden their reading diet. Those in face-to-face book clubs tend to become close friends, and they almost always see each other or communicate outside the scheduled meetings. In contrast, those in virtual book clubs said that their online discussions focus much more on the book—characters, themes, structure—than on related anecdotes from their real lives. Virtual book club members are almost always voracious readers; some are homebound or geographically isolated.

Some particularly passionate readers belong to both face-to-face and virtual book clubs; these readers reported that they talk in more depth about the content, structure, and style of the book in the virtual book club than in the face-to-face club. Sedo conducted her research before video-link book clubs were possible, so these distinctions may be blurrier for contemporary book clubs.

I wonder if the few men who love to read fiction dislike the structured nature of face-to-face or video-link book clubs. A male fiction-loving friend of mine says he hates to attend meetings, especially in the evenings, so book clubs are out for him. Are these men instead satisfying their need to talk about books with the women in their lives, or via online book clubs like *Goodreads*? I follow a Goodreads member named Will Byrnes who writes especially compelling reviews—over 1,000 at last count. I don't always agree with his book choices, but I always learn something from his critiques.[16] During the pandemic, book clubs around the world stayed alive and well through online meetings. My own book club has returned happily to face-to-face meetings, but perhaps an enduring consequence of the pandemic will be a more diverse range of online book clubs, with something for every reader, even including a "silent" book club for introverts.

VISUALIZING WORLDS THROUGH WORDS

Book club membership thus mirrors, even exaggerates, the gender gap in fiction reading. Why do so many women gravitate to books as a preferred way to receive their stories? A clue is buried in one of Raymond Mar, Keith

Oatley, and Jordan Peterson's (yes, *the* Jordan Peterson) earlier papers.[17] They report briefly on the fiction advantage for women, and also on women's higher scores on a measure of transportation in stories that includes items such as "I really get involved with the feelings of the characters in a novel." Essentially it is a measure of "mental simulation"[18]—putting oneself in a character's head and experiencing the sights and sounds, thoughts and feelings of that character. (The brain's default network is activated when we engage in mental simulation, especially when we connect the characters' experiences to our own, even briefly as we're reading.) Some men also had high scores on this measure, and those men in turn reported a strong preference for reading fiction. The few men who love reading fiction, like Joe, are especially good at getting inside the heads of the characters in a story.

But many men have difficulty with narrative transportation. Charlie's score on this same measure of transportation was only 12, compared to Anna's score of 21, and Joe's whopping score of 26, out of a possible 28 points. Mar cites societal pressures as the main reason for men's low rates of fiction reading. From a young age, boys learn that reading fiction is a more appropriate activity for girls and women than for boys and men. Only those boys and men with incredible imaginations are able to withstand these societal pressures and pursue their need for fiction reading, with concomitant benefits for their theory of mind and empathy.

The story can't be that simple.

According to literary theorist Jonathan Gottschall in *The Storytelling Animal: How Stories Make Us Human*, stories are a basic *human* need, not just for women.[19] If most men aren't regularly reading fiction, are they getting their story fix in some other way? As noted earlier, men consistently report reading more history books than do women. After all, history *is* a story, with events shaped by human desires, intentions, and beliefs, false or true. Are men also drawn even more than women to visual stories in movies, TV, and video games?

MEN PREFER VISUAL STORIES

Yes. Men report both watching TV and gaming more often than women. One survey showed that men consistently watch more TV than women, with men in 2022 averaging over 3 hours/day and women averaging 2.5 hours/day.[20] Men also play more video games than women at 2.9 hours/day versus 1.5. For instance, Charlie and Joe both enjoy watching TV and movies more than Anna, who reports viewing only rarely, and Tia, who does not watch movies at all, and only some TV. Charlie and Joe also like to play video games with a storyline, like *Halo* and *Call of Duty*, whereas Anna and Tia seldom play video games. Altogether, Charlie and Joe spend many more hours each week watching TV and movies and playing video games than either Anna or Tia. My own TV-viewing binges while recovering from cancer were the exception; like Anna, I'm now back to reading books much more often than I watch TV or movies, and I rarely game. I'll say more about gaming among young people in Chapters 4 and 5.

In line with their preferred reading genres, men and women also differ in their preferred viewing genres. In one of the few studies to survey adults' reading and viewing habits simultaneously, psychologist Peter Rentfrow and colleagues found that people's entertainment preferences clustered first into either highbrow versus lowbrow.[21] As you might imagine, literary fiction and nonfiction, foreign films, documentaries, and art TV all fell into the highbrow group, whereas romance, thrillers and science fiction, horror and action movies, family dramas, and daytime talk shows all fell into the lowbrow group. Men and women are equally likely to prefer highbrow and lowbrow fare. The gender divide occurs for what *type* of highbrow and lowbrow content they prefer. Regardless of quality, women are more likely to read books and watch shows with social content, whereas men are more likely to read books and watch shows with action content. For instance, Anna's most recent lowbrow movie was *Ever After: A Cinderella Story* compared to Charlie's *Amazing Spiderman 2*.

Reese Witherspoon's Hello Sunshine appeals to highbrow and lowbrow women alike with her book picks, which range from *To Kill a Mockingbird* to *Gone Girl*. She's also enticing women who prefer to consume their fiction on the screen rather than to read. Many of us like to read the book *and* watch the movie. I had already read all of Liane Moriarty's books before I had the pleasure of binge-watching Reese's amazing adaptation of *Big Little Lies*; somehow she stays true to the characters and to the story even with the change in setting from a Sydney suburb to Monterey.

As Tia and Joe show us, individuals' genre preferences don't always fall neatly along gendered lines. In Rentfrow's survey, some men preferred literary fiction, and some women preferred science fiction. Their preferences were linked to personality profiles, with highbrow men *and* women more likely to be extraverted and open to new experiences—highbrow readers, regardless of gender, are highly social creatures who enjoy new intellectual and cultural outlets. Yet highbrow and lowbrow readers of *fiction* (who tend to be women) share higher levels of the personality trait of agreeableness, which is a measure of how trusting, forgiving, warm, sympathetic, and, yes, how empathetic you are toward others.[22] When our *Origins* members reported on their personality traits, it did turn out that Anna, Tia, and

Joe were all somewhat more agreeable than Charlie. Once again, science reiterates the point that those who read fiction are more likely to be compassionate and empathetic people, whether they veer toward highbrow or lowbrow content. Perhaps fiction readers' tendency to be agreeable is also why they enjoy such long-lasting alliances with each other in book clubs. For instance, life story researcher Dan McAdams revealed that he and his wife started a mixed-gender book club that has been going for nearly 30 years.[23]

Yet these broad-brush personality profiles do not fully explain the gap between women's and men's attraction to reading fiction. Although there is an established gender difference in agreeableness, with women overall more likely to report being agreeable than men, it is a small one. We all know highly agreeable men and highly disagreeable women.

VISUALIZING STORIES IN OUR MINDS

I propose instead that each one of us differs in our predilection for mental simulation—the practice of envisioning events in our minds—and that this individual difference can help us better understand the gender gaps for reading and viewing fiction. The events we envision can be real or imagined, with ourselves or others as the central characters. All adults engage in mental simulation on a daily basis, including at night when we dream. While formulating your shopping list in the middle of a boring meeting at work, do you picture yourself walking along the aisles of your favorite grocery store, picking up the items that you need to make a risotto for dinner? In the same boring meeting, do you find yourself thinking back to a dinner party at a friend's house the past weekend, replaying the more interesting conversations in your head and seeing the emotions on your friends' faces? Do you enjoy imagining alternate conversations or experiences, ones that never happened—and perhaps never should happen—in real life?

On a loftier plane, we all also imagine the future course of our lives, with greater or lesser detail, and we replay important life events with some regularity: from childhood memories and first love to accidents and other traumas. These past events are not fiction. They actually happened, and we recall many details of those events with high accuracy. But we now know that the way we remember them is based on a creative process involving mental simulation that is very similar to our acts of imagination.

Do men and women differ in their real-life simulations? Is there a gender gap for real-life simulations that parallels the gender gap for reading fiction?

THE GENDER GAP IN STORIES *(27)*

In a word, yes. Men and women differ in the way they remember *and* tell *and* write about real-life stories. In study after study, women consistently report longer, more vivid, and more detailed memories of real-life events compared to men.[24] From in-depth analysis of these details, it is apparent that women specifically recall more mental states—thoughts and feelings, their own and others'—as well as the sights and sounds and smells of the past event. They also focus more on relationships in their stories of real-life events than do men, and they use reported speech more often: "And *then* she said, 'I'm not gonna get in the car with *you!*' So of course I said, 'Oh yes you are!'" Dialogue enlivens a story by helping the listener take the perspective of the characters.

Let's compare Charlie and Anna talking about their teenage travels.

First, here is Charlie's terse story of his experiences working overseas after high school:

> I went to America for a year and worked over there. It was just an awesome experience. I worked over there and a few hobbies I liked before I left, I like hunting and stuff, so I worked as a hunting guide. Worked in a ranch and did a bit of snowboarding and stuff.

Next, consider Anna's elaborate story of camping at an animal park in the summers:

> We would have like a mini New Year's out there and like we'd throw our glow sticks in the air and have a good time. It was just so fun. We used to, uh, feed the animals as well. So like, um, the guy would, there'd be like specific times of the day, so like at morning and at night or in the afternoon we'd feed the animals and like, we could throw grain over, um, and like feed the horses and stuff. 'Cause like, oh, what's it called, there was a pig, forgot what are they called, it doesn't matter, um, kunekune pig! Um, super cute. And (laughs) his name was Porky, he just ate all the scraps. So basically the whole camp would bring together the scraps and would feed it to Porky the pig, which was great (laughs). Oh yeah, you go on like night walks. So like um, he'd take you on like, just a walk around the park at night and like where you might see more nocturnal animals but not really really. Yeah, but, it was fun anyways. Yeah, it was good. It was the thing that you'd always look forward to at the end of the year. Like, you're like, "Oh my gosh, I'm going camping."

Although Charlie tells us his trip was an "awesome experience," from this sparse account we aren't able to visualize his work as a hunting guide the way we are able to see Anna's campground throughout the day and into the evening. Anna's story is also filled with characters—from the guy who ran the camp to the other kids throwing their glow sticks to Porky the kunekune pig—whereas Charlie doesn't mention a single other creature, human or nonhuman, alive or dead.

Psychologists Azriel Grysman and Judith Hudson conducted a systematic review across all the published studies on gender differences in real-life stories up to the 2010s.[25] They concluded that these differences in the internal landscapes of men's and women's stories exist across a wide range of methodologies and ages (although most of the research so far has focused on European Americans). Women's stories are simply more replete in talk about relationships and internal states than men's. Women even rate their own past emotional experiences—positive and negative—as more central to their lives than do men.

Another study by Grysman helps us understand this female memory advantage.[26] He asked undergraduate men and women to write descriptions of everyday events within a day after they occurred. Two to three months later, he called them into the lab for a surprise memory test. The women recalled the events with greater detail, especially for internal details such as emotions, thoughts, and perceptions. This memory advantage was completely parallel to their richer descriptions of internal states soon after the event had happened. Even as women are living their lives, they are noticing and encoding more emotional and sensory details of events compared to men.

Yet this binary view of gender doesn't begin to capture the individual differences in mental simulation abilities. Because our gender identity does not always line up with our biological sex, Grysman and colleagues also tested the role of each for this female memory advantage in an online sample with a wider age range.[27] Both biological sex and gender identity uniquely accounted for differences in mental simulation in participants' real-life stories. Biological females and people who identified more with stereotypically feminine traits (such as being warm and gentle) were more likely to write personal narratives rich in emotions and factual and sensory details. Biological males and people who identified more with stereotypically masculine traits (such as being competitive and independent) were more likely to write personal narratives light on emotion and high on themes of agency. In other words, the gender gap in their narratives couldn't be reduced simply to either biological sex or to gender identity; both forces work together to create a gender gap in stories.

Altogether, it's clear that many women are reading more fiction than most men and they're talking together about fiction more often. When women do watch TV and movies, they choose shows that focus on people and relationships. They tell real-life stories that are richer in internal states. In short, many women are consistently engaging in mental simulation more often than most men on an everyday basis. The ease with which many women simulate helps explain why they enjoy reading fiction so much more than most men do—it is simply easier for most women to visualize entire worlds from mere words than it is for many men, which may explain why many men are drawn instead to visual stories. In turn, the daily workout many women undergo when they read about their own and others' mental states contributes to their greater theory of mind and empathy.

DO THESE GENDER DIFFERENCES REALLY MATTER?

Are women better than men at reading other people's minds and at empathizing with others? Well, yes. Women consistently score higher on the Mind in the Eyes test than men.[28] It's not a huge advantage—not anywhere near the male advantage for the velocity with which they throw a ball[29]—but it is undeniably a skill at which women are somewhat better. Women (and humanities majors, not coincidentally) also consistently score higher than men (and science majors) on standard measures of empathy,[30] which tap the degree to which we feel what another person is feeling. Try out the most popular empathy scale, the Davis scale, at https://www. eckerd.edu/psychology/iri/. In fact, the transportation scale mentioned earlier is one of four dimensions of empathy on this scale: the others tap perspective-taking (theory of mind), empathic concern, and personal distress at others' misfortunes. Anna and Tia, for instance, both earned high scores of 79 on the Davis scale, well above the average score in *Origins* of 64. In contrast, Charlie's score of 58 fell short, mostly due to his lower scores on perspective-taking and transportation into stories. Mega-reader/ viewer/gamer Joe, on the other hand, garnered the top score of the whole sample at 94.

Recall from Chapter 1 that the default network of the brain is active whenever we are empathizing with others' feelings, taking others' perspectives, remembering past events, and imagining future events, as well as when we are simply "thinking about nothing" (also known as "resting state").[31] Exciting new brain-imaging projects that pool data across research sites around the world, such as the Human Connectome Project, are showing that women on average have greater connectivity in the brain's default network than men.[32] (Think of connectivity as synchronicity of activity across distant brain regions, probably because they are anatomically connected and "communicating" with each other.)[33] The authors of one of these studies suggest that men's lower connectivity across these brain regions reflects a greater tendency to develop specialized skills (such as spatial orientation), whereas women's higher brain connectivity reflects a greater tendency to develop integrative skills that require synchronization across cortical networks (such as language).[34] Understanding fictional and real-life stories requires high levels of integration across the hubs of the default network.

Researchers are now working on connecting these gender differences at the neural level to the gender differences in self-reported empathy and in observed real-life behavior.[35] For instance, women's and men's neural responses of empathy in functional magnetic resonance imaging (fMRI) scans are correlated with their scores on self-report empathy scales. In one important study by neuroscientist Tania Singer and colleagues, both men and women showed neural responses of empathy to the pain of others who had played fairly in an online game.[36] But when actors who had played unfairly in the game received a painful shock, only the women and not the men responded with empathy at the neural level. Men instead had neural responses of satisfaction when the unfair players were punished.

One possible reason for the gender gap in fiction reading is that many women, with their slightly better theory-of-mind and empathy skills, prefer to exercise this capacity on a daily basis by reading about and viewing fictional mental states. We all gravitate toward things we're good at, and if we're good at something, it's more likely that we'll enjoy it and do it even more, a virtuous cycle. (In Chapter 3, I will trace how these skills and reading habits develop from the very beginning of life.) The upshot is that by adulthood, most women have read much more fiction than most men, and they correspondingly have slightly better social understanding skills.

Of course, reading about and watching fictional lives is not the only way to develop social understanding. Tia, who does not read or watch fiction as often as Anna, has equally advanced empathy skills. No doubt she is honing them every day in real life through her work with young children as an early childhood teacher.

Fortunately, the experimental studies show that both men and women accrue the same (small) benefits from reading a short passage of fiction.[37] So although men score lower on average on theory of mind and empathy than women, they grow from reading fiction to the same extent as women. When we can entice men to read fiction or write about their difficult experiences (under duress, it seems, or for course credit), these stories hone their social attunement. It turns out that men also ramp up their empathy when they are paid to do so, showing that the gender difference is *not* due to men's lack of ability to empathize.[38] Parallel benefits of mental simulation for men and women are also apparent in the expressive writing studies. In a meta-analysis by psychologist Joanne Frattaroli of 146 expressive writing studies, men and women experienced similar health benefits from writing about their most difficult real-life experiences.[39]

At first blush, the implications seem large. If we could just get men to read more fiction and to be more expressive about their real-life experiences, they would understand people better, they would feel better, and their health would improve, right? Perhaps, but enticing people who don't like novels to read fiction on a regular basis, and encouraging those who are not naturally expressive to talk or write about their deepest thoughts and feelings, may not be so easy. Baron-Cohen talks about the "male brain" that is more interested in objects and how they work than in people and relationships.[40] In fact, he thinks of autism as an extreme version of the male brain; although autism may be underdiagnosed in women, population studies show much higher rates of autism among males than females. Neuroscientists are now linking the empathy and theory-of-mind deficits of autism spectrum disorder to atypical patterns in the default network.[41] In the general population, these differences in social understanding between men and women are mostly slight. However, trying to get most men to read fiction when they are simply not as interested in understanding others' emotions and intentions may be about as fruitful as trying to get most women to practice their ball-throwing skills. Sure, we would definitely improve with practice, but what if we simply don't care how fast or how well we throw a ball?

Recently, my adult sons, Ben and Dylan, have been trying to help me learn to throw a ball for our labradoodle Tui. Our practice sessions at the local field involve excruciating step-by-step instructions on how to hold my arm, where to step, when to twist. The results? Frustratingly slow for us all, including (and perhaps especially) Tui. I do think I'm getting slightly better, although Ben and Dylan may disagree. Of course, some women excel at reading fiction *and* at throwing balls and other objects, such as my friend Evelyn Tribble—a world-renowned Shakespeare scholar[42] and prize-winning hammer thrower.

As a culture, we should stop shaming and start celebrating the few men, like Joe, who do love to read fiction. As journalist L. V. Anderson writes, "Feminists shouldn't roll our eyes at men-only book clubs. We should applaud them."[43] I hope that knowing about these gender differences in mental simulation will also help women to be more patient with their husbands, male coworkers, brothers, and fathers who don't enjoy reading or watching fiction or talking about the minute details of everyday social interactions. After all, women have to save something to discuss at book club!

Today is the first Thursday of the month, so it's time for book club. In the past 10 years together, we've been through cancer, broken bones and torn ligaments, hookups and breakups, house sales and purchases and renovations, life-threatening mishaps of pets and teenagers, the death of two parents and a sister, and, not least, the birth of three beautiful babies—two girls and a boy. What stories are in their futures?

CHAPTER 3

✺

How Children Grow to Love Stories

"And what is the use of a book," thought Alice, "without pictures or conversation?"
—Lewis Carroll, *Alice in Wonderland*

How did Anna grow up to love reading so much, whereas Charlie is lukewarm about books? All aspects of a child's development arise from a complex interplay of nature and nurture over time, a call-and-response cycle between genetics and environment from before birth and throughout life. Scientists have not yet traced the epigenetics of story, but we do know that nature and nurture interact to create children who love stories. This story starts near the very beginning of life.

THE NATURE AND NURTURE OF STORIES

In the last trimester of pregnancy, the fetus is learning the sound of their mother's voice. (Fathers' voices are farther away and less distinct in utero, so most babies do not learn their fathers' voices until after they're born.) In a classic series of experiments now called *The Cat in the Hat* studies, psychologist Anthony DeCasper tested 3-day-old babies' memories for stories they had heard while still in the womb.[1] Babies cannot tell us about their memories, of course, so first DeCasper needed to help the newborns *show* us what they remembered. He did this by teaching them to suck a pacifier at different intervals, with shorter or longer intervals enabling the babies to turn on recordings of different stories. In that way, the babies were able to choose which of three stories they preferred to listen to: a recording

How Stories Change Us. Elaine Reese, Oxford University Press. © Oxford University Press 2024.
DOI: 10.1093/oso/9780197747902.003.0003

of their own mother reading a "familiar" passage from *The Cat in the Hat* that she had read daily for the last 6 weeks of the pregnancy, a recording of another mother reading that same passage from *The Cat in the Hat*, or a recording of their own mother reading a less familiar passage (from a carefully matched rhyming story) that she had read only once during the pregnancy—when making the recording.

Babies who had received daily reading in utero quickly learned to suck the pacifier in a pattern that turned on *The Cat in the Hat*, regardless of whose voice was on the recording. Other babies whose mothers had not read daily during their pregnancies did not show a preference for *The Cat in the Hat* over the other rhyming story. Of course, at this tender age, babies cannot understand the meaning of the words, but this study shows that newborns are already attuned to the cadence and tempo and sounds of particular stories they heard in the womb, not just to their mothers' voices. Babies are wired for stories.

Soon after they are born, some babies hear more stories than other babies.

In the *Growing Up in New Zealand* longitudinal study, we asked over 6,000 mothers to tell us if they read books to their baby, and if so, at what age they had started reading.[2] By the time their babies were 9 months old, most New Zealand mothers (84%) reported reading books with them at least once a week. But mothers varied in how early they started to read books and how often. Perhaps because of publicity arising from *The Cat in the Hat* studies, 10% of mothers said they starting reading books while their baby was still in the womb. Another third started to read to their babies in the first 6 weeks of life. Over half of the mothers, however, started to read between 6 weeks and 3 months, and the remaining mothers reported beginning after their baby was 3 months old.

I've known only two babies since the very beginning—my sons, Ben and Dylan. Ben was just shy of 6 weeks old the first time I tried to read a book with him. A multitasking mother from the start, I had taken him to a conference in Quebec City with my sister, Jen, to help out. She bought Ben's first book, a French version of *Caillou* (not yet a TV star). Although I was a new parent, I had already logged many hours of reading with young children as a babysitter, Sunday school teacher, aunt, and child development researcher.

Yet my reading debut with Ben felt awkward and mistimed. He could barely focus, and I knew the most he could perceive at that point was face-like configurations on the page. I preferred our face-to-face stories about real life, in which I would ask him a question—"Who had a big sleep today?"—and then wait expectantly for some response, if only a furrowing of the brow, before supplying an answer—"Benjamin Bunny did, that's who." Nevertheless, I persisted in sharing picture books in short bouts with Ben when he was well-fed and alert. Perhaps because book-sharing is not easy with infants, parents in the *Growing Up in New Zealand* study reported reading more often to their first-born children than to their subsequent children.[3] Parents of only one child may simply have more time and energy to pour into these interactions.

From the beginning, babies react in different ways to stories, just as they react in different ways to everything else in their world. Every parent knows that each baby is unique, with his or her own rhythms and reactions to the world. Scientists have shown that by the time babies are a few months old, each has a somewhat reliable temperament.[4] The self is by no means fully fledged, but each and every baby has a consistent way of responding to the world that will later evolve into what we call personality in adolescence and adulthood.

In the first year of life, the most reliable portents are the baby's tendencies to be happy versus sad, to be sociable versus shy, to be fearful versus brave, to be distractible versus attentive, and to be able to regulate their bodies and their emotions (or not). Although there is a great deal of research on these early temperamental differences, there's little research on which aspects might be most vital for children's growing love of stories.

So far, social attention skills are proving to be the most important predictor of how babies respond to stories from books *and* real life.

Babies' social attention skills begin with a focus on the human face. From the start, baby girls focus more on the human face than do baby boys, who focus more on objects. Psychologist Jennifer Connellan, one of Simon Baron-Cohen's PhD students, demonstrated this effect in an elegant study.[5] Connellan visited mothers and their newborns while still in the hospital. When babies were quiet and alert, Connellan either gazed at them with a neutral expression or showed them a ball-shaped mobile which displayed a scrambled but symmetrical arrangement from a photo of her face. (The effect is a bit creepy.) Many baby girls preferred Connellan's real face instead of the scrambled face on the mobile, whereas many baby boys, despite the creepiness, preferred the mobile instead of her real face. Of course, there were some baby boys (25%) who preferred Connellan's face, and some baby girls (17%) who preferred the mobile. For both boys and girls, babies' preference for objects has been traced to higher testosterone levels during pregnancy.[6]

Babies' attention skills continue to develop over the first year, with a milestone at around 9 months when they begin to coordinate their attention to objects with their attention to humans, especially to their parents.[7]

This is the advent of triadic *joint attention*—among self, another person, and an object—a critical social-cognitive skill that is much harder for children on the autism spectrum to develop. By this age, typically developing babies are beginning to share their focus with parents on an object, such as a book. What does this advance mean for book-reading with a baby?

A baby is developing joint-attention skills if, when they are interested in a picture in a book, they point and then look back and forth between their parent's eyes and the picture. Joint attention represents a cognitive leap in their thinking because they are now able to coordinate their attention to two things at once.

Joint attention is also a social leap. When a baby coordinates their gaze between a parent and an object, they are also gauging their parent's reaction and changing their behavior accordingly—shall I touch this new object or not? Do I like it or am I scared of it? In study after study, baby girls (on average) show higher rates of joint attention and more advanced processing of facial expressions than do baby boys.[8] Parents also rate baby girls as better than baby boys at maintaining and shifting attention.[9] Critically, neuroimaging research shows that the development of joint attention in babies and toddlers corresponds with changes in functional connectivity across brain regions, especially between visual areas and the regions of the default network that I described in Chapter 2.[10]

Parents respond in kind. In the *Longitudinal Study of Australian Children*, psychologists Brad Farrant and Stephen Zubrick found that when babies showed higher rates of joint attention at 9 months, their parents reported spending more time reading with them over the next 2 years.[11] When a baby looks attentively at the pictures in the book, it's easy to continue reading books with that baby. It's much harder to keep sharing books with a baby who cries or looks away or even smacks a book out of your hands.

We are the same people with each child that we parent, but we are different parents to each child. Psychologists and co-grandparents Judy Dunn and Robert Plomin talk about the way mothers and fathers parent each child differently as a result of being more experienced, or more tired or stressed, but also because each child's temperament evokes different reactions from parents.[12] These "nonshared" environmental influences within the same family (along with each child's unique experiences in the world) are a powerful force in exacerbating differences among siblings' personalities and preferences. (Dunn and Plomin are also a fascinating real-life coupling of nurture and nature with Dunn's focus on environmental influences and Plomin's focus on genetic influences in child development.)

The few studies that exist on how parents adapt their book-reading to their babies' temperament suggest, fortunately, that parents who rate their

HOW CHILDREN GROW TO LOVE STORIES *(37)*

babies as showing more distress than other babies eventually find ways to read *more* often, not less often, with these children over time.[13] So if you are landed with a book-hating baby, don't give up. With patience and creativity, it's possible to turn even these babies into story lovers.

My second son, Dylan, was an action baby; he started walking at a mere 10 months. From then on, he preferred to do just about anything other than sit quietly with a book. I adapted to Dylan's temperament by reading books to him at bedtime, when he was slightly less active, and by sticking to books that I knew he would like. Dogs, rodents, and rabbits were always safe bets, so we read all the *Clifford* and *Maisie* books, and he adored *Max and Ruby*.

Alongside their growing social attention skills, babies' speech is also progressing rapidly from cooing vowel sounds at about 2 months (*aaah*, *oooh*) to babbling consonant-vowel combinations at about 4–6 months (*ba-ba-ba, do-do-do*). Later in the first year of life, babies are beginning to understand simple words—starting with their own name—even if they can't say these words yet.[14] Coinciding with joint attention at around 9 months, babies start pointing to and showing objects to anyone who will look, an action that powerfully evokes a label from many adults in Western cultures ("That's a _____.").[15]

The real rumpus begins, however, from 12 months onward. It is around their first birthday that many babies produce their first recognizable, referential word, although there are many garbled contenders in the lead-up.[16] Around age 1, babies also start pointing more regularly to people and objects in books[17] and in life, both on their own and when adults ask, "Where's the ___?" All of these new communication skills combine to make book-reading more fun for parents, and this means parents and toddlers alike are going to turn to books more often.

Ben was 13 months old when we took an ill-advised road trip from west Texas to Oregon for my sabbatical at the University of Oregon. I spent most of the ride in the back seat beside Ben as entertainer/soother/feeder/wiper. We had only a few books with us that he'd received for his first birthday party with family. One was a schlocky version of *The Little Red Hen*, complete with a rubber hen on the front that squawked when Ben pushed it, and again, and again. I can't even count the number of times I read that book to him on that trip. What I remember best is one moment when I asked him, "Where's the little red hen?," not expecting an answer. He placed his pudgy finger right on the eponymous hen, not on her chicks or the dog or the mouse or the cat. It had taken a year from that first awkward reading of *Caillou*, but he—and I—were finally hooked on books.

REAL-LIFE STORIES ARRIVE ON THE STAGE

Within a few short months of uttering their first words, toddlers start to refer to the past and the future.[18] At first, these words refer to just-completed actions (*'Nana* [banana] *all gone*) or hoped-for events (*More 'nana*). As a parent, these baby sentences may not seem any more amazing than the first time you heard your toddler proclaim (*'Nana!* for a banana right in front of them. Take a moment—right now—to think about what these past and future references entail for a toddler. The banana itself is no longer in front of them; they must instead be relying on a mental image of a banana, coupling their name for the object (*'Nana*) with a word marking past (*all gone*) or future (*more*), even though they cannot yet use past or future tense. They are also communicating their likes and dislikes, wishes and fears, to another person. These utterances about past and future are simultaneously a cognitive, linguistic, and social milestone—all by a mere 18 months of age. They can now share with others the heretofore invisible contents of their own minds.

These crude sentences about past and future open a floodgate for real-life stories to flow into a child's life, alongside the stories they may already be getting from books.

Soon after referring to events a few moments away from the present, toddlers quickly move on to talk about events from the past day and the next day, last week and next week, last month and next month. By the time they are 2 years old, they are able to refer to events that occurred up to 6 months previously—a quarter of a lifetime for a toddler. This period of 18–24 months is a time of especially rapid language acquisition, often called the "naming explosion," in which toddlers are primed to talk.[19]

Supporting these dramatic changes in language and thinking, toddlers' brain development is also changing rapidly. A notable change is increased functional connectivity in the default network, especially via the posterior cingulate hub that supports higher-order thinking, including remembering.[20] Critically, toddlers who have been diagnosed with autism already show brain differences in functional connectivity compared to neurotypical toddlers or those diagnosed with language delay.[21]

The way parents and other adults converse with toddlers about books and real life is vital for many aspects of their development. Parents' conversational turn-taking with toddlers between 18 and 24 months, even more than how many words parents say, predicts their children's language and IQ scores 10 years later.[22] Psychologist Rachel Romeo and team took the next step to show that children whose parents use more conversational turns show greater activation in a functional magnetic resonance image (fMRI)

HOW CHILDREN GROW TO LOVE STORIES *(39)*

scanner in Broca's area (the language production part of the brain) when hearing a story read aloud.[23] The greater the activation in Broca's area while hearing the story, the more advanced the children's language development. Simple turn-taking between adults and young children spells brain development and language skill.

Another critical feature of adults' speech for children's language learning is to talk about what children are looking at, not to redirect children's attention. When a parent supplies a label for an object their toddler is already gazing at, their toddler will learn that new word much more rapidly than if the parent draws their attention to a new object.[24] When their babies are more attentive, parents converse more often in these supportive ways while reading books and telling stories together. Those babies grow into toddlers with better language skills, and those toddlers eventually grow into preteens with greater verbal skills.[25]

At our first *Origins* visit to 18-month-old Anna at home, she is adorable with blond pigtails sprouting straight out either side of her head. She gazes at her mother raptly as they reminisce about a recent visit to a friend's farm:

MOTHER: *Can you tell Mummy about when we went to the farm?*
ANNA: *Ahhhh.*
MOTHER: *What did we see at the farm?*
ANNA: *Ah dadadadada um.*
MOTHER: *Little baby lamb, lamb. Clever girl. What did you do to the lambs? (pause) What did you do to the lambs at the farm?*
ANNA: *Ahh.*
MOTHER: *What did you give to the lambs?*
ANNA: *Is a baaa (lamb sound)*
MOTHER: *Baby lamb. Did you give them a bottle?*
ANNA: *Yes.*
MOTHER: *You did! What was in the bottle?*
ANNA: *Ah.*
MOTHER: *What was in the bottle?*
ANNA: *Milk.*
MOTHER: *Clever girl. Milk in the bottle.*

Notice how most of Anna's mother's questions require more than a yes-or-no answer ("What did you see?" "What did you give to the lambs?" "What was in the bottle?"). Although Anna isn't contributing many actual words to the conversation, her mother praises her profusely on those few occasions, and then adds a bit more ("Clever girl. Milk in the bottle.") All of these strategies combine to boost children's language skills.[26]

GIRLS GAIN GROUND EARLY

And—you guessed it—the toddlers with the largest vocabularies tend to be girls. In the *Growing Up in New Zealand* study, we found large gaps at age 2 between the vocabulary size of boys and girls: Girls already spoke (on average) nearly 10% more words than boys.[27] Anna and Charlie had similar vocabularies at 18 months, but by age 2-1/2, Anna's vocabulary had shot ahead to be one of the highest in the sample, whereas Charlie's stayed at the average.

To her credit, Charlie's mother tried hard to have conversations with him over the years we visited him. Sturdy, cherubic Charlie would tell her "I wanna play with toys" or "Can I get up now?" instead of sitting still and reminiscing. At one point his mum pleads, "Can you please keep talking to me?" to which his older sister, Jessica, volunteers "I will!" in Charlie's stead. Anna and Jessica were simply more willing than Charlie was to sit quietly and converse.

Remember the finding that women are slightly better on average than men at theory of mind and show higher levels of empathy? Empathy, which relies on the early-maturing limbic structures of the brain, is evident in young children before they are capable of first-order theory of mind (understanding others' false beliefs), which relies on the later-maturing prefrontal and temporal cortices of the default network.[28] In several large longitudinal studies, toddler girls already show more concern for another's distress than do toddler boys, and this gender difference is consistent once it appears.[29]

Add to this advantage the gender differences in play that start to emerge in toddlerhood. Across all mammalian species, not just humans, young males prefer active and rough-and-tumble play, and young females prefer quiet play (such as book-reading—for humans, at least).[30] These early play preferences are linked to testosterone levels in males and females.[31] Of course, some boys prefer quiet play and some girls prefer rough-and-tumble play; there are far greater differences among boys, and among girls, than there are differences between boys and girls. Yet these small overall differences in play preferences combine with girls' stronger attention and empathy and language to create a heady mix for their burgeoning love of stories and, later, of reading.

The gender lines intensify further in the preschool years as children are trying to figure out the categories in their world—starting with the category of gender.[32] What are the rules? Where are the boundaries? At first, young children see the world in strict binaries. Even the children of psychologists who study gender stereotypes are not immune: Researcher

Marjorie Rhodes was surprised when her 3-year-old son announced one day, "Boys play guitars."[33] Preschoolers' rigid gender rules are most often applied to roles in the dramatic play corner ("You be the daddy/prince/husband") and to some highly sex-typed toys ("Boys don't play with My Little Ponies") rather than to books. Fortunately, preschoolers still see books as fairly gender-neutral. But the act of book-reading requires sitting down, so it is quiet rather than active play, which girls gravitate toward more than boys.

Yet another factor that works against preschool boys has to do with the books available to them. Did you know that preschool boys are *six times* more likely than preschool girls to have intense interests in taxonomies of creatures or objects—typically dinosaurs or vehicles (cars, trucks, trains)?[34] This predilection for restricted interests is linked to fetal testosterone levels for both boys and girls.[35] These intense interests can make it more difficult for parents and teachers to find books that boys will like. When I tried to read Dylan a book about anything besides a dog or rodent or rabbit, I had very little success. The mismatch between some boys' interests and the books we read to them works to turn some boys farther away from books and from reading. But do not assume that all boys prefer to read nonfiction. Literacy scholar Margaret Merga showed that it is a small minority of boys (17%) who read mostly nonfiction; nearly half of boys instead read mostly fiction, with the remainder reading roughly equal amounts of both.[36]

The culmination of all of these forces is that parents spend more time reading with their daughters than with their sons in the first 5 years of life. On a daily basis these differences are tiny. When economists Michael Baker and Kevin Milligan analyzed large datasets from three Western countries (the United States, the United Kingdom, and Canada), they found that parents read an average of only 3 minutes longer in each book session with girls than with boys.[37] However, these tiny differences add up to an extra 90 hours of book-reading with girls than boys over the first 5 years of life if parents read with their children once a day, even more if they have multiple sessions per day. Baker and Milligan argue that parents simply find it easier to have extended book-reading sessions with girls than boys, due to boys being slightly more active and less attentive, and girls having more advanced joint-attention and language skills.

For all these reasons, many girls continue to collect more experiences with stories from books than most boys in a cascading cycle of nature and nurture. Book club promoters Jenna Bush Hager and Reese Witherspoon recall with nostalgia their parents and grandparents reading to them from a young age. Both credit their love of books to those precious early stories they heard aloud. Reese Witherspoon remembers her grandmother reading whole novels to her, often Southern literature like *To Kill a Mockingbird*: "I just remember loving storytelling, because she would do all the different voices for me. It made me fall in love with books. She came alive while she was reading."[38]

QUALITY MATTERS, TOO

When parents read a picture book with their young child, they don't just read the text. Parents ask questions about the pictures and talk about the story. We now know through scores of studies that these book "conversations" help children around the world to develop oral language as well as socioemotional and theory-of-mind skills.[39]

Two crucial elements of a high-quality book conversation involve parents discussing the characters' thoughts and feelings and relating the characters' experiences to their children's own lives—a form of reminiscing. In the following example, a mother and her 4-year-old son, Nick, from one of our studies read a book about New Zealand birds called *Ferguson's Night Fright*.

TEXT: *"My name is Ferguson," the fantail said, "and I got lost today.*
My mum, she told me when I went out not to play too far a . . .?"
NICK: *Waaaay*
MOTHER: *I wonder if the mum's worried where Ferguson is, and the mum's gone out searching for him.*
NICK: *Mmmm*
MOTHER: *Because when you got lost at the stadium, we went searching for you. I ran up and down the stairs, and I asked people had they seen a little boy, and I called your name, 'cause I was very worried.*
NICK: *Someone else had already got me.*
MOTHER: *Somebody had found you, hadn't they?*
NICK: (nods head yes)
MOTHER: *Yeah, and then you were brave, weren't you?*
NICK: (nods head yes)
MOTHER: *You weren't crying when you were with the person, were you?*
NICK: (shakes head no)
MOTHER: *No.*

Although girls are engaging more often than boys in these book conversations, when parents of sons do sit down to read a book, their conversations are of a similar quality to parents of daughters.[40] Fortunately, adults and preschool children can have high-quality conversations about e-books, too, even over video chat, as long as the e-book is a basic version without too many "bells and whistles" that can distract children (and parents) from discussing the pictures and the storyline.[41]

For infants and toddlers, who do not learn as well from screens as from face-to-face interactions, print books are still best.[42] There are countless wonderful picture books for babies and young children these days: see Common Sense Media for ideas. But really any book will do—the quality of the conversation is more important for children's development than the quality of the book itself.

Books aren't the only stories that help children's development.

Real life offers countless free opportunities for stories. These ready-made stories that parents tell together with their young children—like the story Anna's mother created about their farm visit or that Nick's mother told about when he got lost at the stadium—also advance children's oral language and socioemotional skills.[43]

For instance, psychologists Penny van Bergen and Karen Salmon and team coached one group of parents to reminisce about emotions when telling real-life stories with their preschoolers.[44] Parents in a control group instead learned to play more collaboratively with their children. Six months later, the children of mothers who learned the reminiscing techniques used more emotion words in their conversations together. In turn, their children were better at understanding what events might cause them to feel certain emotions (happy, sad, angry, scared) compared to children of mothers in the play group. My PhD advisor, Robyn Fivush, argues that reminiscing may be a particularly effective way to help children understand their emotions because the discussions take place when children are calmer and no longer in the grip of the emotion.[45]

Note the way one mother explores her son Jesse's emotions—both positive and negative—during a recent haircut, a commonplace event but one that can be distressing for many young children:[46]

MOTHER: *What was the first thing he [the barber] did?*
JESSE: *Bzzzz (running his hand over his head).*
MOTHER: *He used the clippers, and I think you liked the clippers. And you know how I know? Because you were smiling.*
JESSE: *Because they were tickling.*
MOTHER: *They were tickling, is that how they felt? Did they feel scratchy?*
JESSE: *No.*
MOTHER: *And after the clippers, what did he use then?*
JESSE: *The spray.*
MOTHER: *Yes. Why did he use the spray?*

CHILD: (silent)

MOTHER: He used the spray to tidy your hair. And I noticed that you closed your eyes, and I thought "Jesse's feeling a little bit scared," but you didn't move or cry and I thought you were being very brave.

Together, these conversations about emotions from books and real life are powerful agents for children's budding socioemotional skills. With my colleague, Elizabeth Schaughency, along with speech-language therapist Jane Carroll and former PhD students Amanda Clifford, Shika Das, and Jessica Riordan, we have been trialing different ways of talking about books and real life with preschoolers. We call our program *Tender Shoots*, drawing from a Māori *whakatauki* or proverb, *Grow tender shoots for the days of our world*.[47] The study is a gold-standard randomized-controlled trial in which we compared three groups of children and their parents. In two of the groups, we asked parents and children to read the same 12 picture books over 6 weeks, such as the classic Paul Galdone version of *The Three Billy Goats Gruff*. However, we taught only one group of parents to talk about mental states during and after the reading, linking to children's real-life experiences (called *Rich Reading and Reminiscing*).[48] For instance, after reading *The Three Billy Goats Gruff*, parents in this group reminisced about a time their child was brave. Six weeks later, the children and parents in this group had increased their mental state talk in reminiscing conversations.[49] This increase in talk, particularly for emotions about negative events, later helped children's story and emotion understanding, their conflict resolution skills, and even their impulse control over the next year.[50]

These conversations about books and real life also helped children's oral language skills. One year after the trial had ended, when children were 6 years old, those children in the Rich Reading and Reminiscing group retold a new story they had just heard using more detail compared to children in the other two groups.[51] They specifically used more dialogue in their retellings, indicating a higher degree of mental simulation and vividness in their memories of the story. Children's storytelling skills are in turn linked to better reading comprehension later in primary school.[52]

These positive effects of *Tender Shoots* are a childhood version of the benefits that adults experience when they read fiction and tell and write real-life stories. Children simply need more help accessing the emotional causes and consequences embedded in stories from books and real life.

Cultural differences do exist in how often—and how—parents read books and reminisce with young children.[53] For instance, my former PhD student Tia Neha asked Māori parents, who are oral storytellers par excellence, to reminisce with their children about a time the child misbehaved.[54]

HOW CHILDREN GROW TO LOVE STORIES *(45)*

In their conversations, parents clearly identified what they didn't like about their children's misbehavior, but then resolved the event sensitively with a focus on future good behavior using a practice called *poipoia* that protects children's *mauri* (positive energy). Here is an example from a mother and her daughter, Marama.

MOTHER: *Can you remember the naughty thing that we were gonna talk about?*
MARAMA: *When I hit you.*
MOTHER: *Yeah.*
MARAMA: *And then my dad came.*
MOTHER: *That's right. Why did you do that?*
MARAMA: *'Cause you were do, cause you didn't let me do something.*
MOTHER: *Oh. And what happened when you hit mummy?*
MARAMA: *Went into time out.*
MOTHER: *Mmm. Was that fun?*
MARAMA: *Nope.*
MOTHER: *So what did you decide after that?*
MARAMA: *Say sorry.*
MOTHER: *Yeah. And? Can you remember the other thing you decided?*
MARAMA: *Ah not to hit you again.*
MOTHER: *That's right. Good girl. And have you hit mummy since then?*
MARAMA: *Mmm, can't remember.*
MOTHER: *I'm sure you haven't. I'm sure you've been a good girl.*

Yet despite these cultural differences in the way parents read and reminisce with young children, across cultures shared reading and reminiscing is linked to growth in children's vocabulary, reading achievement, social understanding, and prosocial behavior.[55] In the culturally diverse *Growing Up in New Zealand* study, parents' daily book-reading when their babies were 9 months was the only "modifiable" predictor—meaning something parents can change relatively easily, unlike their education or socioeconomic levels—of children's later flourishing.[56]

When adults explicitly discuss the connections between books and real life, over time children's narrative, social, and emotional skills will grow.[57] Versions of these storybook and reminiscing conversations even help children with autism develop in their communication and theory-of-mind skills.[58] If you are a parent, grandparent, aunt or uncle, or a preschool teacher interested in learning these techniques, please see my book *Tell Me a Story* and my website, https://www.elainereese.org/, for more ideas. For children with autism, see Tiffany Hutchins' and Ashley Brien's (CCC-SLP) guide, *Supporting Social Learning in Autism: An Autobiographical Memory Program to Promote Communication and Connection.*

WHAT ABOUT STORIES FROM TV AND MOVIES?

In our *Tender Shoots* project, would we have found similar benefits from asking parents to talk about movies or TV shows instead of talking about books and real life? Perhaps, but I expect that any benefits would depend on the content of the show and on the quality of the resulting conversation. Psychologist Gabrielle Strouse found that when parents watched slow-paced video stories of popular picture books (such as Kevin Henke's *A Weekend with Wendell*) with their children, pausing throughout the video to have brief conversations, their children's language skills increased.[59] These effects are similar to those of interactive book-reading. But how often do parents watch a movie or TV show together with their children in this painstaking way?[60]

Movies, with their more complex storylines, may be better than TV shows for fostering children's language and socioemotional skills. For instance, psychologist Raymond Mar and colleagues found that preschool children whose parents reported they watched more movies had better theory-of-mind skills—with a similar association for children whose parents read them more books—but they found no association between children's TV watching and their theory of mind.[61] The authors suggest that parents may co-view and talk about movies more often than TV shows, similar to books, but so far no one has tested this hunch.

Of course, the TV shows that preschool children watch solo can also have positive effects on their learning and their socioemotional skills. For instance, there's a wealth of high-quality research now showing benefits of *Sesame Street*, *Dora the Explorer*, *Blue's Clues*, and *Clifford* for children's learning.[62] When children watch TV shows high in prosocial content (old standbys such as *Mister Rogers' Neighborhood* and *Barney & Friends* or new fare like *Special Agent Oso*, Australian hit *Bluey*, and the charming New Zealand show *Kiri and Lou*), a meta-analysis showed they became more altruistic, more positive in their social interactions, and less prejudiced.[63] These effects are stronger when parents co-view the show and discuss prosocial themes, as a recent study of *Daniel Tiger's Neighborhood* showed.[64] Another meta-analysis showed that children have higher language development when they watch more shows with educational content, and co-view more often with adults.[65] One longitudinal study even found that preschoolers who watched more educational TV (especially *Sesame Street*) read more books for pleasure later as teenagers.[66] Some of these effects are stronger for boys. For instance, boys benefit more in their language learning than girls when adults co-view shows with them, and boys who watched *Sesame Street* in preschool later earned better grades in high school English and were less aggressive.

Across Eastern and Western cultures, children who watch more prosocial TV programming become higher in empathy, which then translates to prosocial behavior.[67] These mediated effects parallel precisely those that researchers are finding for adults when they read fiction that is replete with social content. These positive effects of children's TV are often overlooked in our concerns about the effects of violent TV content on aggression, which I will cover in Chapter 5. To foreshadow, the size of these effects of prosocial TV content on children's prosocial behavior is virtually identical (in the weak to moderate range) to the size of the effects of violent TV content on children's aggressive behavior.[68]

New work by neuroscientist John Hutton shows that traditional picture books, however, provide the optimal brain stimulation for young children compared to screen versions. Hutton's study involved healthy 4-year-olds undergoing fMRI brain scanning while they heard or saw three different Robert Munsch stories (of *The Paper Bag Princess* fame).[69] In the audio version, children heard the story read aloud but did not see any images. In the picture book version, children heard the story while seeing illustrations from the book projected onto a screen inside the scanner. For the TV version, children watched and heard an animated version of the story in the scanner. Compared to the audio-only version, the picture book version increased functional connectivity between visual perception areas of the brain and the default network by 55%. In contrast, compared to the picture book version, the TV version actually *decreased* functional connectivity between visual perception and the default network by 37%, and between visual perception and language networks by a startling drop of 82%. Children's visual brain regions were understimulated by the audio version, and so overstimulated by the TV version of the story that they weren't able to integrate the images with the storyline as they were in the picture book version.

Hutton argues that picture books "turbocharge" young children's brain development with a Goldilocks-like effect of just the right level of stimulation. Another of Hutton's studies shows that children's neural responses to picture books depend on their mothers' reading style.[70] When their mothers naturally engaged in book-reading conversations while reading *The Little Engine That Could*, similar to the style we have encouraged in *Tender Shoots*, their children later showed more activation in left-hemisphere brain areas supporting complex language and emotion understanding while listening to an experimenter read short stories. Apparently a history of interactive reading helps children to process stories heard aloud at a deeper and more integrative level, and to connect with stories on an emotional level.

Best of all, these positive effects of reading picture books, and of the conversations parents have with children about books and real life, are similar for girls and boys. These parallel effects are exactly like the adult fiction-reading and expressive writing studies that produce similar benefits for women and men. So, when parents *do* take the time to talk more with their children about people's emotions and thoughts, either from fiction or real life, both boys and girls benefit.

THE GENDER GAP WIDENS

It is in the school years that the gender gap in stories begins to run deep and wide.

For starters, more boys than girls experience difficulties with reading.[71] Some of these children are poor readers because of learning disabilities such as dyslexia. Other children with attention difficulties find it hard to sit still long enough to learn to read. Still other children, predominantly boys, experience difficulties in both their learning and their attention skills that severely hamper their reading. About a third of children who have attention-deficit/hyperactivity disorder (ADHD) also have a reading disability.[72] Even boys without disabilities report that it's hard to find books that they like to read; primary-school classrooms are stocked with books chosen mainly by female teachers. New Zealand's National Library has wonderful suggestions for school librarians when selecting books that children, boys and girls alike, actually want to read.[73]

A less-researched reason is that by school age, some children (often other boys) start bullying boys who like to read, especially those boys who like to read anything that might be perceived as a "girly" book. For instance, in a qualitative study of gender boundaries in reading, researcher Elizabeth Dutro relays an anecdote about a 5-year-old boy who chose *Beauty and the Beast* at library time.[74] He was immediately mocked by other boys: "Ha ha, he's a girl, he's a girl." The little boy rapidly re-shelved the fairy tale and chose another book. When Dutro asked 10-year-old boys about their reading preferences, one told her, "Us boys like to read football and boys' stuff." In contrast, girls are allowed to freely cross gender lines in book choice, along with other activities.[75]

At home, boys see their mothers reading more often than their fathers, especially fiction.[76] According to a prepandemic survey by the United Kingdom's National Literacy Trust, school-age boys already report reading less often than girls in their spare time and enjoying reading less—only 46% of boys reported enjoying reading "very much" or "quite a lot" compared to 60% of girls.[77]

To further exacerbate this gender gap in reading skill and interest, many parents stop reading aloud altogether when their children (girls and boys) enter school. A 2018 Scholastic survey found that 45% of parents in the United States were still reading aloud to their children by the time they were 6 to 8 years old, an increase from 38% in 2016.[78] However, that percentage dipped to 21% of 9- to 11-year-old children. In contrast, nearly all of their children (83%) independently reported that they loved or liked being read to aloud at home, with the top reason that it was a special time with their parents. As one articulate 8-year-old said, "I like it when my mom reads to me. I enjoy the time together and we get to read harder chapter books. I can't wait to see how the story ends."

Think about the limited vocabulary and storylines of the books they're able to read on their own at this age, and it's clear why they wish you still read aloud to them. Psychologist Sebastian Suggate showed that even at ages 8 and 10, children's ability to learn new words from stories was better when they heard an adult read aloud than when they encountered those same words when reading silently on their own.[79] Also, even though "hook books" for new readers have increased dramatically in quality, they can't match the complexity of longer chapter books that children can still only access from someone reading aloud to them, either live or digitally. My favorite hook books are Dav Pilkey's *Captain Underpants* and his hysterical new series *Dog Man*—I wish this one had been around when Dylan was a beginner reader. Hook books targeted to girls exist too; see Gecko Press' beautiful series *My Happy Life*. Gecko Press even has a book list for children struggling with dyslexia.

By age 10, girls outperform boys in international reading tests in countries all around the world.[80]

HOW PARENTS, TEACHERS, AND LIBRARIANS CAN HELP

As babies, many girls start out with more of all of the qualities that promote oral language, and then parents and teachers build on these strengths throughout early childhood, adding up to girls reading earlier and enjoying reading more. But biology is not destiny—state-of-the-art twin studies tell us that the lion's share of young children's oral language skill is due to environmental factors rather than to genetic factors.[81] With patience and creativity and persistence, we can help boys become better talkers *and* better readers.[82]

It is a different story for the origins of women's ultimate preference for fiction in their reading, and men's ultimate preference for nonfiction. It's entirely possible that these preferences stem from girls' early tendencies toward people and empathy and emotional expression, and for boys' early tendencies toward objects and facts and systems. We can shape most children into readers by boosting their oral language skills, but we are unlikely to make them love one genre over another.

Our shared task as parents, teachers, and librarians is to get them reading and to keep them reading. Remember Joe, our enthusiastic male reader in *Origins* at age 20? His very first memory in life is of his kindergarten teacher reading *The Very Hungry Caterpillar* to him. If we foster a love of language in our children, before long, they *will* love to read books. They may not choose the books we envisioned them reading, but that's the wondrous aspect of parenting and of teaching—our children never fail to remind us that they are exactly and entirely themselves. And perhaps through our conversations about books and life, they will come to appreciate the emotional causes and consequences of historical and contemporary events, as well as the events in their own lives.

∽

A sea change happens once your little person can read solo. Dylan started to read on his own at age 6, skipping quickly from *Clifford* to fantasy chapter books like the *Charlie Bone* series, and the real-life based *Horrible Histories* series. Savor these moments when your child finally curls up on the couch with a book, because everything's about to change.

CHAPTER 4

✦

Growing Teens Who Use Stories Wisely

Emma has been meaning to read more ever since she was twelve years old. I have seen a great many lists of her drawing-up at various times of books that she meant to read regularly through—and very good lists they were—very well chosen, and very neatly arranged—sometimes alphabetically, and sometimes by some other rule. The list she drew up when only fourteen—I remember thinking it did her judgment so much credit, that I preserved it some time; and I dare say she may have made out a very good list now. But I have done with expecting any course of steady reading from Emma. She will never submit to any thing requiring industry and patience, and a subjection of the fancy to the understanding.

—Jane Austen, *Emma*

The tween years from 8 to 12 are the golden age of reading. It's that short window when children have the skill and the time to read on their own before they are weighed down with life's responsibilities. When I was 9, Wednesdays were library day at Bowie Elementary. The shelves of books seemed vast to me; the idea that I could pick out *any book I wanted* from that array was dizzying. Which would I choose? Madeleine L'Engle's *A Wrinkle in Time*? Or the *Diary of a Young Girl* by Anne Frank? Wednesdays are still my favorite day of the week—they have become my writing day.

This is the age when some children begin to read like a house on fire. As novelist Haruki Murakami describes his own adolescent years, "When it came to books, I greedily devoured a wide range, like I was busily shoveling coal into a blazing furnace."[1] A 2019 Common Sense Media survey shows that most tweens read for pleasure, and over a third (38%) enjoy reading with a passion.[2] Fortunately, tweens are spoiled for choice—the

How Stories Change Us. Elaine Reese, Oxford University Press. © Oxford University Press 2024.
DOI: 10.1093/oso/9780197747902.003.0004

high-quality options for young readers these days from both mainstream and independent presses are staggering. I was thrilled to see that Common Sense Media's "50 Books All Kids Should Read Before They're 12" still includes *A Wrinkle in Time* and *Anne Frank: The Diary of a Young Girl*. For something a little different, see Gecko Press' series for middle readers, such as the edgy *Harsu and the Werestoat* by New Zealand writer Barbara Else.

But reading at this age isn't just for pleasure.

BENEFITS OF BOOKS FOR TWEENS AND TEENS

It turns out that the tween years are extremely important for cementing reading skills and for creating a lifetime reading habit. Once again, children's oral language skills act as a critical foundation for independent reading to take off at this age. Children can be perfectly fine decoders of words, but if their vocabularies are small, they will not zoom ahead in their reading. Instead, they could experience what reading expert Jeanne Chall called the "4th grade slump" at around age 10.[3] These children stall out in their reading because they are not able to comprehend more advanced texts full of words they wouldn't encounter in everyday conversations: abstract words like *compassion*; technical words like *atom*; literary words like *plot*. To compound the problem, their smaller vocabularies render them less able to learn new words from their independent reading.[4] Think of the last time you tried to learn a foreign language. When you understand 9 out of the 10 words in a sentence, you can likely grasp the meaning of the unknown 10th word from context. But if you can understand only 5 out of the 10 words, you're unlikely to learn a single one of the new words.

Of course, oral language skills alone are not enough to turn children into readers: they also need to become skilled at decoding print. Journalist Emily Hanford brilliantly dissects the dangers of an exclusive focus on oral language over phonics (learning letter sounds) in beginning reading instruction in her podcast *Sold a Story*. Yet the age-old "reading wars" show us that a pendulum swing back toward an overemphasis on phonics could do children an equal disservice in terms of dampening their enjoyment of reading.[5] The best approach to reading instruction is one that is tailored to an individual child's needs and that will help them read accurately, with understanding, as quickly as possible.[6]

If reading is slow and frustrating, whether due to difficulties in comprehension or decoding, the outcome is identical: Children will read less and less. The gap between poor and good readers widens over these years. At age 12, *Origins* participant Charlie's reading was perfectly fine; his comprehension score for a fictional passage was right at the average for our sample. Anna's reading comprehension, however, had shot ahead to the gifted range. In *Origins*, the two best predictors of children's reading comprehension by age 12 were the size of their vocabularies as toddlers and their word-reading skills in the first year of school.[7] Children's language skill still matters even after they crack the code, because larger vocabularies and better narrative skills help them make sense of what they're reading. Theory-of-mind skills also support children's reading comprehension, as psychologist Serena Lecce and colleagues showed in a longitudinal study with 9-year-olds.[8] Most likely, a better theory of mind helps young readers understand story characters' intentions and motivations; this deeper insight in turn inspires them to read even more fiction, which further sharpens their theory of mind.[9]

The other reason that it's important to support children's reading for pleasure in the tween years is that it's about to drop off. Not just decrease gradually, but fall precipitously. Even voracious readers, like my son Ben, read less often for pleasure as teens. In the same 2019 US Common Sense Media survey, only 24% of teens aged 13–18 reported enjoying reading "a lot" compared to 38% of tweens aged 8–12.[10] Scholastic Books surveys have tracked this drop at ever-earlier ages over the past decade such that they now call it the "decline by nine."[11] In Scholastic's 2018 survey, only 35% of 9-year-olds report reading a book most days of the week versus 57% of 8-year-olds. Many children lose their enthusiasm for reading books soon after they've learned to read.

This dip in book-reading when crossing the threshold from child to teen is not a new phenomenon. According to Jane Austen, this pattern of teens reading books less often for pleasure than their younger counterparts goes back even to 19th-century England. In a more modern UK National Literacy Trust survey, over half (54%) of 5- to 8-year-olds reported reading daily outside class, compared to a negligible 16% of 14- to 16-year-olds.[12] Likewise, in an annual survey of American adolescents called *Monitoring the Future*, in 2016 only 16% of US high school seniors reported reading books or magazines for pleasure on a daily basis.[13]

Book-reading among today's teens is so rare that the authors of that study call it "Legacy Media," lumped together with reading magazines and newspapers, as well as with watching TV and movies. This trend of teens reading books or magazines less often for pleasure is apparent across Organisation for Economic Co-operation and Development (OECD) countries. Ironically, in 2015, *Time* magazine claimed that "We're living in a golden age of young-adult literature, when books ostensibly written for teens are equally adored by readers of every generation."[14] So why are teens reading fewer and fewer books? And what are they doing instead?

Everyone who's spent time around a tween or teen these days knows what they're doing instead. They're looking at YouTube clips and TikTok, they're scrolling and posting on social media, they're gaming. *Monitoring the Future* tracked increases in every form of digital media that correspond directly to the precipitous drop in reading. For instance, high school seniors in 2016 reported spending an average of 2.2 leisure hours a day on the Internet, up from 1.4 hours a day in 2010. Drilling down, social media and gaming have risen more modestly, from averages of around 1.4 hours a day in 2013 to 1.8 and 1.5 hours a day in 2016. The situation is similar in the United Kingdom. Since 2005, UK teens' consumption of every form of print media has decreased: fiction, magazines, newspapers, comics, poems, and technical manuals. The latest US Common Sense Media survey was conducted in 2021, still in the thick of the pandemic. Tweens' and teens' screen use had increased by 17% from 2019, but the activities they enjoyed were the same: online videos, followed by video games and social media.[15]

Yet the news is not all dire. The 2019 Common Sense Media survey reported a significant increase in teens' e-book reading from 2015 once they included books read on any device, such as a phone or tablet.[16] Over that same period, teens' book-reading time (including print and e-books) seemed to have stabilized at about 20 minutes a day. Okay, only a small portion of their total media time is spent reading books, but at least their book-reading is not continuing to go down as dramatically as it did right after the introduction of portable devices.

Teens simply have too much going on in their minds and their lives to read books for pleasure, especially when that means spending hours alone. As one 16-year-old stated, "I really don't have time to read any books that I want. I liked it better when I was younger and could read whatever I wanted." They want instead to be with their friends, whether virtually or in real life. As psychologist G. Stanley Hall noted among early 20th-century adolescents, "Some seem for a time to have no resource in themselves, but to be abjectly dependent for their happiness upon their mates."[17]

Should parents accept this dip in teens' book-reading as normal, and hope that they will return to reading for pleasure as young adults? To some extent, yes. For instance, Charlie reported hardly ever reading for pleasure at age 16; when he did read, it was mainly car magazines. In his early 20s, however, perhaps because he's no longer in school, Charlie reported he's finally reading books. As I mentioned in Chapter 2, he could recall only two books that he'd read recently, but they were actual books, not magazines. One bright spot from the pandemic was a temporary return to book-reading for young people. Children and teens in the United Kingdom reported reading books more often during lockdowns and enjoying reading more.[18] But by 2021 in the United States, tweens' and teens' reading rates were similar to prepandemic levels.[19]

Parents already have so many things they must encourage/coerce teens into doing: go to school, do their homework, help out around the house, dress semi-appropriately, participate in extracurricular activities, learn to drive, prepare for university, maintain a modicum of respect for their parents and teachers, spend a minuscule amount of time with their siblings, sleep, stay away from drugs and alcohol, and so on. What parent of a teen wants to add "make them read more books" to that to-do list?

Yet the research on what reading books for pleasure does for tweens and teens is compelling. For instance, what about all the reading and writing they say they're doing on the Internet? Does it actually contribute to their reading skill? Psychologist Lynne Duncan and colleagues classified younger and older adolescents' reading habits and measured their ability to comprehend literal and inferential information from fiction and nonfiction texts.[20] A strong pattern emerged across ages—only adolescents' reading of fiction books (excluding comics and graphic novels) and their leisure writing of texts/emails uniquely predicted their reading comprehension skills. Reading fictional books uniquely predicted higher levels of inferential text understanding. In contrast, nonfiction reading preferences were unrelated to their reading skill, and computer gaming predicted lower reading comprehension.

Fortunately, e-books do not seem to hamper older children's and adolescents' reading comprehension. Several well-conducted studies show that although children and adolescents take slightly longer to read the e-version, they comprehend just as much or even more from an e-book versus a print version.[21] And adolescents with dyslexia read even faster and comprehend more when a passage is on an e-device than in print; eye-tracking studies show that it's easier for them to attend to the shorter lines of text on smaller e-readers than on tablets or on the printed page.[22]

Critically, young people's book-reading habits can even translate into prosocial attitudes and behaviors. With over 8,000 children, the UK *Millenium Cohort Study* documented that reading for pleasure at age 7 uniquely predicted lower levels of hyperactivity and inattention and higher prosocial behavior at age 11, even for a subset of children who started out with higher levels of hyperactivity and inattention.[23] Moreover, an experimental study with young adolescents in a classroom setting found that a weekly discussion group of prosocial scenes from *Harry Potter* novels, in which Harry helped a stigmatized outgroup (such as biracial Mudbloods), reduced students' real-life prejudice against immigrants.[24] However, these benefits were present *only* if the young people identified with Harry instead of with evil Voldemort.

There are also hints that teens' enjoyment of reading is linked to better psychological well-being. A 2018 UK National Literacy Trust report documented higher life satisfaction, positive coping, and self-esteem among teens who enjoyed reading outside class, and especially those who had positive attitudes toward reading.[25] The US *Monitoring the Future* study showed that non-screen activities—such as reading print media, real-life social interactions, and sports/exercise—were linked to lower levels of depression. In contrast, screen activities—electronic device use, social media, and Internet news—were linked to higher levels of depression.[26] And the 2022 Scholastic Kids & Family Reading found that teens who read more experience better mental health, reporting fewer symptoms of anxiety, depression, and loneliness.[27] I'll say more about the dangers of gaming in Chapter 5 and of the dangers of social media in Chapter 6.

Luckily, these potential benefits for teens of reading do not seem to be based solely on reading skill but on enjoyment. In a very large sample of adolescents from two UK cohort studies, the positive links to well-being were apparent for teens who enjoyed reading more, regardless of their reading skill or how often they read.[28]

Yet so far these links between reading and well-being for teens are merely associations—we need longitudinal and experimental studies to show that reading fiction actually fosters teens' well-being. It could simply be that teens who already feel better are able to do more of these "effortful" activities of reading, engaging in live social interactions, and exercising. Perhaps books need to be specifically targeted to the problems tweens and teens might be having to make an impact. A review of nine experimental studies of such fictional "bibliotherapy" is promising; children and teens who participated in school-based book discussion groups about specific problems, compared to a control group, subsequently showed small to moderate alleviation of their symptoms of depression, anxiety, stress, and aggression.[29]

What we know so far is that reading books on any platform is good for teens' cognitive and social development, that reading fiction is uniquely important for teens' reading comprehension and theory of mind, and finally that the micro-reading/skimming they're doing on the Internet is a poor substitute at best—the reading equivalent of junk food.

For all these reasons, it's too soon for us as parents and teachers and librarians to give up on encouraging tweens and teens to read more fiction.

THE GENDER GAP IN READING CONTINUES TO GROW

The other reason we can't give up is that this dearth of reading appears to be affecting our sons more than our daughters, widening a gender inequity that has existed since before they started school. For instance, the 2019 Common Sense Media survey found that among 8- to 18-year-olds, girls reported reading for pleasure 6 minutes more each day than boys. Not surprisingly, the latest international reading studies of tweens and teens continue to show a large gap between boys' and girls' reading achievement for nearly every participating country.[30] Although this gap is narrowing in some countries, the overall trend is for this shrinkage to be due to a decline in girls' reading skill, with boys staying at the same low levels.

By the teenage years, the disparity in how girls and boys view reading is vast. In PISA 2018 (OECD's Programme for International Student Assessment), with a massive survey of 15-year-olds from around the world, 44% of girls and only 24% of boys agreed that "Reading is one of my favorite hobbies," whereas 60% of boys and only 39% of girls agreed that "I read only to get information that I need."[31] The pandemic has served to widen the gender gap in reading even further.[32]

Ireland is a positive example in the latest findings, with reading scores that top those in Europe, combined with a narrower gender gap.[33] Among other initiatives in Ireland over the past 10 years, one change was introducing graphic novels to the curriculum in an attempt to entice boys to read more often and to enjoy reading. We still need to know more, however, about whether reading graphic novels improves teens' reading comprehension skills as well as does reading traditional novels.

Reading in the teen years matters because it can open up—or shut down—a young person's future.

Being able to read well is essential for every academic subject in high school. Anna achieved at a top level in her final year of high school (called Year 13 in New Zealand), which meant she was guaranteed entry to university. Charlie performed well in high school in Years 11 and 12, but decided not to go on for that final critical year. He received a high school diploma, but not at the level required for university entry. Once he decides what he wants to do, however, Charlie should be absolutely fine. New Zealand has a thriving apprenticeship system for young people who want to become builders, mechanics, midwives, or electricians. In other countries, like the United States, not going to university severely restricts job prospects. In developed countries around the world, young men are attending university at lower rates than are young women. Experts point to teenage boys' lower rates of reading comprehension as one of the main reasons.[34]

WHAT ARE TEENS DOING INSTEAD?

In stark contrast to reading, gaming has become a nearly universal activity for teens all around the world. Boys are particularly avid gamers. In fact, the gender divide for gaming is even larger than that for reading. In 2019, 70% of US boys said they enjoyed playing video games "a lot," and gaming rated as boys' favorite media activity (and one of girls' least-favorite activities—their favorites are instead listening to music and using social media).[35] For instance, in the Program for International Student Assessment (PISA) 2018, 53% of 15-year-old boys versus only 10% of 15-year-old girls around the world stated that they played online collaborative games "every day or nearly every day."[36] Boys are still getting their stories, but they're rarely getting them from books.

Are there any positive effects of this pervasive gaming among teenage boys? Because of public concern of the effects of video game violence, for many years researchers did not even bother studying the possible advantages of video games. Psychologist Tobias Greitemeyer and others have steadily rectified this imbalance with their high-quality research on the precise effects of prosocial video game content on prosocial attitudes and behaviors. Given the bad rap that video games often receive, the results are surprisingly optimistic. In a meta-analysis of 98 recent independent studies with over 36,000 participants, Greitemeyer found that people who played video games with more prosocial content had more prosocial thoughts, feelings, and behaviors, and fewer aggressive ones.[37] The effect sizes were all in the small to medium range. And, lest you think that it's simply the case that people with prosocial tendencies are drawn to prosocial video games, these effects were exactly the same for experimental studies, in which participants were randomly assigned to play the prosocial games, as for correlational studies, in which participants chose their own games.

Now, you might argue that teenage boys are rarely playing prosocial video games, so it's a moot point that these games can be beneficial. It's true that there are very few completely wholesome video games out there that appeal to teens. In some of Greitemeyer's experimental research, their prosocial video game is *Lemmings*, a retro game with crude graphics in which the goal is to guide a bunch of lemmings out of a maze.[38]

I honestly do not know any teenage boys who would bother playing a game like *Lemmings* when there's much more action-packed and exciting fare available. Charlie's favorite at age 16, for instance, was the violent *Call of Duty*. According to the Entertainment Software Association report in 2022, the American video game industry alone was worth $60.4 billion in

2021, up from $35 billion in 2018.[39] The top five PC/console games were (1) *Call of Duty: Vanguard*; (2) *Call of Duty: Black Ops—Cold War*; (3) *Madden NFL 22*; (4) *Pokémon: Brilliant Diamond/Shining Pearl*; and (5) *Battlefield 2042*. I suppose it's reassuring that the relatively benign *Pokémon* is in the top five, and that the new *Battlefield 2042* has a T rating rather than M. I'll say more about the effects of these popular games in Chapter 5. For now, suffice to say that gaming—at least with the violent content which comprises most of the video game market and toward which teenage boys are drawn—is not a substitute for reading books when it comes to promoting story understanding, empathy, or theory of mind.

Let's look at gaming culture to understand why many boys like it so much compared to reading books: (1) gaming involves technology; (2) gaming is constantly stimulating, and thus less effortful; (3) gaming is social, or at least boys consider gaming to be social. Most popular games that teenage boys play are online and collaborative.[40] Whether the other player is beside them or next door or in another country, these games give teens the feeling of connecting with others and sharing common interests and goals.[41]

HOW PARENTS, TEACHERS, AND LIBRARIANS CAN HELP

Can reading books ever compete? Probably not. But we can try to make reading more enjoyable and less effortful for boys if we align reading with the reasons they love gaming. First, we can involve technology with tablets and e-readers (although, as literacy scholar Margaret Merga argues, we still need to offer print books, too).[42] A National Literacy Trust survey reported that 8- to 16-year-old boys are reading e-books even more than girls are, which could work toward closing the gender gap in reading enjoyment and skill.[43] In fact, the gender gap was erased completely for boys' and girls' leisure reading of fiction on screens, at around 30% for each. As a bonus, children are far more likely to look up unfamiliar words online than via a print version.[44] Media scholar Federico Pianzola lists some excellent suggestions for rendering reading more social with new technologies in his book, *Digital Social Reading: Sharing Fiction in the 21st Century*.[45] Finally, a boy reading from a tablet or even a phone is seen as less nerdy than a boy reading a print book. Hey, he could be looking at YouTube videos—who needs to know he's reading an actual book?

The same National Literacy Trust report also noted that the privacy of e-readers was appealing for less confident readers, who don't want others to know the level of the book they're reading. Boys are also listening to audiobooks even more often than are girls.[46] With their earbuds inserted, no one would know that they are listening to a novel instead of rap music. Listening to stories is soothing at any age, and it is obviously less effortful than reading. I'll say more about audiobooks in Chapter 8.

We don't know yet, however, if teens who hear stories rather than read them, or who read graphic novels or use social story apps like Wattpad, benefit in terms of their reading comprehension or social understanding. Nor do we have much neuroscience research yet on what reading fiction looks like in the typical teenage brain,[47] probably because it's very difficult to entice teens to go to any appointment, especially one that involves going into an magnetic resonance imaging (MRI) scanner when they haven't even broken a bone. I hope that someone will soon conduct that research. In line with John Hutton's ground-breaking neuroscience work showing that young children receive optimal brain stimulation from print picture books over animated stories,[48] will we find that teenagers experience optimal brain stimulation from any extended work of fiction, regardless of platform, as long as it is complex and engaging?

Second, it's important to give boys and girls as much choice in books as possible: action, adventure, science fiction, fantasy, book versions of movies and video games, and graphic novels like Philip Pullman's new version of *The Golden Compass*. Parents are vital for helping tweens especially to find books; no one knows a child's preferences as well as a parent. The 2018 Scholastic survey showed that parents often underestimate the difficulty their children have finding books they'll like.[49] But be careful to offer them an array of choices instead of foisting your own picks onto them, as *The New York Times* parenting writer Jessica Grose found when she tried to get her daughter to read her own childhood favorites.[50] Mother and daughter compromised on Lois Lowry's heartbreakingly beautiful novel *Number the Stars* about a Danish family hiding a young Jewish girl during World War II. Teachers and librarians are also influential, because they are able to offer children a wide range of books from which to choose.[51] Once tweens and teens finally do choose, make books easily accessible on as many platforms as possible.

Another way parents can encourage a love of books in tweens is by continuing to read aloud to them. The same Scholastic survey showed that although 60% of parents of 9- to 11-year-olds believed it was still very important to read aloud to their children, only 21% of them actually read to their children most days of the week.

Parents and teachers can be good role models for tweens and teens by reading for pleasure themselves, and by talking about what they read with tweens and teens.[52] This role-modeling may be especially important for fathers of sons. Based on gold-standard time-use survey data in the United

Kingdom and Germany, the best predictor of 8- to 19-year-old boys' leisure reading was their *fathers'* own reading for pleasure, not their mothers'.[53] (The converse was true for girls' leisure reading, with their mothers' own reading for pleasure the strongest factor.) The National Literacy Trust's recommendation is for "dads and lads" to read together from a young age.[54] Obviously, most teens wouldn't allow their dads to continue this practice, but even reading a book in the same room with a teen is a positive predictor of their own leisure reading.

The final task of making reading more social is perhaps the hardest of all to tackle. Is there a teenage boy version of the Man Book Club? Fortunately, there's book-tubing on YouTube and now TikTok's #BookTok—a new wave of young people vlogging about their favorite books. Most of these book tubers and Tok-ers are young women, such as Whitty Novels, which started in 2013 and at last check had over 55,000 subscribers. This young woman is indeed witty. She's also a great role model; she's open about her diagnosis of generalized anxiety disorder and talks about how she's coped through her college years. But there are a few brave young men out there book-tubing too; one of the most popular is Jesse the Reader with over 395,000 subscribers. My personal favorite book tube channel ViktoriaReads belongs to my son Ben's partner Viktoria, who reads everything from classics to science fiction/fantasy to romance. For teenage boys, the best book-tubing site I could find is an educational website called ThugNotes, with over 3 million subscribers. Comedian Greg Edwards (aka Sparky Sweets) uses rap and hysterical graphics to promote classic literature like Shakespeare's *Hamlet* and George Orwell's *1984*. Check out the comments, almost all of which are from boys. Even teachers are recommending this channel.

No matter what kinds of books a teen likes best or hates least, and whether they're cis-gender or queer, there's a book-tuber out there to talk up books to them—and sometimes to even have a virtual discussion with them via the comments, which seem ultra-supportive compared to a lot of YouTube channels. These sites are about as close to a book club as most teens will ever get. There's no empirical research yet on whether book-tubing is good for teens' empathy, theory of mind, and well-being, but I envisage the effects will turn out to be mostly positive, whether a teen is watching, commenting upon, or creating one of these sites.[55] These sites connect teens to others with similar interests whose presence reminds them that they are not alone,[56] and that reading books can be fun and (gasp) maybe even cool.

If you are a parent, teacher, or librarian, Margaret Merga's accessible books *Reading Engagement for Tweens and Teens* and *School Libraries Supporting Literacy and Well-Being* offer a host of evidence-based, practical strategies for encouraging young people to read, including how to capitalize on BookTok trends![57]

TEENS ARE DOING REAL LIFE (SORT OF)

In stark contrast, teens who refuse to read a book will spend countless hours writing about themselves on social media.[58] I'll say more about social media in Chapter 6 when I discuss the dangers of real-life stories. To give you a taster, the jury is still out, but it's looking as if reading and telling personal narratives over social media does more harm than good for teens and especially tweens. As a researcher of teens' life stories, I also know firsthand that teens will spend literally hours telling their life story to interviewers they've just met. Why? Because teens are busy doing real life, not books. They're trying to figure out who they are and how to be, and reading fiction is an indirect route at best to that goal. They simply can't afford the 5–10 hours it takes to read a real book about fictional people's lives. In that time, major events will have occurred in their friends' lives that they will have missed. They'll be behind the curve.

For the past 15 years, I've been putting myself into the minds of adolescents on a daily basis through my research, my fiction reading, my movie and TV viewing, and my home life. It's not always a fun or pleasant place to be. But it has given me some insight into why teens are the way they are and why they do what they do. Most of the time, what they're doing is testing out possible selves—through social media or gaming—and books are not immediate enough to satisfy this need.

THE TEENAGE BRAIN ON STORIES

You've probably heard many times over that teenage brains are undergoing massive remodeling. The showpiece of this remodeling is a fine-tuning of the prefrontal cortex, which translates to better planning, wiser decisions, and inhibition of some undesirable behaviors. But you may not be aware that prefrontal cortex development also underlies the dramatic changes in theory of mind that are happening in adolescence.[59]

For instance, neuroimaging researchers asked over 150 11- to 15-year-olds while in the MRI scanner to watch videos of young adults talking about real-life emotional events, such as the death of a grandparent or winning a sporting event.[60] The adolescents' task was to judge which emotions the person in the video was feeling, compared to the experiencers' own ratings.

GROWING TEENS WHO USE STORIES WISELY (63)

Adolescents who were better at these emotion judgments—and, yes, girls were better on average than boys—showed greater activation in the brain regions involved in theory of mind (such as the medial prefrontal cortex), not the brain regions involved in coexperiencing emotions (such as the inferior parietal lobule), which develop earlier. These results suggest that cognitive processes are particularly crucial for the advances in theory of mind we see in adolescence.

Recall that both of these regions are major hubs of the default network. The default network is also continuing to develop over adolescence, mainly via greater connectivity across hubs; adolescents with high-functioning autism show less connectivity across hubs compared to typically developing adolescents.[61]

If you are a parent of a teen, you will be able to hear these brain changes happening in the stories your adolescent tells about real life, which make a startling leap in maturity between ages 12 and 15, especially in terms of connecting causes and consequences.[62] This jump in insight is most apparent in the way adolescents talk about turning points in their lives—events that changed who they are or how they see themselves as a person.

For instance, Anna's turning point at age 12 was her cousins' move to Australia:

> I think that if my cousins didn't move to Australia, I'd probably see them more often, but I didn't really see them that often any way. But I probably would see them more. And I used to get birthday presents from them, but now I don't 'cause it costs lots.

At age 16, Anna demonstrated much more sophisticated reasoning in her turning point of starting high school:

> I got way more confident in like, my brain, and like what I could do with everything. Like everything I enjoy I just became . . . way more confident and I was actually good at it. And I think when I got to high school, I became closer with my brother because we were already quite close in age, but like when you get older the age gap kind of shrinks. So it wasn't really high school that did that, 'cause we're at different high schools, but more the fact that I was high school age, I suppose. And that's really nice.

One way adolescents make these links is through mental time travel, in which they use their default network to connect past and present to future via simulating those possibilities in their minds—before, or instead of, acting them out in real life.[63] Psychologist Tilmann Habermas calls these insights "autobiographical reasoning."[64] Teenagers become able to draw inferences about who they are based on past events in their lives. This change in their thinking in turn has a dramatic effect on their identity and well-being.

Habermas and co-author Susan Bluck go so far as to claim that teens are finally "getting a life."[65] Within a few short years, their ability to make these connections and to create more coherent life stories will translate to being more satisfied with their lives and to higher self-esteem.[66]

For instance, Anna demonstrates deep insight in her turning point of a relationship breakup at age 20. The story goes on for several pages, but these are the key bits:

> And so basically um I'm with another person now and it's a lot better and I just, it's kind of made me realize like that, I don't know, I just need to not do that again. Like it's just hard to kinda just go, but it's just made me realize like what's more important, I suppose in our relationship. Like it doesn't matter how long you've been together if you feel like you're not happy.

When older teens and young adults show us through their real-life stories that they understand how events in their past have shaped who they now are, they also report greater well-being at that time and up to a year later.[67] As a young adult, Anna reported above-average satisfaction with her life. Exciting new experimental work by Dan McAdams and Brady Jones demonstrates that when 15-year-olds are guided to write about these connections between past and present when telling stories of successes and failures, their goal persistence improves, as do their grades.[68]

TEENS *DO* LISTEN TO FAMILY STORIES

It is in the realm of these real-life stories that parents can continue to make their greatest contribution to teens' story understanding. Unlike the books parents try to push on their teens without success, teens still want to hear parents' real-life stories—family stories of parents' childhoods and adolescence, and of their own infancy and early childhood. Kate McLean's book *The Co-Authored Self: Family Stories and the Construction of Personal Identity* is a lovely source of knowledge about teens' experiences with family stories.[69] (A word of warning: Teens do listen to these stories, and they *will* remember them, so select family stories with care.)

The teenage years are the start of what is known in the memory field as the "reminiscence bump"—the years from about ages 15 to 30 in which we remember events more vividly than from any other time of our lives.[70] We know teenagers listen to their parents' stories closely, because when we ask them to tell us these stories in the lab, they can produce them on the spot for us, and tell them in great detail, with enjoyment.[71]

Here's an eloquent example from a New Zealand Chinese adolescent girl in one of my studies that illustrates the power these family stories can have:

> I always like umm hearing about the story about how my mum and dad got together. Because it's like a story of two most unlikely people. Umm my dad was from the countryside, and my mum was from the city, and umm and during that time you know how in China there is a lot of like aversion to people who come from the countryside and things. Umm, and so my mum, and because she was so beautiful she had heaps of people chasing after her. And my dad was, to put it bluntly, not very attractive, and poor, and a nerd because you know he was working really hard. But for some reason, umm like they fell in love and stuff. And yeah, the story of the two most unlikely people, and yet you know it somehow worked, and yeah. I do not believe in love at first sight. But for my parents, it was love at first sight.

When my collaborator Yan Chen tested the contributions of teenagers' own life stories versus their parents' childhood stories to their well-being, she found that both types of stories contributed to adolescents' well-being across three cultures (New Zealand European, New Zealand Chinese, and Māori), but in different ways.[72] Whereas the insight with which teens tell their personal life stories links mainly to their overall satisfaction with their lives, their parents' stories instead contribute to their sense of self-worth—their self-esteem. From their mothers' stories, the important element for the teens' self-esteem was talk about emotions and intentions and perspectives on the childhood event. From their fathers' stories, the important element for the teens' self-esteem was the overall coherence of the story, with a clear beginning, middle, and end. The "love at first sight" story illustrates both of these patterns. Remembering and understanding their own stories and their parents' stories is yet another way that teens can improve their inferential capacity.

How do teenagers become so wise by mid-adolescence?

Their brain development helps, of course, as does the way parents have told stories with them throughout childhood and early adolescence. In *Origins*, my collaborator Sebastian Suggate found that 16-year-olds with better reading comprehension were those who as 4-year-olds were better able to retell a fictional story they had just heard.[73] Preschoolers' story-telling skills are in turn shaped by the way their parents have read fictional stories and told real-life stories with them from even younger ages.[74] Recall from Chapter 3 that young children whose mothers read picture books to them in more interactive ways showed more activation in language, socioemotional, and memory areas of the brain when hearing stories read aloud while in a scanner.[75] Although there's no research yet linking adolescent brain development to family storytelling, I predict that adolescents who have heard more family stories will show more mature connectivity across brain networks when hearing a fictional story while in a scanner.

Our findings in *Origins* reveal the most supportive style for parents of conversing about important events in young adolescents' (11- to 12-year-olds) lives is to thoroughly *explore* children's negative emotions, *validate* their point of view on the event, and only then *expand* with their own observations. In this excerpt from a conversation with Anna at age 12, her mother gently explores the reasons behind Anna's "meltdown" when she repeatedly lost matches at a tennis tournament, but she kept going to finish out the day:

MOTHER: *How did you feel at the start of the tournament?*
ANNA: *It was alright, I was kind of nervous.*
MOTHER: *It was your biggest tournament ever, wasn't it?*
ANNA: *Yeah. And then I played someone and I lost, but I knew I'd lose so it didn't matter. And then I played someone else and I thought I'd win, but I didn't, and I was sad.*
[intervening turns about differences between the matches]
MOTHER: *And it's not easy to talk about those really bad things, is it? But do you want to say what happened in the middle? It's like a meltdown. Really, wasn't it? Yeah, kind of. And there were tears.*
ANNA: *Yeah.*
MOTHER: *There were tears because it just wasn't a good day at all, was it?*
ANNA: *No, not really.*
MOTHER: *And you didn't want to do it.*
ANNA: *No.*
MOTHER: *And did your mum say, "That's okay, Anna, you don't have to do it?"*
ANNA: *No* (laughs).
MOTHER: *What did mum say?*
ANNA: *She said, what did you say?*
MOTHER: *That you had to finish the match.*
ANNA: *"You have to finish" and so I did, and then I got a present 'cause I kept going.*
MOTHER: *It's really important, we thought, to have acknowledged the fact that you kept going on, it was really . . .*
ANNA: *Persevering.*
MOTHER: *Perseverance in the face of extreme difficulty.*

In early adolescence, both boys and girls still need this exploration and validation of emotions when discussing negative events, and they need help creating positive resolutions. In *Origins*, the 11- and 12-year-olds who were able to talk openly with their mothers about these negative events, and who were able to reach a consensus about their emotions, were later able to tell their own life stories at ages 15 and 16 with more insight and maturity.[76]

We now have experimental verification of the importance of these early conversations about life experiences between mothers and children in a study with my former PhD students Claire Mitchell and Sean Marshall. In a subset of over 100 families from *Origins*, our *Growing Memories* study is a gold-standard randomized controlled trial in which we coached one group of mothers to reminisce in richer ways with their toddlers, compared to mothers and toddlers in a control group. Those toddlers whose mothers reminisced in these elaborative ways grew into tweens who told stories about difficult life experiences in more coherent ways at age 11.[77] At age 15, they were teens who told more insightful turning-point stories.[78] By age 20, they were young adults who not only continued to tell more insightful life stories; they also reported lower levels of depressive symptoms and greater self-esteem.[79] Talking with your toddler about everyday events, as frustrating as it can be at times, pays off in spades in the long term.

WHAT ABOUT WRITING?

From about age 14, teens are better equipped to do their own reasoning about negative life events. The evidence so far is that expressive writing— using Pennebaker's techniques of writing about difficult or traumatic events for 10–15 minutes a day for 3–4 days—has at least small benefits for teens in terms of physical and mental health, and for school attendance.[80] As with adults, expressive writing is equally helpful for teenage boys and girls.

However, expressive writing is contraindicated for young adolescents. In one study, 9- to 13-year-olds who were instructed to engage in expressive writing about negative experiences actually got more depressed and anxious over the next 2 months.[81] Preteens and young adolescents do not yet have the reasoning skills to benefit from solo expressive writing, which underscores how vital it is for parents to pay special attention to how they talk with younger teens about their more difficult life experiences.

Parents and teachers can capitalize upon older teens' love of writing about themselves to create some coherence out of the emotional chaos in their lives. An impressive 32% of US teens report writing for pleasure (including stories, articles, poems, and blogs).[82] Those teens who write actually prefer pen and paper to writing on a device.[83] If you are a parent of an older teen, make sure they have special notebooks or journals to write in, and don't *ever* peek. Expressive writing works best when it's completely private.

The main task for teens is to grow a story about who they are, to "get a life." Carving out an identity was the main task of adolescence in Jane Austen's day, and it is still the main task of adolescence today. But the way that today's teens are discovering who they are is through presenting virtual versions of themselves to others on a daily basis, trying on different selves and casting them off just as quickly, as if they were trying on clothes at the mall. Today's teens are using a plethora of entertainment and social media sites to learn what they *think* they need to know for how to become a person in this century. They're using these virtual versions because they're easy, available, and captivating. Are there any dangers to these stories?

CHAPTER 5

The Dangers of Fictional Stories

The medium is not the message: the message is.[1]
—Daniel Anderson

I've spent the first half of this book telling you about all the ways that stories are good for us. Stories teach us to be kinder and more empathetic to others; stories shore us up to be healthier and to feel better about our real lives; stories enrich our knowledge of ourselves and of the world. We use stories to escape from the constraints of everyday life, to sustain a happy mood, to wallow in a sad mood, or to drag ourselves away from despair. Stories help us understand who we are and who we could be. It doesn't seem to matter whether we're reading or watching or talking about fictional stories, or whether we're telling or hearing or writing about real-life stories—all are linked to benefits. Nonetheless, with my own addiction to fiction, and my public promotion of stories to parents, I am constantly on the lookout for any detrimental effects.

So, is there a downside to stories?

Yes. The evidence is now crystal-clear that certain stories, or too many stories, can be harmful to our health. This evidence comes from research conducted with all ages, from young children through to older adults, and from all kinds of research designs—correlational, longitudinal, experimental—even a few brain-imaging studies. There are so many studies on this topic, in fact, that it would be impossible to tell you about them all in a single chapter, so I'll focus on a few landmark studies that best illustrate the dangers of stories.

How Stories Change Us. Elaine Reese, Oxford University Press. © Oxford University Press 2024.
DOI: 10.1093/oso/9780197747902.003.0005

THE PITFALLS OF STORIES FROM BOOKS

Let's start with stories from books. The good news is that children's picture books are more culturally and racially diverse than they were in the 20th century. Researchers in the United States first documented this problem in the 1960s, when only 7% of children's books contained even a single Black character.[2] Nancy Larrick, the president of the International Reading Association in 1965, noted that in some of these books, "The litho-pencil sketches leave the reader wondering whether a delicate shadow indicates a racial difference or a case of sunburn." Unfortunately, a 2019 study called "The Cat Is Out of the Bag" found Dr. Seuss books to be some of the worst offenders, containing only 2% non-White human characters, most of whom are depicted in negative and stereotypical ways.[3] By 2021, however, over a third of children's picture books contained Black, Indigenous, Asian, Latinx, Pacific Island, or Arab characters.

The bad news is that, even in these "diverse" picture books, the central characters are often still White children, and Asian and Muslim characters are often portrayed as exotic and foreign, not as typical children living everyday lives.[4] Moreover, some children's books are still as sexist in the 21st century as they were in the late 20th century.[5] For instance, in-depth analyses of popular children's books from the 20th and early 21st centuries showed no change in sexist representations over time. Children's book characters are still nearly twice as likely to be male as female, whether human or nonhuman. In fact, animal and inanimate characters, such as Thomas the Tank Engine, are even more likely than human characters to be male. Female characters tend to be portrayed in stereotypical occupations and are more likely to appear in indoor than outdoor scenes. Award-winning books are no less likely to contain these biases than lower-quality books. Crucially, counter-stereotyped male characters are also under-represented in children's books, as are fathers.

Some wonderful exceptions exist, of course. I applaud the work of brave publishers like Abrams Books for their counter-stereotyped books such as Andrea Beaty's *Rosie Revere, Engineer* and *Ada Twist, Scientist*. Books like these are making great strides in the right direction and are hugely appealing to girls and boys alike. When children are exposed to less stereotyped literature, they become less willing to endorse gender stereotypes about occupations and activities, and they are more willing to play with counter-stereotypical toys (for example, girls playing with dump trucks).[6] Check out the nonprofit organization We Need Diverse Books for recommendations for books portraying racial and gender diversity as well as people who are differently abled and from a range of religious backgrounds.

Nor are we protected as adults against bias in the fiction we read. In a fascinating big data study of gender stereotypes in over 5 million published books of English-language fiction in the 20th century, men were even more over-represented than they were in children's literature, with over twice as many adult male characters as adult female characters.[7] Men were also described more positively than women throughout the century.

Although these disparities are not surprising, they do underscore how vital it is to promote books for children and adults alike containing diverse, strong, positive, and empathetic characters. I urge authors, publishers, and readers to do better in this decade. Try reading Bernardine Evaristo's Booker Prize winner *Girl, Woman, Other*, a beautifully written and provocative book that is spurring great discussions about gender, culture, and identity.

The newest concern about children's books is that the characters are almost all anthropomorphic, featuring nonhuman animals or hybrids acting, thinking, and feeling in human ways. Can children learn as well from nonhuman characters and from fantasy books as from realistic fare? A growing number of studies now shows that anthropomorphism in picture books and stories impairs young children's learning about animals, evolution, and technology.[8] For instance, one study found that children who heard *Thomas the Tank Engine* books 3 days in a row were more likely to endow real trains with human qualities. Another study showed that anthropomorphism impairs children's sharing behavior: Children who heard the storybook *Little Raccoon Learns to Share* later shared fewer stickers with another child compared to those who heard a version of the same storybook with Photoshopped human characters.[9] Moreover, although parents think that young children prefer fantasy storybooks, they actually prefer stories based on real life.[10] And when stories are of the fantasy variety, older children and adults prefer more realistic characters—like Harry, Ron, and Hermione—populating those books. Perhaps children's book authors need to listen to the children and create more real-life themes and realistic characters. Whenever I visit bookstores to choose new children's books for projects like *Tender Shoots*, it's hard to find a picture book that *doesn't* include anthropomorphism.

Personally, I love children's books with anthropomorphized characters and would not ever want to see them supplanted entirely. Where would children's literature be without *Where the Wild Things Are, Corduroy*, and *Peter Rabbit*? In fact, I'm currently creating my own children's book based on our Flemish Giant rabbits Poppy and Hoppy. It's a tale of biting and how to repair a friendship after all goes horribly wrong—but that's another story. Researchers Gabrielle Strouse, Angela Nyhout, and Patricia Ganea point out that books with anthropomorphized characters may help instill empathy in children for animals and for nature.[11]

Perhaps these hybrid characters will be especially useful in this century. Children's literature theorist Maria Nikolajeva predicts that "Today's children and young people are likely to be the first generation to co-exist with and possibly be threatened by the new species of superhumans, and fiction can potentially prepare them for this challenge."[12]

Children aren't the only ones who enjoy fictional books about real-life events. Many adults love to read historical fiction. One of our top reasons is to learn about history without having to read a dense history book or watch a documentary.[13] My all-time favorite author of historical fiction is Geraldine Brooks, writer of Pulitzer Prize–winning *March* (the *Little Women* story rendered from the father's point of view) and *Year of Wonders*, an imagining of life in the time of the bubonic plague—particularly relevant pandemic reading.

Fortunately, studies show that we do learn true historical facts very effectively from stories.[14] On the other hand, the whole point of historical fiction is for the author to bridge the gap, via imagination, between what is known and what has escaped historical record. Such bridging may create problems. In studies in which people read stories containing true and fantasy facts about a historical event, they often later rate the fantasy facts as true—even when this knowledge contradicts their own prior correct knowledge (such as learning incorrectly from a story that the Atlantic is the largest ocean).[15] Later, we feel as if we have always known these "facts" and that we merely reencountered them in our reading.

This misinformation effect from reading stories is so powerful that it can occur after a single reading. Our belief in the fantasy fact gets even stronger over time as we forget that we learned the "fact" in a story.[16] General warnings before reading that the stories contain errors do not help. In fact, highlighting statements containing possible errors in the story actually increases the amount of misinformation learned, because we then process those statements more deeply.[17] Lead researcher Elizabeth Marsh claims of her experiments that "story reading led to an illusion of truth."[18]

The ease with which false facts from fiction can enter our knowledge base came home to me recently. Our book club's monthly assignment was *The Sound of Things Falling* by Juan Gabriel Vásquez, a young Colombian hailed as the next great South American writer. It is indeed an excellent book that quietly wends a story of two couples, 20 years apart, both struck by drug violence in Colombia. A crucial part of the narrative is that young, not-so-idealistic Peace Corps volunteers played a large part in the origins of the Medellín drug cartel. It was not until I was telling my friend David excitedly about the book that I came to realize that this plot element was a false fact, or rather, a fictional creation on the part of the author. David asked, "Did that actually happen?" (A reluctant reader of fiction, David once said to me, "Fiction is just bad information.") I had to quickly consult the Internet because I had assumed that the novelist had based that part of the story on documented incidents, given that there were many other facts woven into the story, such as Nixon first publicly using the term "war on drugs" in a press conference in 1971. But a search revealed that there is indeed no good evidence that Peace Corps volunteers encouraged campesinos to grow marijuana and to later process coca leaves for export, nor (spoiler alert) was a Peace Corps volunteer in Colombia ever murdered as in the book.[19] Yet this misinformation had insidiously crept into my mind as fact, because it seemed so plausible. In this case, the false fact is so compelling that notable reviewers of the book accepted it unquestioningly as well. This experience has made me wary of "facts" embedded in fiction.

Unfortunately, older children, teens, and young adults are even more prone to these misinformation effects from reading than are young children and older adults.[20] They are victims of their stronger memory abilities— their sponge-like ability to absorb facts means that they retain more false facts, as well as true facts, from what they read.

To combat the misinformation effect, the only technique that seems to help even slightly is to ask readers to stop to evaluate each fact as true or false, as David prompted me to do.[21] What reader of historical fiction is going to do that for every purported fact? After all, the main reason we read fiction is to experience a great story. If we wanted historical accuracy, we would be reading nonfiction.

Luckily for science fiction/fantasy lovers, however, these misinformation effects are less likely to occur when we read science fiction or fantasy stories.[22] It seems that we're better able to cordon off the information learned from less realistic stories so that false facts don't seep into our general knowledge base.

THE DARK SIDE OF VISUAL STORIES FROM SCREENS

Let's move on to the dangers of watching fictional stories from TV and movies. The big question here is whether children and teens imitate the violence they see on film, whether it has no effect whatsoever, or whether it even decreases their aggression.

A new analysis shows that movies are currently the most violent of prime-time media: They are more likely than TV shows to contain at least one violent act and are more likely to be "saturated" with violence.[23] At age 16, nearly all of our *Origins* participants had at least one R-rated movie in their top three, mixed in with blander fare. For instance, Anna and Tia both loved the aptly named *Donnie Darko*; Charlie and Joe liked road trip movies *Due Date* and *Hit and Run*. But some teens' favorites were all at the outer bounds of violence. For instance, fellow *Origins* member Marco listed science-fiction action thrillers *Predator 1*, *Predator 2*, and Stanley Kubrick's *Full Metal Jacket* as his top three movies. For perspective, Common Sense Media lists *Predator 1* as age 16+, and both *Predator 2* and *Full Metal Jacket* as age 18+ for graphic violence. What is the effect on young people of a consistently violent diet of visual stories?

We now know the answer to this question, and it's not benign.

This research began in the 1960s, soon after TVs became household items in the United States. The most famous studies were psychologist Albert Bandura's "Bobo doll" experiments. (The infamous Bobo doll was a 5-foot-high inflatable punching bag.) Bandura's design was simple: One group of 4-year-old children watched a film clip of an adult woman punching, kicking, and hitting the Bobo doll with a mallet while talking aggressively (*Sock him in the nose*; *Kick him*; *POW*).[24] Another group of 4-year-olds viewed the same woman committing the same hostile acts on poor Bobo in real life in the lab playroom. (I'm pretty sure that, as with many early psychology studies, this one would no longer pass an ethics board.) A control group of children did not see any aggression. All children were then escorted to a different laboratory playroom while being surreptitiously filmed. The playroom contained a range of toys of the era—tea sets, trucks, dolls, dart guns—and of course, the eponymous Bobo doll.

You guessed right—those children who saw aggressive acts, whether on film or in real life, engaged in nearly twice as many violent acts in the playroom compared to children in the control group. Their violent acts were verbal and physical—some directly imitated from the film, some invented on the spot (*Shoot the Bobo*). In fact, children in the film condition were even more likely to engage in aggressive gun play than children in the real-life condition. Girls and boys alike were more aggressive after seeing either filmed or real-life violence. These findings supported Bandura's theory of social learning that children model the behavior they see, whether in real life or on film. This notion now seems obvious. At the time, however, influenced by psychoanalytic theories of catharsis, TV executives actually promoted violent programming for children as a way to let off steam and reduce aggression.[25]

Many studies from the subsequent five decades support and extend the findings of the original Bobo doll experiments. For instance, strong

THE DANGERS OF FICTIONAL STORIES   (75)

longitudinal research shows that children who view more violent TV and movies grow up to become more aggressive adolescents and adults, even after controlling for children's initial aggression and other factors that go hand in hand with children's excessive viewing of violent TV, such as poverty and parents' own aggressive tendencies.[26] This hostility does not always manifest in physical or verbal aggression; it can be subtle, such as a tendency to interpret other people's ambiguous actions (for example, knocking against someone in a crowd) as hostile rather than accidental. Updating Bandura's theory, media theorists Craig Anderson and Bradley Bushman added a cognitive component with their General Aggression model (GAM) in 2002.[27] The idea is that viewing violent media creates a script for violence through which the real world is filtered, making it more likely that those who ingest violent media will react in aggressive and hostile ways. The GAM has held strong for two decades in explaining human aggression more broadly.

A compelling recent experiment from Bushman's lab had 8- to 12-year-olds watch 20-minute clips from two older PG-rated movies (*The Rocketeers* or *National Treasure*), both of which contain gun violence.[28] The clips were shown either in their original form or in edited versions with the gun violence taken out, but with the rest of the action sequence left intact. Then the children, who had arrived in pairs with a friend, were allowed to explore the lab playroom. Most of the children soon discovered that there was a *real* semiautomatic 9-mm handgun in a drawer. (Of course, the gun was modified so that it could not fire, and parents were fully informed of the gun before they gave consent. However, I am certain that this study would never pass an ethics board in New Zealand.) The children who had earlier viewed the original versions of movie clips containing gun violence were more likely to hold the gun, pull the trigger on the gun, even pretend to shoot their friend with the gun at point-blank range, than children who had viewed the versions with the gun violence edited out. And this havoc was wreaked with a short clip from a PG-rated movie that we now see as mild, even family-friendly—parents on Common Sense Media rated *National Treasure* as suitable for ages 9+.

Perhaps in response to the now-conventional wisdom that TV violence begets violence, current popular children's programming contains low rates of violence.[29] So as long as parents let children watch Nick Jr. or the Disney channel, TV is fine, right? After all, children learn from educational TV like *Sesame Street*, and they become more altruistic after watching prosocial programming like the popular Australian show *Bluey* (see Chapter 3).

I'm sorry to disappoint harried parents of young children, but *Bluey* and *Daniel Tiger's Neighborhood* are exceptions to the rule. Although most children's programming today contains low rates of violence, TV shows also have low rates of prosocial and educational content.[30] In addition, virtually all of children's contemporary visual media is supernatural (fantastical) in content, meaning that thanks to computer-generated animation, nearly all shows depict events that could never happen in the real world. A silver lining to TV streaming is that most young children are no longer subjected to adult content, but they're still subjected to a great deal of visual media with little or no educational value for real life.

Researchers are just starting to understand how this fantastical content affects children's learning and behavior. Does fantastical content deplete children's attention, resulting in short-term decreases in their self-regulation?[31] For instance, a series of studies by psychologist Angeline Lillard and team showed that after watching only 9 minutes of a highly fantastical show (*Sponge Bob*, *Fan Boy*, or *Little Einsteins*), 4- and 6-year-old children's self-regulation deteriorated compared to children who had instead watched a more realistic cartoon (*Little Bill* or *Phineas and Ferb*) or who drew a picture, played with toys, or heard a book. These findings are important because the short-term dips in self-regulation occurred even after children watched educational TV shows if the program also contained high amounts of fantastical content (like *Martha Speaks*). Crucially, children didn't show decreases in self-regulation after hearing a fantastical storybook.[32] Self-regulation skills in childhood are key to later success in life: Children who are able to regulate their emotions and behavior go on to have better grades, more stable relationships, and career success.[33]

So far, neuroimaging studies support the view that watching fantastical content depletes young children's self-regulation because it requires more cognitive effort for children to process these unrealistic events. In one study in which preschool children watched either highly fantastical (*Tom and Jerry*) or less fantastical cartoons (*Mickey Mouse Clubhouse*), those who watched the highly fantastical cartoons showed increased activation in the prefrontal cortex.[34]

At first blush this prefrontal cortex activation while watching a cartoon may seem like a good thing—what if passively viewing fantastical content actually improves young children's self-regulation over the long term by giving their prefrontal cortex a workout? However, children who watched *Tom and Jerry* performed more poorly on self-regulation tasks later than those who watched *Mickey Mouse Clubhouse*, indicating an overtaxing of cognitive resources, not a boost.[35]

Although there are not yet any experimental studies on the long-term effects of watching fantastical content on young children's self-regulation, these short-term effects could be an important indicator. Early and heavy doses of entertainment and adult TV programming (aka background TV) are also linked over time to lower levels of self-regulation and less growth in young children's thinking and language development.[36] In contrast, the time that slightly older children spend reading books and engaging in extracurricular activities is instead linked to higher self-regulation.[37]

It may be safest to think of fantastical content as overactivating the young brain, similar to John Hutton's study that viewing a TV version of a story overactivated the preschool brain compared to the "just-right" activation of a picture book version. Plus, babies who start out poorer in self-regulation—those who are frequently irritable or fussy, or who need a lot of help falling asleep—are allowed more TV/video time as toddlers, probably as a way to help soothe them.[38] This vicious spiral of screen time and self-regulation difficulties begins from the first year of life. These early habits then lead to ever more excessive viewing at older ages.[39]

A special word of warning about the dangers of visual media for infants and toddlers—given the risks, the American Academy of Pediatrics recommends no screen time *at all* for infants under 18 months, with the exception of live video chats.[40] For toddlers between 18 and 24 months, although there are a few benefits of watching educational TV, these are diminished compared to real-life interactions and book conversations.[41] Due to what is called the "video deficit effect," infants and toddlers have difficulty transferring knowledge from the two-dimensional screen world to three-dimensional real life.

The negative effects of visual media are lessened when adults co-view and converse about the show, but research shows that this co-viewing happens only about half the time, and it is decreasing with the widespread use of tablets.[42] It's simply easier to watch a TV together than to huddle with your child over a tablet. Even when these co-viewing interactions do take place, they're of lower quality than non-screen interactions.[43]

For preschoolers, the evidence is clearer that they benefit from educational and high-quality programming, as I discussed in Chapter 3. Yet excessive amounts of screen time displace valuable face-to-face interactions and pose problems for children's self-regulation. Since the pandemic, young children's screen time around the world has gone up and stayed up—the new normal.[44] There are some hints, however, that this increase on its own may not be problematic: A longitudinal study in Israel showed that although *during* the pandemic this heavy viewing was linked to children's emotional and conduct problems, it no longer predicted problems after the lockdowns ended. Instead, other factors, such as mothers' ongoing distress, best accounted for children's post-lockdown difficulties.

Unfortunately for tweens and teens, many popular TV shows and movies feed them with a steady diet of gender and racial stereotypes.[45] The most striking pattern is that female and non-White characters are given less airtime than male and White characters. Consistently, there are 2 to 3 times as many male to female characters in a TV show. Latinos, who make up nearly 20% of the US population, appear in children's programs only 8% of the time. Visual media also portray female characters as more passive and less capable than male characters, and they highlight females' physical attractiveness rather than internal qualities. Male characters are rarely portrayed in ways that are seen as more feminine, such as showing affection. These same stereotyped patterns are apparent—and even more limiting—for non-White characters, and non-White children consume even more visual media than do White children.[46] Although there's no longer as much overt racist content in contemporary TV and movies, there are still subtle and not-so-subtle racial stereotypes: Asians as nerdy, Black women as tough, Jews as smart and sly.[47]

What are the effects on young people? Tweens and teens with a heavy diet of visual media are more likely to endorse gender and racial stereotypes.[48] A longitudinal study with US tweens showed that TV exposure predicted dips in self-esteem over time for White and Black girls and for Black boys.[49] In stark contrast, for White boys, TV exposure predicted increases in self-esteem. In an experimental study, after watching stereotypical TV clips from *Sadie J* or *Life With Boys*, tween girls were less likely to see themselves entering STEM occupations and more likely to endorse stereotypical occupations, such as teacher or florist, compared to girls who watched counter-stereotyped clips from *Ask An Astronomer* or *Smart Girls at the Party*.[50] In yet another study focusing on tweens, girls *and* boys with more exposure to tween TV (such as *Violetta* or *Austin and Ally*) were more likely over time to hold unrealistic expectations for their own appearance.[51] When coupled with stereotyped visual media, body dissatisfaction can lead to eating disorders.[52]

Tweens and teens can also adopt unrealistic expectations about relationships from popular TV shows and movies. Idealistic, romantic content can lead to unrealistic beliefs, such as love at first sight. Young adolescent girls may be particularly prey to these fairy-tale notions. In one study, 11- to 14-year-old girls watched either the romantic *High School Musical* or the more neutral children's movie *Over the Hedge*.[53] Younger girls who watched the romantic fare were afterward more likely to ascribe to romantic beliefs such as "There will only be one real love for me" than girls who had watched *Over the Hedge*. Older girls were less influenced by the movie, perhaps because they had more real-life experience with relationships. But even older girls and young women can be subtly influenced by constraining and stereotypical scripts in TV and movies. For instance, as much as I love *Gilmore Girls*, and despite the many positive mother–daughter themes it contains, the generation of young women raised on it were implicitly led to believe that career and motherhood are an either/or proposition.[54]

Let's say you've found a family-friendly movie that is low in violence and stereotypes, and it's one that you think your tween or teen may actually want to watch with you. It's based on historical events, so you and your family may even learn something from it. Similar to reading historical fiction, will you all learn *accurate* information? Psychologist Andrew Butler's fascinating research on popular films based on historical events shows that they contain inaccuracies small and large. Undergraduates who watched clips from popular movies containing inaccuracies were later highly likely to recall the false information as true, even when they read a text passage containing the correct information in the same session.[55] However, Butler did find that giving a specific warning about the misinformation *before* participants watched the film cut down on their memory errors.

Because popular children's books and movies that are used to teach science and history in the classroom are often rife with errors, teachers need to carefully fact-check any books or movies before using them in their curriculum. In reaction to Butler's findings, veteran high school teacher Judith Raizy Nathan has decided to stop showing popular movies in her classroom as a standard part of her social studies curriculum.[56] Alternatively, teachers can rely on recommendations from reputable organizations such as The National Science Teachers' Association, which publishes lists each year of high-quality science trade books.

Similar misinformation effects occur from watching popular science fiction movies, such as the 2020 science-fiction horror film *Underwater*.[57] The film is about deep-sea drilling but at a depth that is simply not practical with current technology. Among the many other inaccuracies in the film, one is that divers at such a depth could quickly resurface safely. In reality, they would experience decompression syndrome or "the bends" and would die. Research shows that people are able to detect only 35% of the science errors in such films.[58] Recall that this misinformation effect was not as strong for science-fiction books: Apparently we are less able to cordon off inaccurate information when it is presented in vivid visual detail in a science-fiction movie.

The take-home message is that visual stories are highly persuasive and memorable, whether the events depicted are accurate or biased.[59]

ACTION STORIES: THE MOST DANGEROUS OF ALL?

Violent, stereotypical, and inaccurate content from TV and movies, however, is the least of our worries for today's tweens and teens. Recall that TV and movies are now classed as "Legacy Media" because today's teens watch so little. Most of their media diet, especially for boys, is now in the form of online videos on YouTube or TikTok and video games.[60] TikTok wasn't around for the participants in my *Origins* study, but YouTube and video games were, with similar gendered preferences. For instance, 16-year-old *Origins* participant Marco vastly preferred gaming to either reading books or watching movies, as did Hayden, whose favorites were *Halo* and the ultra-violent *Gears of War*, and Jeremy, whose top pick was the hyper-realistic *Call of Duty*, with its controversial mass shooting of civilians in an airport. In response to public concern about the role of violent video games in mass shootings around the world, there has been a veritable explosion of research on the effects of video gaming, with even more controversy than surrounded the earlier work on TV violence.

I should note that along with the swell in video games for entertainment there has been a corresponding surge in serious games—mostly simulation-type video games expressly designed for learning new knowledge or skills, or adopting healthier habits. High-quality research on these games shows that they can be as effective or even more effective than face-to-face teaching for all sorts of skills, ranging from executive functioning to problem-solving to learning CPR techniques.[61] New rigorously trialed e-therapy games created specifically for teenagers, such as the New Zealand-made SPARX (Smart, Positive, Active, Realistic, X-Factor thoughts), are even helping to decrease adolescents' depression and anxiety.[62] My focus instead is on less serious games with a storyline, because that's what most young people are playing.

An especially lively debate has emerged between anti-gaming researchers Brad Bushman and Craig Anderson and pro-gaming researchers Chris Ferguson and Patrick Markey. In Markey and Ferguson's book, *Moral Combat: Why the War on Violent Video Games Is Wrong*, they describe a David and Goliath scenario, in which the young and underfunded pro-gamers are David, and the senior anti-game researchers are Goliath, throwing around their weight and their masses of government funding. Only a few researchers like Tobias Greitemeyer occupy the dangerously vacant middle ground, open to shooters from both sides.

When I delved into the latest research, what I found was very much like unzipping a teenager's duffel bag after being at school camp for a week in the rain. It's an absolute mess. So I sorted through the extremely dirty

THE DANGERS OF FICTIONAL STORIES *(81)*

laundry in this jumbo duffel bag to find a few studies that were not quite as muddy as the others. There is now a whole host of meta-analyses on the effects of video game violence, but it's difficult to trust the results of meta-analyses when many of the original studies are so flawed—the old "garbage in, garbage out" problem.[63]

My pick is Tobias Greitemeyer's and Dirk Mügge's meta-analysis of 98 studies published between 2009 and 2014, which shows a small effect of violent video gaming on aggressive thoughts, feelings, and behaviors[64]—in fact, the size of the effect is almost identical to that of the benefits of prosocial games for helping behavior. Another recent meta-analysis that included only well-designed longitudinal studies revealed a similar small but reliable link between violent video game play and later physical aggression.[65] These well-designed longitudinal studies show that children and adolescents who consistently play violent video games do indeed become more aggressive over time than those who play nonviolent video games (puzzle, art, and world-building games like *The Sims*), even after controlling for family functioning and for children's earlier aggression. A final new meta-analysis of high-quality longitudinal studies shows that this association between violent video game play and aggression increases over childhood and peaks between the ages of 14 and 16.[66] After age 16, violent video games are only weakly linked to higher aggression.

These longitudinal studies are all correlational, which means we cannot identify the specific impact of violent video games on aggression. However, they do track changes in young people's aggression over time in response to their gaming habits, controlling for earlier aggression and many other family factors. The emerging pattern is a warning sign for us as parents and policymakers: We must be especially vigilant about protecting children and adolescents under 16 from violent content in video games.

Even nongamers and adults are not immune to the negative effects of video game violence. A new longitudinal study with adult players shows that merely having friends who play violent video games—even if you don't play them yourself—can lead to higher aggression in nonplayers over time through a social networking effect, in which aggression becomes normalized among friend groups.[67]

These findings are backed up by neuroscience research, which shows that playing violent video games specifically results in decreased prefrontal cortex activity, the brain region associated with higher-order thinking and inhibition of aggressive impulses.[68] For instance, a longitudinal experimental study with young men who normally didn't play many video games produced compelling effects: After a baseline functional magnetic resonance imaging (fMRI) scan, one group was randomly assigned to play

Call of Duty 4: Modern Warfare at least 1 hour a day, whereas a second group abstained from all video game play. After only 1 week, the *Call of Duty* players had decreased from baseline in their prefrontal cortex activity when performing a test of inhibition in the scanner, whereas the abstainers' prefrontal cortex activity stayed the same or showed slight increases. Decreased prefrontal cortex activity indexes lowered inhibitions, which in an altercation (at a university party, for instance, while drinking) could lead to aggressive language and behavior. We do not know yet how long-lasting these neural effects may be, however, or whether they lead to aggressive actions.

Immediately after playing a violent video game, adolescents' limbic activity is also reduced.[69] This effect is so specific that in one experimental study using the "hack and slash" video game *Dynasty Warriors 5*, every time a player killed an enemy, less blood flowed to the player's limbic region, which helps regulate thoughts and emotions.[70] Violent video game play also reduces communication between the prefrontal cortex and limbic regions.[71] Communication between the prefrontal cortex and limbic regions improves self-regulation by helping adolescents put on the brakes instead of being impulsive or aggressive.

Over time, the result is a clear desensitization to violence by which the empathy response is blunted, and aggressive responses become more likely. This desensitization is even stronger when playing first-person shooter games, such as *Halo*, than third-person games. (I suppose that's one point in favor of third-person shooter *Gears of War.*) Almost always, the participants in these neuroscience studies are young men because they are the ones who most often play violent action games. Although the *Dynasty Warrior* study from earlier contained both men and women, it was only the men who showed the desensitization effect.

These effects are especially concerning for adolescents, whose prefrontal cortex is in a period of rapid development.[72] Other toxins like drugs and extreme stress have a disproportionate impact on brain development when encountered during adolescence compared to later in life.

Armed with this knowledge, the only ethical experimental design on violent video gaming with children and adolescents is an intervention, in which one group of young people is somehow encouraged to reduce or replace their violent video game play with nonviolent games, and any changes in aggressive behavior or neural responding are compared to another group of young people who continue to game as usual.

Unfortunately, I could not find a single contemporary study that successfully reduced violent video game play among children or adolescents. Either researchers have gotten so caught up in the debate about whether

THE DANGERS OF FICTIONAL STORIES *(83)*

or not video game violence causes aggression that they're not doing this crucial but more difficult research, or they've tried and failed. Perhaps they couldn't even recruit a sample of young people who wanted to be in such a study. With the splendors of gaming options available today, what teen would sign up for a study in which they volunteer to reduce their gaming time, or replace their favorite action games with blander fare, like the *Lemmings* game I described in Chapter 4?

To make matters worse, many popular video games are strewn with sexist content and violence aimed at female characters. For instance, one study showed that simply viewing violent content against women in video games such as *Grand Theft Auto* led young men to be more likely to endorse rape myths, such as "A lot of women lead a man on and then they cry rape."[73] Another study with 12- to 15-year-old adolescents found that playing as a hypersexualized female character in a warrior adventure game for only 15 minutes increased acceptance of rape myths and tolerance of sexual harassment—among both boys and girls—compared to adolescents who had played the same game as a nonsexualized female character.[74]

New research is highlighting creative ways to dampen the effects of video game violence. One solution is to encourage teens to play video games cooperatively. In one study, young people teamed up to play a violent video game (*Halo* or *Time Splitters 2*) either cooperatively—by protecting each other and killing only the enemy—or competitively, in which they were encouraged to kill their partner along with enemies.[75] Those who played cooperatively were later less likely to "punish" their partner or a stranger with unpleasant blasts of white noise (a standard lab measure of aggression) than those who had played competitively. In fact, the cooperative players' aggression was at similar or even lower levels to a third, control group who had not yet played the game. Cooperative play essentially erased the short-term aggressive effects of violent video games.

This effect of cooperation works even if it's embedded in the storyline rather than with a real-life partner. The *Regeneration* version of the zombie-killer game *Evil Dead*, with its prosocial goal of protecting another character, reduced male players' aggressive behavior compared to *Fistful of Boomstick*, another version of *Evil Dead* in which every man is out for himself.[76] However, aggression was still not as low as for a third group who played the nonviolent video game *Tetris*. These experiments show that a prosocial context and storyline for violent video game play can protect gamers (somewhat) from becoming more aggressive.

Pulling together all of these strands, the evidence is now unequivocal that violent, sexist, racist, and idealistic content in fictional stories nudges people of all ages toward more hostile and stereotyped thoughts and aggression (verbal, physical, relational) and away from empathetic thoughts and prosocial behavior.

Given these small but real negative effects, it's important to treat screen time and gaming as a public health issue. However, it is only one among many issues affecting young people today. It's not the least of our worries, but nor is there cause for moral panic in which all the ills of society are blamed on video games. Sorry, parents and policymakers—that position is simply too easy, and it keeps us from focusing on other serious underlying issues such as child poverty, family violence, youth mental health, and gun control.[77] As neuroscientists Daphne Bavelier and Shawn Green concluded, "Violent video games alone are unlikely to turn a child with no other risk factors into a maniacal killer."[78]

TOO MANY STORIES?

Regardless of content or platform, how harmful is excessive screen time? (Unsurprisingly, a search did not reveal any contemporary research on the harmful effects of excessive book-reading.) A small minority of young people—up to 10%, depending upon how it's measured—develop into problem gamers, defined as gaming so much that it harms their relationships, their work or studies, and their health. In 2013, Internet gaming disorder (IGD) was listed in the American Psychiatric Association's *DSM-5* as a "condition for further study."[79] In 2019, the World Health Organization voted to include IGD in their *International Classification of Diseases*.[80]

Problem gamers are 8 times more likely to be male, to have preexisting symptoms of attention-deficit/hyperactivity disorder (ADHD), depression, or anxiety, to have had problems in school, and to have a negative family climate, coupled disastrously with lower social competence, empathy, and emotion regulation.[81] Female gaming is on the rise, however, so we shouldn't restrict our concerns to male gamers—about 20% of those with IGD are women.[82] The preferred game matters, too. IGD is more frequent among those who play massively multiplayer online role-playing games (MMORPGs) such as *World of Warcraft*, first-person shooter games such as *Call of Duty*, and real-time strategy games such as *Warhammer*. These games share addictive features of complex and unpredictable rewards as well as the opportunity to form social alliances with others online that collectively glue gamers to their seats.[83]

Fortunately, neither Anna nor Charlie was a problem gamer as a teen or young adult. Anna was too busy reading, studying, and playing music;

THE DANGERS OF FICTIONAL STORIES *(85)*

Charlie was too busy hunting, fishing, and playing sports to game to excess. However, 10% of the young people in *Origins*—most of whom were young men, including Marco and Hayden—reported gaming 4 hours or more every weekday.

Excessive gamers like Marco and Hayden are the ones we urgently need to understand and help. What else is happening in their lives that motivates them to spend so much time playing video games? As with young children's excessive screen time, we must consider their use in the larger context of familial, peer, and societal factors such as poverty and limited opportunities. Just as critical, we must take into account the features of the games and the platforms themselves that are promoting addictive use for some people.[84] New interdisciplinary research collaborations with game publishers are promising both for increasing the quality of the data and for designing prevention efforts for this generation and future generations of gamers.[85]

For the current cohort of middle-aged adults, excessive binge-watching of TV shows may instead be the most serious danger of fictional stories. Dubbed the Netflix effect, streaming services have wrought a dramatic change in the past decade in the way all of us now watch TV. At the height of my Scandi-noir obsession, I had to rein myself in from hitting "next episode" again and again.

The popular press is divided on whether binge-watching is a good or a bad thing. On the one hand, journalist M. Willens calls it "binge-bonding." On the other hand, Matthew Schneier of *The New York Times* has identified what he calls "Unseasonal Affective Disorder: Post-Binge Malaise."

What is the scientific answer? We simply don't know yet; the Netflix effect is so new that psychological research is only beginning to tackle it. Researchers have only recently converged on a definition of binge-watching as clicking ahead to that third episode in a single sitting.[86] (Some early studies included even two back-to-back episodes as a binge.) Only one systematic review exists so far, and with only 24 studies,[87] but more research is streaming in every month. In line with the discovery phase of this research, most of these studies are online, cross-sectional surveys, not higher-quality longitudinal or experimental studies.

So far, however, the picture is mostly positive. Most of us do binge-watch these days, and occasional binge-watching doesn't appear to be a problem for most people. For instance, one study found that binge-watching was linked to positive feelings of relaxation immediately after, with no negative effects.[88] Motive matters: Those who are binge-watching out of loneliness or to escape are more likely to develop problematic use over time, whereas those who are binge-watching for fun or relaxation are able to keep their use in check.[89] A high-quality experimental study, in which participants watched either a single episode or three episodes in a row of turn-of-the-century hits *Felicity* or *Everwood*, showed that binge-watching does increase the viewer's transportation into the narrative.[90] By now, readers will be aware that transportation into a narrative can maximize the benefits *and* the detriments of viewing.

Moreover, binge-watching by definition means long hours spent sitting in front of a screen. Heavier binge-watching is associated (albeit weakly) with sleep problems, anxious attachment and depression, and with avoiding interactions with family and friends in order to watch a favorite series.[91] All of the dangers of any sedentary behavior also apply: In a very large longitudinal study of older adults, the risk of chronic disease, obesity, and even death increased with every 2-hour increase in daily TV viewing, after controlling for other variables.[92] Another potential danger of binge-watching is that we are more likely to binge on other substances, including food and drink, while we're watching.[93] There's a growing (pun intended) literature on how all of us, at all ages, lose self-control over our appetites while watching a screen.[94]

I expect the answer to the question of how binge-watching affects adults will be, as for many forms of media, "it depends": on how we're using it, for what reasons, and on our own characteristics and situations. It's intriguing to me that some of the personality traits associated with problematic binge-watching—lower agreeableness and lower openness—are the exact opposite of those linked to fiction reading and book-club membership.[95]

It's possible that there are healthy and positive ways to binge-watch, or binge-bond as Willens puts it. As with all addictive substances and activities, those healthy ways will probably be more social (either with real live people or virtually—the new date night), intentional, and for reasons of engagement and restoration rather than merely passing the time and escaping. Perhaps a new version of face-to-face streaming clubs will supplement book clubs and will attract more men. Perhaps fathers and sons who don't like to read books will watch shows together and discuss them, and mothers and daughters will bond while watching new mother–daughter shows together as they used to watch the latest *Gilmore Girls* episode together each week in the past. Pretty much any activity between parents and teenagers that involves being in the same room and talking—not arguing—has got to be a good thing, and it may even spark some much-needed conversations about difficult topics.

What is the antidote to these violent, sexist, racist, anthropomorphic, fantastical, unrealistic, misleading, and addictive fictional stories? Are real-life stories the answer? In my younger and more idealistic days as a memory researcher of family stories, I used to think so.

CHAPTER 6

The Dangers of Real-Life Stories

Well, this, and this, and this have happened. It would not be accurate as told. She thought nothing could be told and be accurate.

—Elizabeth Strout, *The Burgess Boys*

Unlike fictional stories from books or screens, real-life stories are inescapable. Throughout history and in all cultures around the world, humans tell stories of their personal experiences to themselves and to each other every single day of their lives.[1] At family dinnertimes, we tell one of these stories every 5 minutes![2] Although these stories are based on real events, they are never slavishly accurate. They are at best partial, usually partially invented, and always interpreted. Through my own and others' research on autobiographical memory, I now know that the way we remember and misremember events, and the way that we invent ourselves through the stories of our lives, are replete with dangers.

THE SCIENCE OF MEMORY FOR REAL-LIFE EVENTS

Because our ability to encode and retain events is limited, and our memory fades rapidly, we fill the gaps in our real-life stories with what is generally true or seems plausible. Later we believe that those insertions actually happened. We also seamlessly fuse details of similar events without realizing we are doing so.[3] Occasionally we are misled (intentionally or

How Stories Change Us. Elaine Reese, Oxford University Press. © Oxford University Press 2024.
DOI: 10.1093/oso/9780197747902.003.0006

THE DANGERS OF REAL-LIFE STORIES *(89)*

otherwise) about the true details of events, as when police officers or lawyers question eyewitnesses about a crime scene using leading questions.

Psychologist Elizabeth Loftus and colleagues have amply demonstrated the fallibility of our memories for real life in the face of misleading questions in a massive body of research since the 1970s.[4] Ironically, many of these misinformation studies are based on participants' memories of staged and filmed events, because that's the only way to know with certainty what actually happened in the original event.

For instance, the classic Loftus study involved young people viewing a film of a car accident.[5] Immediately after the film, they were asked about the accident using factual questions ("How fast was the white sports car going while traveling along the country road?") or misleading questions ("How fast was the white sports car going *when it passed the barn* while traveling along the country road?"). In fact, there was no barn in the film. One week later at a memory test, those who had received the misleading question were over 5 times as likely to incorrectly answer "yes" when asked "Did you see a barn?"

A number of features increase these errors. For instance, repeated exposure to misinformation makes it even more likely that it will get incorporated into the memory as fact.[6] Errors also grow the more time has elapsed between the original event and the misinformation, or between the misinformation and the memory question. Unfortunately, people who are more cooperative (aka potential fiction lovers) might be more suggestible in the face of misinformation than those with lower levels of cooperation—but only if they are also lower in cognitive ability.[7]

When we're recalling the past, it's not just nonexistent objects like barns that we get wrong. Loftus and colleagues went on to show that we can be misled to believe that an entire false event actually happened.[8] In these studies, experimenters "implanted" false memories by sending young adults a booklet of family stories that they had prepared with the help of a parent. Three of the stories were true memories from childhood, but the fourth was a false memory of getting lost in a local mall. Each faux *Lost in the Mall* story was crafted with real details supplied by parents. Here's a story the researchers tailored to a 20-year-old Vietnamese American student:

> You, your mom, Tien and Tuan all went to the Bremerton K-Mart. You must have been 5 years old at the time. Your mom gave each of you money to get a blueberry Icee. You ran ahead to get in the line first, and somehow lost your way in the store. Tien found you crying to an elderly Chinese woman. You three then went together to get an Icee.

The false stories worked on some people, not others. At an interview 1 month later, a full 75% of the young people resisted the misinformation, claiming they remembered nothing about getting lost at the mall. But a quarter of the young people claimed to remember at least something about the false event, sometimes inventing new details about it. Even after they were debriefed that the event never really happened, they continued to experience the memory as true. For instance, one participant said, "I totally remember walking around in those dressing rooms and my mom not being in the section she said she'd be in." The fact that these fabricated events are about one's own life (rather than a staged event from a film) can make them particularly memorable.

One criticism, however, of the *Lost in the Mall* study is that many children may have temporarily experienced feeling lost on a shopping expedition, even if parents weren't aware this had ever happened to them. However, later studies have replicated the effect with events that could never have happened, such as seeing Bugs Bunny at Disneyland (Bugs Bunny is a Warner Brothers character so could never have been at Disneyland).[9] Psychologists Maryanne Garry and Devon Polaschek showed that even imagining a false event increases the likelihood that we think that event actually happened.[10]

We construct our memories not just from what we saw and experienced at the original event but also from any relevant information we've encountered since the event, whether that information is true or false. Neuroimaging studies suggest that this false information gets incorporated into the memory as actually experienced, as revealed by activation of the medial temporal lobe—the brain's memory hub.[11]

Given the pervasiveness of real-life stories in our everyday lives, the implications are weighty. Many innocent people end up going to prison on the basis of false eyewitness testimony. The Innocence Project was founded in 1992 as an attempt to overturn these wrongful convictions using expert testimony about the prevalence of false memories, in addition to DNA evidence.

In everyday life, parents may also unwittingly mislead their children into developing false memories when they ask leading questions about an event for which they have little or no knowledge, or even hold false information themselves.[12] Parents' rich reminiscing about an event, such as Anna's mother's reconstruction of their farm visit in Chapter 3, is a double-edged sword. Parents who use an open-ended and accepting reminiscing style, like Anna's mother, help children to later remember those events better.[13] But parents who focus too much on the accuracy of specific details

THE DANGERS OF REAL-LIFE STORIES *(91)*

can end up asking leading questions that cause children to later falsely remember events.[14]

A tragic example of this phenomenon happened in the Little Rascals daycare case in 1989, when parents, police, and therapists repeatedly interviewed young children about suspected sexual abuse by two teachers.[15] Whether or not the abuse actually happened, the adult questioners may have unintentionally implanted memories of sexual abuse in the minds of the children, who came to believe that the horrific events actually happened.

Young children are not the only ones who can be misled by leading questions.[16] Adolescents and adults, too, can come to believe false memories of sexual abuse, usually at the repeated suggestions of an incompetent therapist, with devastating results for families. Loftus' compelling book, *The Myth of Repressed Memory: False Memories and Allegations of Sexual Abuse*,[17] should have put recovered memory techniques into the firepit of damaging therapies once and for all, but unfortunately some clinicians still use them.[18] Given the high rates of documented childhood abuse and the devastation it can cause, psychologist Gail Goodman maintains that clinicians do need to ask their clients about that possibility.[19] However, reputable therapists do not repeatedly question a client about suspected child abuse just because someone presents with symptoms of depression and anxiety.

The ease with which false memories can be created seems maladaptive. Shouldn't our brains be wired to ferret out truth? Psychologist Dan Schacter argues that our memories are so malleable because we need to constantly update the original event with new information—such as the location of a food source in our hunter-gatherer past.[20] It would be maladaptive if we were stuck with the original memory, rigidly refusing to accommodate new information. So we have to live with this malleability; the best we can do is to be aware of the insidious effect that misinformation after an event can have on our memories.

So far this pattern is all sounding very similar to the misinformation effects from books and movies from Chapter 5—when we're exposed to inaccurate information in a book or movie or from a misleading question, even when it conflicts with what we previously knew to be true, we incorporate those errors effortlessly into our memories. But although children and older adults are *less* likely than young adults to incorporate errors from books and movies into their memories, children and older adults are up to 10 times *more* likely than young adults to incorporate errors from misleading questions after a real-life event into their memories.[21]

Why are these misinformation effects for fictional and real-life events so radically different across the lifespan?

The answer lies in the development of two memory systems: semantic and episodic.[22] *Semantic memory* consists of the facts that we know about the world, such as that Paris is the capital of France. *Episodic memory* is instead our memory for particular events or experiences, such as the time we went to Paris and waited in a long line in the summer heat at the Musée d'Orsay. The traditional view was that semantic and episodic memory are distinct in the brain, with the hippocampus and surrounding medial temporal lobe playing a more central role in episodic than in semantic memory, which is served by a larger number of brain regions supporting multimodal processing. Semantic memory continues to accrue over a lifetime and is much more durable than episodic memory, which peaks in young adulthood and then declines. For instance, older people may have trouble remembering what they did last week, but their knowledge about the world, and their words for that knowledge, are mostly intact and still accumulating.

The contemporary view is instead that the line between semantic and episodic memory can be blurry, with more overlap than previously believed.[23] Both semantic and episodic memory rely on the hippocampus and on the more extensive default network. Every word and concept in our semantic memory began with an episodic memory: We first learned that word or concept at a specific time, in a particular place, even if we can no longer recall those episodic details. And every episodic memory also contains elements of semantic memory. It's impossible to describe a traffic accident to another person without relying on shared world knowledge about cars, physics, and the legal system.

With that backdrop in mind, let's revisit the misinformation effects from books, movies, and real life across the lifespan. The memory tests in the misinformation studies of movies and books tap semantic memory— *What is the capital of France?* Young children don't yet have an extensive knowledge base about the world in which to attach new information, and the misinformation provided is almost always new. When coupled with their poorer episodic memory for learning and retaining new details, young children simply learn fewer facts overall, whether true or false, compared to older children and young adults.[24] And although older adults have a more extensive knowledge base than children and young adults, their episodic memory for new details has declined—leading to older adults also remembering less true and false information from books and movies than young adults.[25]

In contrast, the memory tests in the real-life misinformation studies rely on episodic memory for event details—*Did you see a barn?*—as well as "source memory" —knowing where or when we saw or learned something, whether from the original event or from the question afterward.

THE DANGERS OF REAL-LIFE STORIES (93)

Children and older adults have relatively poor episodic memory and particularly poor source memory.[26] So, when confronted with a misleading question about a detail from a real-life event (or a film of one), young children and the elderly are more likely to be suggestible because they blur together their memory of the original event with their memory of the information in the misleading question. Young adults, however, possess both stronger episodic memory for the details of the original event *and* better source memory, which combine to make them less suggestible in the real-life misinformation studies.

Despite these age differences, young and old alike are prone to misinformation effects across all sources. Psychologist Steven Frenda stated it succinctly: "Nobody is immune to the distorting effects of misinformation."[27]

THE CONTAMINATED STORIES WE TELL
ABOUT OUR OWN LIVES

Remembering events and facts inaccurately, or creating entire false memories, is clearly harmful when someone's life or liberty is at stake. Fortunately, most of us never have to provide eyewitness testimony in court. A pervasive memory bias that can affect us all is how we interpret and evaluate the events in our lives, small and large.
Dangers lurk in the stories that we tell ourselves and others about our experiences.

Remember the positive effects for well-being of redemption narratives, in which we take a bad experience and find something good about it? The opposite pattern is what Dan McAdams calls the "contamination" narrative, in which we create a story in which something good happens in our lives and then sours.[28] A classic example of a contamination narrative is a relationship gone bad, with no silver lining. For instance, the narratives we tell about our lives soon after a divorce can easily fall into this trap.

Fortunately, Charlie and Anna from *Origins* told healthy life stories as young adults that did not contain themes of contamination, mirroring their rareness in the general population. But not all of the *Origins* participants were as fortunate. Here, 20-year-old Alex describes the way a breakup tainted all aspects of his life, especially the way he felt about himself:

Before it happened, I feel like I was really happy with pretty much everything in my life. There wasn't really anything that made me unhappy at all. I was happy with university, I was doing well, I had a girlfriend that was going well prior to things starting to go bad, I was happy with my circle of friends, everything was

going well. And then afterwards, I don't know, I just, obviously I was unhappy
'cause I was no longer with her, but I noticed my university results started not
being as great, bickering with friends. Arguments, things weren't necessarily
making me happy the way they used to. It made me lose a lot of confidence in
myself. Just, I wasn't happy with who I was as a person anymore, really. I started,
the breakup made me look at myself and start to notice, just little things that
I wasn't happy about with myself.

Contamination narratives are not just about personal issues, however.
They can also crop up in the aftermath of a more public disaster, such as
this story from psychologists Jon Adler and Michael Poulin's study of
9/11 narratives:[29]

I have always lived in New York, and the towers were around for all of my adult
life. I saw them being built as a child. Their loss to me is akin to the loss a parent
feels when he/she loses a child. I also feel the country lost some of its sense of
innocence on that day. I now wake up each day dreading what may happen.

Contamination narratives creep insidiously backward into one's past to
negatively color events from before the downturn. Not surprisingly, people
who tell contamination narratives suffer from higher levels of depression
and lower life satisfaction and self-esteem.[30] When bad things happen to
us, and we ruminate obsessively about why, we can sometimes create unhealthy and unhelpful storylines.

Even though life's tribulations accumulate as we grow older, this tainting
of life's events is not inevitable.[31] There *are* healthy ways to craft life stories
about negative experiences. These healthy ways are to focus on redemption
in the face of death and destruction, to seek the silver lining in any cloud,
and to savor the small good things in our lives even when the big things are
going terribly wrong.

I can tell you that it's a tall order to find a silver lining when grieving the
unexpected death of a parent, when coping with the aftermath of divorce
on your children, or when you've just been diagnosed with cancer. It may
take years to pull together a positive story in the face of tragedy. It's not
just the passage of time that helps. As Holocaust survivor Edith Eger says
in her memoir *The Choice*, "Time doesn't heal. It's what you do with the
time."[32]

Young people in particular may not yet have the maturity or life experience to put tragic events in perspective. In our cross-cultural studies with
over 400 New Zealand Chinese, Māori, and European adolescents from
ages 12 to 20, we did not find strong evidence of redemption themes in

their stories.[33] Some of them had already experienced tragedies, such as seeing a younger sibling run over by a truck. (Note that a clinical psychologist was always on call when these tragic events came out in an interview.) Instead of full-fledged redemption, most of their attempts at drawing meaning from these negative experiences were smaller and more localized, as when they talked about the perspective they had gained as a result, or the ways they had changed as a person. When young people like Alex draw more of these negative connections between the event and the self, they experience higher levels of depression and lower self-esteem.[34]

Telling stories in these negative ways may increase depression and lower well-being, but it could also be the case that depressed individuals, with their dark view of life, are predisposed to tell stories with contamination themes. There are only a few longitudinal studies so far on this important phenomenon, and little experimental evidence.[35] If we were to do an experimental intervention study on this topic, we would need to first help people reshape these polluted tales in more positive ways and then track any resulting increases in well-being.

Some adolescents, and most adults, will experience much more stressful events than Alex's relationship breakup. The incidence of experiencing a traumatic event at some point in one's life is as high as 90%, depending on the definition of trauma.[36] But fewer than 10% of us will go on to develop posttraumatic stress disorder (PTSD), with more women than men suffering from PTSD. Symptoms of PTSD include involuntarily recalling the traumatic event despite attempts to avoid thinking about it, trouble concentrating, negative mood, and hypervigilance about potential dangers in the environment. Memories of traumatic events can cause great distress and dysfunction.

The type of traumatic event experienced makes a difference. The traumatic events most commonly linked to PTSD are being sexually or physically assaulted, being in combat, experiencing the sudden unexpected death of a loved one, or having a child with a chronic illness.[37] These events don't happen to most people, and for this reason they are sometimes not talked about with others. When we don't talk about an event, either out of shame or because we don't think others will understand, we may not fully process the traumatic event in a way that will loosen its hold on our lives.[38] And when we actively try *not* to think about a traumatic event—to push it away—it paradoxically comes to mind even more.[39]

Another danger of these memories is that sometimes the traumatic events are integrated too well, to the extent that they become central to the individual's life story. In their landmark paper on this phenomenon, psychologists Dorthe Berntsen and David Rubin use the example of a student who reportedly still suffered from the trauma of being in a serious car accident.[40] The student recounted how an ill-informed therapist had helped her to see that the horrific event was symbolic of a lack of control that extended to every aspect of her life, including her relationships. When a person places a traumatic event as a turning point in their lives—the linchpin to their identity—that event comes to define them, with disturbing consequences.[41]

Some people are more prone than others to experiencing PTSD symptoms after trauma. Young adults who are high in the personality trait of neuroticism—people who react strongly to events in a negative way, and who are likely to be anxious, to ruminate often, and to become depressed—may be more likely to place a traumatic event as the cornerstone of their life story.[42] Although rates of PTSD overall are higher in women than in men, those men who are high in neuroticism are especially prone to developing PTSD.[43]

In contrast, young adults who rate themselves as higher in agreeableness are *less* likely to experience PTSD symptoms as a result of trauma.[44] Recall that many fiction lovers, especially women, are high in agreeableness, which could be a protective factor against PTSD symptoms after trauma. For those of us who are high *both* in neuroticism and agreeableness, perhaps the risk of PTSD cancels out, or perhaps the risk from neuroticism remains. We just don't know yet. We need longitudinal studies to find out more about the way our personalities can predispose us toward, or protect us from, these damaging effects of the way we frame negative and traumatic events in our lives.

We also need careful clinical studies of how best to help people who place traumatic events into a central role in their identities. Fortunately, PTSD can be treated successfully with trauma-focused cognitive behavioral therapy (TF-CBT) and with eye movement desensitization and reprocessing (EMDR).[45] If you or a family member is experiencing PTSD symptoms after a traumatic event, seek help from a licensed clinical psychologist.

We also know that adolescents who have experienced trauma or tragedy are even more vulnerable to developing PTSD than are adults.[46] In their first forays into independent life storytelling, young adolescents may be especially susceptible to drawing these negative connections to the self. Several research groups around the world are finding that young adolescents (under age 14) who tell the most coherent real-life stories, with the clearest connections to their identity, are those who also report the lowest levels of well-being.[47] Researchers and clinical psychologists are now trying to figure out why.

In a heartbreaking example from one of my studies, 13-year-old Tony chooses as his life's turning point "the first time my father hit me in the face for not doing my homework."[48] Tony has the disquieting insight that his dad's violence has made him act aggressively toward others, including girls and women.

> All right, since my father's probably hit me I given a piece of him to me so I'm now a bit yeah like my dad, um does it make sense? I'm kind of very aggressive towards other people . . . like ah, she's doing the wrong thing, I—I react, I don't mean to over-react, I mean to [not] do it again, but I just stressing out and kind of . . . doing what my dad does. And I just don't normally trust people . . . the way I should.

It's possible that these young adolescents with clearer insights have been forced by difficult life events to grow up before they're ready. It's also possible that the way their parents or other adults frame real-life stories with them has contributed to their negative self-concept.[49] We know that people who have experienced trauma are prone to casting a negative light on the events of their lives; for instance, they are especially susceptible to creating false negative memories.[50]

Critically, the neuroscience of trauma reveals that those suffering from PTSD exhibit altered connectivity of the default network.[51] This altered connectivity is apparent in both adults and adolescents with PTSD, with reduced cohesiveness of the default network linked to impaired episodic memory and to more severe symptoms of PTSD.[52]

A strong predictor of PTSD is a tendency to ruminate.[53] What's the difference between rumination and reflection? Rumination involves repetitive, restricted, and often unwanted thoughts about the causes and consequences of a negative event. The unfortunate result of rumination about a traumatic event can be for individuals to place that event as an anchor to their burgeoning life story, or to view themselves as damaged and vulnerable as a result of the trauma.[54] These ways of framing a traumatic event create a great deal of distress and do not bode well for the future. Adolescents and young adults are particularly prone to ruminative thinking because their prefrontal cortex (governing cognitive control) is still developing, in contrast to their subcortical amygdala (governing emotional responses), which has come online in childhood.[55] Simply put, it's difficult for adolescents to use more sophisticated strategies of cognitive reappraisal and acceptance in the face of strong negative emotions.

Older adolescents and young adults with more cognitive and emotional resources are instead able to move to a second stage of true reflection on the traumatic event. This more productive thinking can lead to posttraumatic growth instead of posttraumatic stress.[56] Even for adults, this kind of thinking takes time—in one study of adults who had achieved posttraumatic growth, the traumatic event had occurred, on average, 15 years earlier.[57] My cancer diagnosis was a turning point in my life, but ultimately for good: It still helps me to appreciate each and every day that has been given to me since.

These ruminative patterns for young adolescents are evident when they use Pennebaker's expressive writing techniques. Remember how adults' health improves when they write about difficult or traumatic experiences?[58] The same expressive writing techniques that make adults healthier appear to make younger adolescents (ages 9–13) more depressed and anxious over time.[59] As I noted in Chapter 4, solo expressive writing is contraindicated for young adolescents. They do not appear to be able to pull positive meaning yet from these difficult life experiences in the same ways as older adolescents and adults.

The good news is that for older adolescents (14 and up), expressive writing about difficult events has positive effects on objectively good outcomes in their lives—increasing not only mental health but also school attendance and performance, and decreasing physical complaints and doctor visits, with even stronger effects for troubled teens.[60] Perhaps expressive writing could become part of more comprehensive memory therapies, administered by a clinician, to prevent or treat symptoms of PTSD in older teens and adults who have experienced trauma.[61]

THE DANGERS OF FAMILY STORIES

So far I've been focusing on the pitfalls of stories we all tell about events we personally experienced. What about stories of others' lives—our family's stories? Should some be rated PG-13, R, or even NC-17 and not told to our children until they are adults, or left untold altogether?

On the whole, family stories are good for young people. Recall from Chapter 4 that adolescents who know more of their family's history report better well-being. Yet researchers are finding that vicarious family stories— those that parents or grandparents have told us about their own lives—are sometimes linked to adolescent depression and low self-esteem.[62] In our lab, these negative links between family stories and ill health were more prevalent for Māori adolescents, whose families had experienced greater social and economic difficulties, than for New Zealand European or Chinese adolescents. We are still digging down into the content of the stories to figure out the exact reasons for these negative connections. In her eloquent book, *Family Narratives and the Development of an Autobiographical Self*, my PhD advisor, Robyn Fivush, advocates that negative family stories *do* need to be told, but with great care and sensitivity.[63] When told honestly and carefully, tragic family stories can be healing and can bring families together. Bart van Es has achieved this beautifully in his memoir, *The Cut Out Girl*, of his Aunt Lien's time in hiding as a Jewish child in the Netherlands in World War II.[64] Van Es intimates that the telling of Lien's story has brought the younger generations of their family together.

We now know, however, that young people are particularly prone to experiencing PTSD even from traumatic events that weren't personally experienced. For instance, Simon Baron-Cohen opens his book *The Science of Evil* with a story that his father told him at age 7 about a girlfriend's mother who was a concentration camp survivor.[65] Nazi doctors had performed an experiment on her hands, detaching them and then reattaching to the opposite arm, so that her thumbs forever stuck outward instead of inward. This horrific image was indelibly etched on young Simon's mind as an illustration of pure evil that had been directed at a member of his tribe. Perhaps particularly traumatic family stories should be left until older adolescence or even young adulthood to be told. But if those stories are never told, the gap in the family history and the silence surrounding the events may ultimately be even more damaging.

In *The Choice*, one of the best memoirs I've ever read, Auschwitz survivor Edith Eger tried for many years to shield her children from the traumas she experienced.[66] Eventually she realized that "silence and denial aren't the only choices to make in the wake of catastrophic loss." She asks, "What if telling my story could lighten its grip instead of tightening it? What if speaking about the past could heal it instead of calcify it?"

TELLING IT LIKE IT ISN'T: STORIES OF OURSELVES AND OTHERS ON SOCIAL MEDIA

These days, we tell many of our real-life stories over social media in addition to—and often instead of—telling them face to face. With new platforms popping up all the time like heads of the Hydra, scientists are scrambling to figure out the impact of social media on our well-being. Like all other forms of sharing stories, social media appears to be a double-edged sword, with both benefits and dangers. Most of the psychological research is on Facebook; at the time of writing, it is still the most popular platform, with nearly 3 billion users worldwide.[67] My focus is primarily on text/story-based platforms such as Facebook, Twitter (now X), and TikTok as opposed to image-based platforms such as Instagram and Snapchat.

The first danger of all forms of social media is excessive use. The algorithmic basis of all social media platforms virtually ensures that we stay on longer than we intended—our news feed has been carefully curated to appeal to our unique interests.[68] Johann Hari's book *Stolen Focus: Why You Can't Pay Attention* offers a fascinating insider look at these algorithms, as does the 2020 docudrama *The Social Dilemma*. I experienced these algorithms firsthand when, after clicking on a few baby videos on my Facebook feed and some others of kittens, I was soon seeing videos only of babies *with* kittens!

It would be wonderful if baby and kitten videos were our most pressing concerns about social media.

Early social media studies were crude, looking only at how often we use social media in relation to our current well-being. See psychologists Jonathan Haidt and Jean Twenge's valuable list of key studies of social media and well-being at https://jonathanhaidt.com/social-media/ for in-depth summaries and commentary. These early studies can't tell us whether we're depressed because we're using social media or whether we're using social media because we're depressed. Nor were these simplistic associations even consistent. Some studies found that social media was linked to a greater sense of connection to others, whereas other studies found that social media was linked to loneliness, depression, anxiety, and sleep problems. So many social media studies now exist that researchers are not just at the stage of conducting meta-analyses; they are now conducting meta-reviews *of* meta-analyses. These umbrella reviews consistently show a weak negative link between how often we use social media (mainly Facebook) and diverse aspects of well-being.[69] No matter how you slice it, there is a small but real connection between text-based social media use and increased loneliness, depression, and anxiety.

But are young people at greater risk than the rest of us, parallel to the concerns with violent video games? Brain development is especially rapid in the teen years, and thus vulnerable to insult and injury. "Moving parts get broken," claimed the authors of a seminal paper on adolescent brain development.[70] There is a grave concern that excessive online interactions are especially damaging for teens. Soon after social media was launched, a related worry was that teens' online interactions might someday supplant their real-life interactions.

Teens have already reached that tipping point.

A Commonsense Media survey showed that in 2012, real-life interactions still won out: Teens preferred to communicate with friends in person than online via social media, texting, or video-calling.[71] Since 2017, however, they now prefer interacting with their friends through a screen rather than in person. A 2021 Common Sense Media report showed that these trends intensified in the pandemic, with screen time ballooning for all, especially among preteens.[72] And from the preteen years, girls are using social media significantly more often than boys.[73]

And, yes, young people are at greater risk of experiencing the downsides of social media. A massive UK analysis of over 84,000 participants from age 10 to 80 identified adolescence as a sensitive window in which young people's social media use was more likely to be linked to lower life satisfaction—a key indicator of well-being.[74] When the authors drilled down into these associations for young people over time, it became clear that heavier social media use was especially risky at certain ages: for girls at ages 11–13, and for boys at ages 14–15. These different sensitive windows for boys and girls map roughly onto pubertal changes. At these young ages, there was no "Goldilocks effect" for either boys or girls such that moderate use of social media was best. Instead, the relationship was linear, in which increasing use of social media was increasingly bad for their well-being. In keeping with their greater use of social media, effects for young adolescent girls were much stronger than for young adolescent boys.[75] But note that nearly all these studies are based on Northern Hemisphere adolescents, whereas 88% of the world's adolescents live in the Global South (now more aptly called the Majority World).[76] We urgently need to know if these same patterns are present for the bulk of the world's adolescents.

Fortunately both Anna and Charlie were temperate users of social media throughout their teens, at about 1 hour a day. However, nearly 15% of the participants in the *Origins* study at age 16 were heavy social media users, defined as 3 hours or more on a typical weekday. The top two users were young women—Katie and Rosa—who clocked up over 5 hours each school day on social media. These young people indeed reported significantly higher levels of depression and lower levels of self-esteem and life satisfaction compared to those who were lighter users.

For the rest of us, it turns out the dangers lie more in the *way* we're using social media—and how it uses us—than *how often* we're using social media.

Again, the psychological research has focused primarily on Facebook to date. The negative effects seem to be due to a perfect storm of Facebook's features: People often disclose intimate details on Facebook that are then permanently recorded and evaluated (or ignored) by peers. When looking at others' profiles, we often engage in negative social comparisons and end up feeling that everyone else's life is perfect in comparison to our own blotchy real-life version.[77] We may also experience the green-eyed monster of Facebook envy. Then we start ruminating on the multitude of reasons our life doesn't match up to our friends' lives, and this rumination leads to Facebook depression.[78]

The way we present ourselves on social media also makes a difference. In a high-quality experimental study, media researcher Eric Jang and colleagues encouraged adults to use Facebook in different ways: One group was encouraged to present themselves honestly, warts and all, whereas another group was instead encouraged to present themselves "strategically" in an idealized, exclusively positive way.[79] Then participants reported on their happiness. The immediate effects on happiness depended on one's self-esteem at the start of the study: The authentic presentation led to happiness only for those users who already had high self-esteem at the start of the study. For people with low self-esteem, it was instead strategic self-presentation that was more likely to lead to happiness. When we're feeling vulnerable, it does seem that a little polishing of the rough edges of our lives makes sense before we post.

But that doesn't mean we should present ourselves falsely or lie. Another study explored the degree to which we outright lie on Facebook—about our age, gender, achievements, jobs, relationships—as well as how often we pretend to like a post that we don't actually like. People with low self-esteem were more likely to lie and false like; false liking in particular was linked to higher levels of depression, stress, and anxiety.[80]

The content that we experience on social media makes a difference, too. A review of 70 studies (mainly of Facebook use) showed that negative online interactions are consistently linked to depression.[81] For instance, one study found that *all* types of negative content on Facebook—meanness, bullying, unwanted contact, misunderstandings—were associated with higher levels of depression, particularly if the incident occurred in adolescence.[82] This effect seems to work both ways: Depressed young people are at especially high risk of being bullied by peers on Facebook in reaction to their pleas for social support, and the resulting bullying then exacerbates their depression.

Social media can also be a source of well-being for people, but often for those who are already feeling good about themselves.[83] Social networkers who do experience positive interactions, social support, and feelings of connectedness report lower levels of depression.

What is the moral here? Most of us need to use social media with extreme caution. When we do go on social media, it is important to be positive in our posts and likes but to stay true to ourselves.[84] We can start by cultivating a smaller number of real friends on Facebook instead of adding

THE DANGERS OF REAL-LIFE STORIES *(103)*

scores of acquaintances. When looking at a close friend's profile, we know the bumpy realities and are less likely to engage in negative comparisons with our own lives than we would with an acquaintance. These days, we can restrict our news feed to real friends and family.

If we really want to be happier and more satisfied with our lives, however, we should consider taking a break from social media altogether or reducing it to the bare minimum. That's what health psychologist Jeff Lambert encouraged UK adults to do for a week in a high-quality experimental study.[85] Then he tracked their well-being, depression, and anxiety compared to another group of UK adults who used social media as usual. The result? Those who took a social media break reported increased well-being and less depression and anxiety by the end of the week, especially for those who reduced their time on Twitter and TikTok, specifically. Benefits in a similar study specifically with Facebook were even greater for those who had been heavy users at the outset, for people who often experienced Facebook envy, and for those who mostly used Facebook passively rather than actively.[86]

Why do we keep returning to social media if it's making us feel worse? The problem is that we're pathetic at predicting what's going to make us happy. Psychologists Tobias Greitemeyer and Christina Saglioglou conducted a study that helps us understand why Facebook and other social media platforms cause unhappiness.[87] Before using social media, we think that it will help us feel better, but in actuality, social media makes us feel worse because we realize afterward that it's mostly a meaningless activity, particularly if all we've been doing is passive scrolling. We continually forget this insight and keep coming back to social media in what is called a "forecasting error" in our thinking.

As of the time of writing, there is not a single published experiment of social media reduction with adolescents. What teen will volunteer to cut down on their social media use? My urgent recommendation is that researchers need to conduct a longitudinal prevention study *before* tweens get onto social media, with random assignment to an incentive group for delaying the start of social media compared to an "as usual" control group. Only then can we begin to discover the long-term benefits of delaying social media for adolescents' health and well-being.

It's important to note that any psychological research is going to be based on the social media of the past, not present. Researchers can't keep up; by the time we collect longitudinal data, analyze it, and publish it, social media platforms have changed dramatically. Indeed, Facebook present is now more like TikTok than like Facebook past. We must supplement traditional psychological research with interdisciplinary research, big-data analyses, and insider knowledge from industry experts.[88] Our young people are too valuable for us to be conducting a worldwide social experiment upon them without any controls.

Regardless of age, all of us can also fall prey to misinformation in the form of fake news reports over social media. For instance, we're more likely to believe fake news we've seen repeatedly—the "illusory truth effect"— or when we are imbibing news while in a more emotional than rational state.[89] Psychologist Daniel Kahneman, winner of the Nobel Prize, distinguished between our intuitive System 1 thinking and reflective System 2 thinking in his must-read book *Thinking, Fast and Slow*.[90] Intuitive System 1 thinking is fast and efficient but can be faulty; it must be balanced by reflective System 2 thinking when discerning fact over fake. A study entitled "Fake news, fast and slow" demonstrated that people's initial intuitive belief in fake news headlines could be corrected when encouraged to deliberate about its truth value.[91] Unfortunately, when we're scrolling through our social media feed, most of us are in intuitive System 1 mode and are not applying the brakes with our System 2 thinking.

Of course, people's credulity of biased journalism existed long before social media. A huge body of research shows that even slight differences in the way ingroup and outgroup members are described in a news story can lead to biased and prejudiced beliefs and intentions.[92] Yet in the past decade, the transmission of fake news via social media has accelerated.[93] Fake news really does travel faster than true news on social media and can have devastating real-life consequences.[94] For instance, after reading on Twitter that the owners of a pizza joint called Comet Ping Pong were running a child-sex ring (purportedly organized by Hillary Clinton), Edgar Welch fired an assault rifle into the shop.

Fake news moves us away from empathy for others and toward entrenched beliefs about our own group's superiority. Fake news thus works in the opposite direction to the social benefits of reading and watching fiction.

Psychologists are working hard to combat fake news at the individual level through debunking and prebunking efforts. Debunking is easy to understand: These efforts focus on helping people to stop and reflect on the truth of a story before sharing it. But some fact-checking exercises have the unintended consequence of firmly embedding false facts in memory via the same mechanism by which any false memory forms—via repeated exposure and eventual forgetting of the source of the false memory.[95] Later, it is easy to believe the false fact as true because it feels so familiar.

New efforts highlight the value of prebunking or inoculating people against misinformation before they even encounter it. Inoculation can occur through information campaigns about an issue—such as those about the benefits of COVID-19 vaccinations—or through innovative online games. Prebunking does work.[96] There are even indications that prebunking helps most for those who are most susceptible to fake news.

Unfortunately, older adults are especially vulnerable to fake news. Despite their larger general knowledge base, older adults are more likely to forget the source of fake news.[97] This factor, when combined with their greater trust in others, difficulty detecting deception, and lower levels of digital literacy, makes older adults more likely to believe and share fake news. But older adults aren't the only ones who need help. We must also teach children critical literacy skills from a young age so that they can decide which news stories to trust and which to distrust. We can't wait until they're in high school or university to begin to teach these skills.

The antidote to fake news and extreme content in the era of social media must come from psychologists working together with computer scientists, tech companies, governments, and international organizations to combat it at all levels.[98] In a shining example of such a global collaboration, former New Zealand Prime Minister Jacinda Ardern and French President Emmanuel Macron created the Christchurch Call in 2019 to combat extremist online content after the terrorist mosque shooting in New Zealand.

Real-life stories are rife with gaps, outright errors, unhealthy scripts, and lies. But unlike stories from books, movies, TV, and video games, which we can choose to experience or not, we can't escape from creating stories about our lives and interpreting the real-life stories of others. So we must try to be extremely wary of the stories we're told and to craft the stories we tell in the healthiest of all possible ways.

The latest social media studies have been a wake-up call for me personally. I've never been a heavy Facebook user, but I used to be a classic passive user; while waiting in the car for a teenager or before an appointment, I would scroll through my news feed as a way to fill in time. I'm now trying hard to restrict my Facebook use to staying in touch with distant family and true friends, and to be more active than passive when I do hop on. I've substituted Duolingo as my waiting game; maybe someday I will *finally* learn to speak Spanish. Most of all, I'm trying to spend more time with my family and real friends in person—along with a few fictional friends.

CHAPTER 7

✧

The Thin Line Between Reality and Fantasy in Stories

Most of us, I suppose, have a secret country.
—C. S. Lewis, *The Voyage of the Dawn Treader*

I was 3 years old when my brother, Andrew, started school. My sister, Jen, was only a baby, so suddenly I had no one with whom to play. According to my mother, I invented a friend called Bucky. Apparently Bucky always wore a purple dress, my favorite color. I have a singular memory of Bucky sitting beside me on my bedroom floor, wearing her purple dress and doing a puzzle with me. Whether the memory came later from my mother's stories of Bucky or from my own 3-year-old mind is impossible to know. The fiction feels very much like a fact of my life.

Were these early imaginings a sign of my later love of stories of all kinds? Was Bucky a healthy response to feeling lonely or a portent of dysfunction? As a developmental scientist, I'm fascinated by continuity and discontinuity across the lifespan in imagination. As an advisor to educational agencies and to parents, I need to know whether story play is central to children's learning and development. If so, how can teachers and parents best support children's play?

How Stories Change Us. Elaine Reese, Oxford University Press. © Oxford University Press 2024.
DOI: 10.1093/oso/9780197747902.003.0007

THE FUNCTIONS OF FANTASY

The impulse to replay and create fictional stories is essentially an urge to simulate, to act *as-if* instead of *as-is*. This impulse is present from toddlerhood onward, as soon as mental simulation becomes possible.[1] But fantasy is not just for children—most humans engage in story play in different guises throughout their lives. At all ages, people differ in the time they devote to fantasy simulation and the novelty of those simulations.

The two main functions of story play are to connect to others (real or imagined) and to use those imaginings to shape our future—the *as-it-will-be*. These stories may not always be played out with or for other people, but they are always "parasocial" in that we are either acting as another version of ourselves, we're role-playing as a fictional character, or we're interacting *with* a fictional character (as I did with Bucky).[2] Across the lifespan, we engage in story play when we're bored and need a challenge, or when we're feeling lonely and need to connect. Whether for toddlers, teens, or octogenarians, story play is an intricate weave of imitation and elaboration, theme and variation. Across ages, story play confers a host of cognitive and social benefits.

THE STIRRINGS OF STORY PLAY

Story play dawns in that magical and momentous second year of life.[3] At the same age that toddlers' memory abilities allow them to begin to understand and tell real-life stories, they are also starting to understand and produce fictional stories. At first, these pretend stories contain only a single action—such as a toddler slurping loudly from an empty cup—much like the one-word stage of language development. Just as these one-word utterances turn into two- and three-word sentences, these single pretend actions quickly progress to combinations: first stirring imaginary liquid in a pitcher and then pouring that invisible liquid into a cup before pretending to drink.

By the age of 2, toddlers play in more elaborate ways with real and imaginary others. For instance, now they can pretend to feed a doll and put it to bed, or offer their parent a cup of imaginary tea. In fact, a lack of social imaginative play in early childhood is a hallmark of autism.[4] The underlying brain development for all this simulation of past and future and fantasy is, once again, in the default network, which supports mental imagery about the minds and actions of imagined others and of the self.[5]

In the preschool years, children all over the world start engaging in role-play in earnest, pretending to *be* others for hours, even days, on end.[6] Remember the kid in *Daddy Daycare* who wouldn't take off his Flash Gordon costume? The most popular alter egos in Euro-American cultures are still animals, parents, superheroes, and princesses; in less industrialized cultures role-play is more realistic.[7] Children of this age can coordinate roles with adults or other children toward a common goal, albeit with a heavy dose of bossy on-stage direction—"Stop snoring! You're not the daddy." They readily assign emotions to their characters—"The dragon's mad now so it's breathing fire." Psychologists Jerome and Dorothy Singer (parents of life-story researcher Jefferson Singer from Chapter 1) refer to ages 3 to 6 as the "high season" of pretend play.[8] These dramas occur on a daily basis in preschools that allow children time and materials for such play. If you are a preschool teacher, Vivian Paley's books are a source of inspiration, especially *The Boy Who Would Be a Helicopter* and *A Child's Work: The Importance of Fantasy Play*.[9]

Children who engage in more pretend play have more advanced language development.[10] This relationship likely goes both ways, with richer language deepening the possibilities for collaborative fantasy play, and pretend play in turn enriching children's language. For instance, experimental studies show that introducing children to new storybooks and subsequent role-play boosts their language development, with the more fantastical the content of the book, the better.[11]

Many prominent child development experts like Kathy Hirsh-Pasek and the late Edward Zigler (of Head Start fame) are united in the belief that play is not a luxury line in the early childhood curriculum. Instead, it is absolutely essential for children's learning and development.[12] Others argue that although play is not necessary for children to learn, it should be included in early childhood curricula simply because it's fun.[13]

FRIENDSHIPS, REAL AND IMAGINED

Nearly all young children in industrialized societies also form attachments to media characters from as early as 18 months.[14] These attachments are children's first parasocial friendships. Whereas role-play involves *being* someone or something else, parasocial friendships entail wanting to *be with* fictional characters, from the real people in *The Wiggles* to puppets like Elmo and animated characters like Bluey. These parasocial relationships are especially likely to develop with TV characters such as Dora who attempt to interact directly with the child. Parents support these early parasocial

THE THIN LINE BETWEEN REALITY AND FANTASY *(109)*

friendships when they encourage children to interact ("Tell Dora where the map is"), implicitly telling the child that forming a relationship with a fictional character is valued. Giving children toy versions of their favorite media characters is yet another way to facilitate these fantasy friendships.

Why would parents want to foster parasocial friendships? Isn't it hard enough to teach children how to have real friends?

It turns out that young children show better understanding of storylines and learn more from educational TV if they have a strong parasocial relationship with the main character, such as Dora or Elmo.[15] Parasocial friendships also provide valuable, low-risk practice that will help children form real friendships. However, cultures differ dramatically in how supportive adults are of children's pretend play, with Euro-American culture representing the peak of support in terms of resources and facilitation by adults.[16] In other cultures like the Kpelle people of Liberia, adults tolerate play but do not actively support it, and in a few cultures, like the Yucatec Maya people, adults actively curtail play, allowed only when no other productive activity is possible.

I'LL MAKE UP MY OWN FRIENDS

The epitome of imaginative play in the preschool years, however, is the creation of wholly imaginary friends, such as my friend Bucky. Imaginary friends are much more common than was once thought—nearly half of all young children across cultures create one or more.[17] Psychologists Marjorie Taylor and Stephanie Carlson invented the Imaginary Companion Interview as a way of asking children about their imaginary friends and of getting independent corroboration from parents.[18] Although the classic imaginary friend is one that is completely invisible to others, they argued that the definition needs to include personifications of stuffed toys if those personalities go beyond the stereotypical (think stuffed tiger Hobbes from *Calvin & Hobbes*).

Certainly some of children's parasocial relationships with media characters can also evolve into true imaginary friendships if the child consistently interacts with the same character, endowing that character with a personality that extends past their portrayal in the book or show, and inventing new scenarios to engage in together. My former PhD student (and former researcher at Facebook, Pinterest, and Google) Gabriel Trionfi and I found that 48% of the *Origins* children at age 5 professed to having an imaginary friend when interviewed.[19] The exact same prevalence of imaginary companions existed in a separate sample of Māori children.[20]

Their friends ranged from the mundane (a pretend puppy with the anodyne name of Brown Puppy) to the truly fantastical (Giant Strongman, a 1-million-year-old wrestler with no toenails). Same-sex friendships dominated: Of those imaginary friends reported to have a gender, all of the boys' friends were male, and nearly all of the girls' friends were female (although one progressive friend was "a girl and a boy"). For instance, Tia at age 5 had an imaginary friend called Marka, whom she described as a girl "just like me" with brown hair and brown eyes.

Imaginary friends are more common among firstborn and only children, which indicates that their function is to create a friend when one is not readily available or is too young to play with yet.[21] In many studies, girls are more likely than boys to create imaginary friends,[22] probably due to girls' early predilection for simulation. Not surprisingly, children with high-functioning autism are less likely than neurotypical children to have imaginary friends, especially of the invisible variety. Some children with autism, however, do have imaginary friends.[23]

We asked all the teens in *Origins* at age 16 who had previously reported an imaginary friend at age 5 whether they recalled their pretend friends.[24] Only 22% of the teens (all girls) remembered the specific imaginary friend they had previously told us about, almost always with fondness. For instance, although fiction fanatic Joe was one of the 5-year-olds who reported an imaginary friend, at age 16 he could no longer recall ever having had one. The girls' memories of their friends were stronger if their parents knew about the friend at the time. It's possible that these parents talked more often at the time or later about the imaginary friend, and perhaps were more supportive of the disruptions to family routines that can arise (setting an extra place at the table; buckling the imaginary friend into an invisible car seat each and every time you venture out).

For instance, when we asked 16-year-old Tia about her former imaginary friend Marka, she recalled a conversation with her mother at the dinner table in early childhood. "I had Marka with me sitting at the table beside me and Mum was setting dinner and she asked if Marka needed a plate and I was like, 'She doesn't need food, Mum.'" Marjorie Taylor's book *Imaginary Companions and the Children Who Create Them* is a classic on this topic, and is still the best source available for parents on these fascinating friendships.[25]

The contemporary view of imaginary friends is that they are a "good thing" for young children and are evidence of creativity—I would add resourcefulness—rather than dysfunction.[26] Based on my own research in New Zealand and others' research in the United States, United Kingdom, and Australia, young children who have imaginary friends are not necessarily more intelligent than children who do not have imaginary friends.[27] In some studies, however, children who have imaginary friends are more advanced in their theory-of-mind skills and are more creative.[28] They definitely tell better stories: Their fictional stories include more character dialogue, and their real-life stories include more causal and temporal connections—both markers of more sophisticated narratives.

Countering earlier concerns that children with imaginary friends are socially delayed in some way, they are actually more likely than children without imaginary friends to describe their real best friend's thoughts and feelings.[29] Children with imaginary friends also report interacting with their fantasy friends in similar ways to how they interact with their real friends.[30] Finally, children with imaginary friends have just as firm a grasp on reality as other children their age; they know perfectly well that their imaginary friend is not real. Young Tia scoffed at her mother's offer of food for invisible Marka. In our interviews with children in *Origins*, they sometimes ended up reassuring us that their imaginary friends were not real, thinking we had lost our own grip on reality.

Imaginary friends tend to disappear when they're no longer needed. Some meet violent ends: One child reportedly threw her imaginary friend off a ski lift. Other children, however, retain their imaginary friends into the preteen years or pass them down to younger siblings.[31]

SECRET COUNTRIES

In middle childhood, fantasy play appears to go underground as children have less free time and engage in more scheduled activities (e.g., music lessons, sports, Scouts). At least, this form of play becomes less obvious. Experts on children's imagination agree that fantasy play has simply become more private, and takes on different forms, but has not disappeared.[32] Instead, tweens' and teens' parasocial relationships with media characters and celebrities intensify (including YouTube and TikTok celebrities).[33] Most young people report at least one of these attachments, usually to a same-gender celebrity.

Another way children at this age immerse themselves in imaginary worlds is to read book series (*Harry Potter* or *Clarice Bean*) or to watch TV series or movie sequels (again, *Harry Potter* but also *Star Wars* and *Hunger Games*) and then to reenact these dramas with their siblings and friends.[34] Series work better for this purpose because parasocial friendships with characters from extended dramas are more intense.

Young adolescents may also start keeping a diary (40% of one sample of German 12- to 17-year-olds) in which they privately record their troubles, triumphs, and fantasies. Most of these diary-keepers are girls who use their diary as an imaginary friend (such as Anne Frank's *Kitty*, who was a character from one of Anne's favorite books).[35]

The epitome of imaginary play in middle childhood and early adolescence is the creation of whole imaginary worlds, called "paracosms." Marjorie Taylor and Michele Root-Bernstein are the world's experts on paracosms.[36] These imaginary worlds are rarer than children's imaginary friends and much rarer than children's attachment to media figures, but not as rare as once believed.

The best-known example is the Brontë siblings' "Glass Town," inspired by their play with brother Branwell's toy wooden soldiers, in which they spun an imaginary world in West Africa, oversaw battles, created a language (based on Yorkshire dialect), and even created roles for themselves as godlike spirit figures.[37] As young adolescents, Charlotte and Branwell wrote down their stories and created maps and drawings of Glass Town in miniature hand-sewn books, which can be viewed in the Brontë Parsonage Museum in Haworth and in other museums around the world. Their Glass Town play continued for an estimated 8 years, with the last few years veering off into each sibling's private daydreams about the imaginary world, before evolving into new offshoot worlds of Angria and Gondal when Charlotte was 18 and Branwell 17.

As 8- to 12-year-olds, whenever my sister and I weren't reading, our favorite childhood activity was to immerse ourselves in imaginary worlds in which we became our favorite book characters. The imaginary world that Jen and I most often inhabited, and that we never shared with our friends, came from Sydney Taylor's *All of a Kind Family* series. This world of a Jewish family with five sisters, set in turn-of-the-20th-century New York City, was about as far from our world of two Catholic girls in 1970s West Texas as we could get. I was the older sister, Ella, and Jen was the younger sister, Sarah. In an instant—whether we were on a family car trip, at a swimming lesson, or playing in the backyard under the blazing Texas sun—we could seamlessly slip into the 1900s lower East Side. When in the Ella-Sarah world, we would go about our everyday activities through the imagined eyes and voices of early 20th-century Jewish girls in New York City.

Taylor's contemporary studies of 8- to 12-year-old children show that just under 20% of children will create extended imaginary worlds.[38] In an interview with Marjorie Taylor, I described our Ella-Sarah world and asked if it would count as a paracosm.[39] Sadly, she confirmed my hunch that as intense as this world was for us, Ella-Sarah was a "pre-paracosm," because it was originally taken from a book. Nor did we invent a back story or create external documentation like maps and languages. Jen reassured me, "Having a paracosm sounds like a disease, so maybe it's for the best." Our motivation was not to systemize, but instead to strengthen our bond with each other, and to practice our mind-reading by seeing through the eyes of others who differed from us so dramatically.

Boys' and girls' childhood paracosms exhibit different qualities. For instance, in Taylor's case study of two boys' paracosms versus two girls' paracosms, she noted that "the boys' paracosms were at war with each other, whereas the girls' paracosms worked together to fight a common enemy."[40] In Charlotte and Branwell Brönte's Angria paracosm as older teens, Branwell handled the political and military aspects while Charlotte was in charge of the personalities and relationships. In several studies, girls are more likely to report paracosms than boys.[41] Once again, girls engage in imaginative play more than boys, and the qualities of their imaginary worlds differ. So far, no study has ever shown the reverse—with boys more likely than girls to create imaginary friends or imaginary worlds.

Taylor's contemporary study also highlights the social nature of paracosms. In contrast to the long-held belief that these are solitary pursuits, often these paracosms—for boys and girls alike—are created among siblings or close friends who have the opportunity to spend many hours together in unstructured play. Like Christopher Paolini's *Eragon* world of Alagaésia and the Brönte siblings' Glass Town, some paracosms last well into adolescence or even into adulthood, even becoming the impetus for published novels.

My own pre-paracosm with Jen was nowhere close to turning into a novel, nor did it make it to our teenage years. I remember at age 12 half-heartedly playing Ella-Sarah—yet again—with Jen, but my mind was definitely elsewhere. Ten-year-old Jen stormed out of our bedroom, accusing me of "acting like a teenager before you even *are* one!" That was the end of the run of our 4-year play. In Root-Bernstein's study of undergraduates' and MacArthur Fellows' paracosms, only 20%–25% survived childhood into the teenage years.[42]

Like younger children's imaginary friends, tweens' and teens' parasocial relationships and paracosms are mostly a good thing. Indeed, many of the older children with paracosms (over 80% in Taylor's studies) were the same children who had had an imaginary friend as a young child.[43] These children excel at storytelling. They are not necessarily more intelligent than other children, but they do consistently tell more creative stories and draw more creative pictures than children without paracosms. Adolescents who keep diaries also report higher self-esteem, better social relationships, and more active coping strategies than those adolescents who do not keep diaries.[44] Young people who develop intense parasocial relationships with celebrities report greater social support from their real friends, and they appear to use these relationships to boost their self-esteem when feeling low.[45] Although the social and cognitive benefits of collaborating with other children in creating paracosms have not yet been measured, teachers take note: Michèle Root-Bernstein has some fantastic ideas in her book *Inventing Imaginary Worlds* for how paracosms could be incorporated into the curriculum at all levels to boost students' creativity and critical thinking skills.[46]

EVEN ADULTS HAVE PRETEND FRIENDS

Our engagement with fictional worlds doesn't even end with adolescence. Many adults remain highly invested in their parasocial relationships with celebrities and with fictional characters from books, TV shows, movies, and video games. Psychologist/novelist Jennifer Lynn Barnes estimated that people around the world have collectively spent 235,000 years engaging with Harry Potter books and movies alone.[47] And that was a conservative estimate, based on reading each book in 3 hours and never rereading or rewatching. In a study intriguingly titled "Who needs friends?," psychologist Jaye Derrick and colleagues found that introverts were more likely than extraverts to engage in fictional worlds and to have parasocial relationships, suggesting once again that adults turn to these fictional friends when real friends are not readily available.[48] Just like real friendships, parasocial friendships help us feel better about ourselves and give us a sense of belonging.

These relationships are one-way, but they feel reciprocal. Some of us may even find ourselves having imaginary conversations with our favorite characters. One reason we engage in these interactions is to cope with the sadness and emptiness that we feel at the end of a book or series, with the *Game of Thrones* discussion thread between seasons as proof. These "parasocial breakups" can even cause actual grief.[49] Bereaved fans of the TV series *House* expressed this grief in online memorials after character Dr. Lawrence Kutner's suicide, even though actor Kal Penn was alive and well. "I will miss Dr. Kutner on House," one fan posted. "I can't believe that he's gone . . . G-dspeed, Dr. Kutner."

Adolescents and adults who are insecurely attached in their real-life relationships are more likely to form intense parasocial friendships and to experience grief when the celebrity or character dies or the series ends.[50] (Test your own attachment style at https://openpsychometrics.org/tests/

THE THIN LINE BETWEEN REALITY AND FANTASY *(115)*

ECR.php if you're curious.) Good real-life changes can arise, however, from these parasocial breakups. Although Facebook memorial pages for dead TV characters may indeed be a media marketing strategy, they appear to help people process their parasocial grief and to know that they're not alone. In one study of over 350 adults in the wake of comedian Robin Williams' death by suicide, those who professed a stronger parasocial relationship with Williams before his death reported they would now be more likely to seek treatment if depressed and also to support help-seeking for others.[51]

A growing number of people simply avoid the breakup altogether by reading or writing fan fiction (aka fanfic), in which every conceivable ending occurs for their favorite characters. Did you know that bestseller *Fifty Shades of Grey* began as fan fiction for the *Twilight* series? Another version of fanfic is to reimagine a contemporary version of a novel from centuries past. Even Alexander McCall Smith can be considered a fanfic writer with his adaptation of Jane Austen's *Emma* into modern-day Norfolk. (I've read and enjoyed both versions, despite the mixed reviews for the modern-day reworking.)

Most of us, however, do not take our fandom to these extremes. In a survey of *Star Wars* fans, around 20% read or watched fanfic, but only 1% were fanfic writers.[52] It makes sense that more fans are consumers than producers of fanfic, in line with the ratio of readers to writers of fiction more generally. I predict that teens and adults who write fan fiction were highly likely to have had an imaginary friend as young children and to have created a paracosm in middle childhood, but research has not yet explored the characteristics of fan fiction writers in that depth.[53]

The power of parasocial relationships is also evident in the blurring of boundaries many of us experience between character and author, or between character and actor. A prime example is of adult fans who act with hostility toward actors who play dastardly characters. Comic-Con fans literally steer clear of actress Lena Headey, the evil Cersei in *Game of Thrones*, lest she curse them in real life. This tainting can go the other way, too, when celebrities are pilloried for their offscreen exploits. Their real-life actions shouldn't affect how we feel about their acting, but nevertheless they do, and in an incredibly costly way. If these effects weren't real, Netflix would not have cancelled Kevin Spacey in *House of Cards* to a reported loss of $39 million.[54] I know formerly staunch *Mad Max* fans who will no longer consider going to a Mel Gibson movie because they abhor the actor's drunken, anti-Semitic behavior over 10 years ago. Of course, we all know that actors are not actually their characters, and that celebrities adopt public personas, but the emotion circuits of our brains respond in similar ways to our interactions with parasocial and real friends.[55] The result is a visceral carryover of emotions across the fictional divide.

The peak of adult parasocial relationships is to create or inhabit imaginary characters—becoming a novelist or an actor, or engaging in cosplay. Many of these highly imaginative adults had imaginary friends and paracosms as children and adolescents. It is no coincidence that the real-life Juliet from *Heavenly Creatures* paracosm fame later became a crime novelist under the pen name Anne Perry. Marjorie Taylor surveyed 50 contemporary novelists and noted that nearly half of them (42%) recalled having imaginary friends as children, whereas in the general population, fewer than 20% of adults recall having imaginary friends.[56] And nearly all the novelists (92%) reported that their characters have wills of their own. For example, J. K. Rowling revealed that she tried to turn Harry into Harriet so that she could have a female protagonist, but "it was too late. . . . He was very real to me as a boy, and to put him in a dress would have felt like Harry in drag."[57]

Not all children with paracosms grow up to become writers or actors, of course. In a study of MacArthur Fellows by Root-Bernstein, the 26% surveyed who described having paracosms were fairly evenly spread across careers in the arts, humanities, social sciences, and natural sciences.[58] Root-Bernstein argues that children who create paracosms are likely (but not assured) of growing up to become adults who are highly creative in their chosen fields.

Why do adults spend such vast swathes of time in fantasy worlds?

Cognitive scientists Edgar Dubourg and Nicolas Baumard assert that engagement with these "fictional superstimuli" is increasing around the world, such as with the explosion of Chinese fantasy genres *xuanhuan*, *xianxia*, and *wuxia*.[59] Their explanation is evolutionary: Across cultures in a more sedentary age, imaginary worlds satisfy our human need for exploration.

Revisiting imaginary worlds through rereading or rewatching also induces nostalgia, which is rejuvenating—nostalgia helps us feel happier, less bored and lonely, and closer to our true selves.[60] Rereading childhood favorites is particularly satisfying, as literary scholar Patricia Meyer Spacks found when she spent her first year of retirement rereading her favorite books rather than exploring new ones.[61] No wonder the rates of rereading favorite books, rewatching series, revisiting favorite video games, and fanfiction writing all went through the roof during pandemic lockdowns.[62]

How much do we all *need* these imaginary worlds? Michéle Root-Bernstein argues that world play is critical for nurturing children's creativity, and that it's no longer being supported via unstructured free time for children: She claims that since the 1970s, children's unstructured outdoor free time has been cut in half, and their total play time by 25%.[63]

Marjorie Taylor agrees that imaginary play is essential for creativity, but disagrees that it's disappearing: She believes that imaginative play is still alive and well—as shown in her recent study of children's paracosms.[64]

My own view is that with the rise in time spent on screens, and the tendency for screenplay (especially video games) to produce focused attention rather than mind-wandering, truly imaginative world play is at risk.[65] As researchers, we need to better understand how imaginative play is supporting children's and adolescents' brain development, learning and creativity, and well-being. As parents and early childhood teachers, we need to treasure imaginative play by providing children with the gift of unstructured (and less supervised) time that does not include screens.

Even as adults, we still need world play. According to Root-Bernstein, we are engaging in world play whenever we read history or play simulation computer games like *The Sims* or imagine alternate future scenarios in our personal lives or for a work project. Another everyday form of parasocial relationship is a desire to get behind the story to know its creator. It makes sense that people who love to learn about others' minds, whether they're characters in a book or in real life, will become especially fascinated by the minds of their favorite authors. Literary scholar Brian Boyd, in his book *On the Origin of Stories*, talks about "readers of others and readers of authors."[66]

As adults, Jen and I have transformed our childhood love of stories into an adult tradition of weaving fiction into real life—prior to the pandemic, we ventured together on literary pilgrimages to the settings of the beloved stories of our childhood, and a few from adulthood. It began with our *Sound of Music* bike tour in Salzburg, followed a few years later by a trip to the Betsy-Tacy house of author Maud Hart Lovelace in Mankato, Minnesota. Our very special pilgrimage someday will be to take the *All of a Kind Family* walking tour of the lower East Side in New York City, sponsored by the Museum at Eldridge Street. These sister trips give us a chance to relive our make-believe play from childhood and to reconnect with each other, as well as giving us a much-needed respite from everyday life.

THE DARK SIDE OF IMAGINATION

Are there any downsides to all of this creative play?

During childhood, there do not appear to be any negative effects. However, new research by psychologists Paige Davis and Charles Fernyhough found that adults report more visual or auditory hallucinations if they had childhood imaginary friends *and only if* they also experienced extremely adverse childhood experiences such as sexual or physical abuse.[67] A very small number of people who experience these prodromal psychotic symptoms (less than 10%) will go on to experience full-blown psychosis in adolescence or young adulthood.[68] But which comes first? Are some children creating imaginary friends in response to their early hallucinatory tendencies? I interviewed voice-hearing expert (and novelist) Charles Fernyhough to ask why. Fernyhough acknowledged that "there are reasons to believe that the unusual experiences might be there first, and that the imaginary companions are created to make sense of them, but also that it could work in the other direction. . . . I suspect it's a bit of both."[69] Of the four highly imaginative Brönte siblings, all the girls went on to become accomplished writers. Tragically, Branwell succumbed to a laudanum and alcohol addiction in his 20s, which some believe was secondary to schizophrenia.[70]

The tendency of those with strong imaginations to hear voices may not always be a bad thing, especially for those who do not find the voices distressing, or even enjoy them.[71] For further reading, I recommend Charles Fernyhough's authoritative book on this subject, *The Voices Within: The History and Science of How We Talk to Ourselves*.

In a fascinating survey of over 1,500 adults aged 18 to 81 as part of the Edinburgh International Book Festival, courtesy of *The Guardian*, psychologist Ben Alderson-Day and colleagues found that those readers who report higher levels of hallucinatory experiences are able to hear book characters' voices more vividly and thus to immerse themselves more completely in a work of fiction.[72] As one participant described: "I become so engrossed in a novel that the characters become real to me. I know that they are not real, but they feel real. It is as vivid as watching the characters in a film on TV where the screen is my mind's eye." Some participants even described hearing book characters' voices as they went about their everyday lives—a phenomenon the authors call "experiential crossing"—which is almost certainly activating the default network.[73] And, before you ask, women in this study did report somewhat more vivid imagery while reading compared to men.

As one young woman described:

Last February and March, when I was reading "Mrs. Dalloway" and writing a paper on it, I was feeling enveloped by Clarissa Dalloway. I heard her voice or imagined what her reactions to different situations. I'd walk into a Starbucks and feel her reaction to it based on what I was writing in my essay on the different selves of this character.

For most people, having a rich imagination is a blessing rather than a curse.

RIFFING ON REALITY

So far I've talked only about our engagement with fictional worlds. But nowhere are the lines between reality and fantasy as wafer-thin as when we read or tell real-life stories. The genres of autobiography, memoir, and historical fiction—and of course, autofiction—all rest on the blurring of real and imagined. With my fascination for real-life stories, I enjoy these genres immensely, with recent favorites being Michelle Obama's *Becoming*, Maggie O'Farrell's *I Am, I Am, I Am: Seventeen Brushes With Death*, and Lily King's *Euphoria*, which is a fictionalized account of anthropologist Margaret Mead's love life. I've already talked about the way all of us cast the events of our lives through stories that are redemptive or contaminative, ruminative or savored, and how this framing affects our well-being. Every life story is a form of presenting an idealized or demonized self, with written autobiographies the pinnacle of the carefully constructed and coherent ideal self.

The fictional nature of self-presentation is especially apparent in our portrayals of ourselves and others on social media. Teens and adults alike surgically remove the bad bits to present an embellished, Photoshopped version of their lives.[74] There are exceptions, of course, when we bare all and show the dark side, but this is just another way of fictionalizing our lives—in this case with an emphasis on the underbelly. This demonized self-view is linked to depression, whereas positive and even idealized self-views on social media are linked to well-being.[75] Similar to the benefits of idealizing our partners in intimate relationships, it is healthy and adaptive to idealize ourselves.[76]

The hallmark of our idealized self lies in our imagined stories of the future. As children's detailed memories for real life grow, so, too, does their ability to imagine detailed versions of the future.[77] At the end of Dan McAdams' life story interview is the future story, in which the interviewer asks the person to project themselves into the future to tell a story of what's to come. By now, I don't need to point out that these future stories are a form of simulation, a type of mental time travel to a future self in which we are drawing upon our autobiographical memories. Younger and older adults alike who tell more detailed and positive future stories that include intimacy goals report better well-being.[78]

Conversely, impoverished future stories spell dysfunction. In one study that my former PhD student Hadar Hazan and I conducted with clinical psychologist Richard Linscott, we found that undergraduates with schizotypy—a personality type predisposed to hallucinations or delusions (about 10% of adults)—had sparser future stories than undergraduates without schizotypy.[79] Here's an example of a future story from one of the undergraduates with schizotypy:

> I have no idea what my future will look like after the next 3 years. However, over the next 3 years I see myself living with my friends and finishing my degree.

In stark contrast, here's an example of a typical undergraduate's future story:

> I am hoping my future will be successful, as defined by getting into various courses (and if I don't get in then finding an alternate pathway to some sort of job in the health and well-being industry that I am passionate about and that I can help make changes through). I am hoping that I will get into clinical psych, spend the next 3 years here in Dunedin with a few of my friends who are also in post-grad courses. I want to eventually be involved in positive psychology and the sort of health and well-being industry. . . . I also want to get married and have a family, two or three kids. I want to be able to work part time while my kids are growing up, but also be in a very secure position financially. Both my husband and I will need good jobs for this to be a possibility. I want to travel, but am not fussed about when. I'm in no hurry, preferring to concentrate on setting myself up for a comfortable life before I indulge in luxuries like traveling. I hope to own my first house by the time I am 28.

In contrast, the undergraduates with schizotypy did not differ as starkly from typical undergraduates in their stories of the past. Because the main point of the past is to live well in the future, it makes sense that these future stories are even more diagnostic of dysfunction than are stories about one's past. In extreme cases of ill-being, psychologist Michael Chandler noted that 85% of the actively suicidal teenagers he interviewed were unable to envision any connection between their past and future selves.[80] They could no longer use their past to project themselves into the future, either to imagine something good or bad.

Fortunately, most of us can learn to imagine our future in greater detail. Memory expert Dan Schacter and colleagues have created an "episodic specificity" technique that encourages people to first recall minute details about a film they just watched, then to imagine future events that they're worried about with the same level of detail, and finally to imagine those future events again with detailed positive outcomes.[81] Not surprisingly, the episodic specificity technique activates the default network. This 7-minute process per dreaded event leads to improved problem-solving skills, decreased anxiety, better mood, and more adaptive coping skills. A next step will be to test episodic specificity coaching with clinical samples.

IMAGINING WHAT COULD HAVE BEEN

Another way that we all use imagination every day to project ourselves beyond the present moment is to engage in "counterfactual thinking"—*what might have been*. Upon missing the bus to work on the day of an important meeting, I think back to my morning and imagine if I had just spent less time reading the news, I would have made it on time, and the rest of my day would have been better. Especially in response to a negative event, we create an instant replay—but we alter key details in the chain of events in our minds to end up with a different present and future. With more significant events—such as a divorce—we can (and do) entertain a whole host of possible worlds in which we rewind the past to alter the path that led to the breakup.

Counterfactual thinking is an essential part of being human. Counterfactuals rely on causal thinking, plus imaginative and future thinking, with more than a dollop of executive functioning to temporarily suppress the real world and to switch back and forth between the alternate and real universe.[82] The neuroscience of counterfactual thinking is accordingly complex.[83] These reflections on actual and imagined past, present, and future engage the default network, as well as the cognitive control and emotion processing networks.

Counterfactual thinking is arguably more advanced than children's early pretend play.[84] Although even simple pretend play starts with a counterfactual—an *as if*—from that moment forward, the child (mostly) stays in the imagined reality until the play has ended. The pretend world (again, mostly) doesn't impinge on the actual world; they peacefully coexist. True counterfactual thinking instead involves actively comparing the actual past to the alternate past, and the alternate past to an imagined future.

Given this sophistication, it's not surprising that counterfactual thinking appears relatively late on the developmental stage.[85] Exactly how late is highly contested among researchers.[86] More important than *when* counterfactual thinking emerges is *how* counterfactual thinking affects children's and adults' everyday lives.[87]

By adulthood, people in all cultures studied so far engage in counterfactual thinking, but those in cultural or religious groups with a stronger emphasis on divine forces appear to use less counterfactual reasoning overall.[88] Even in those cultures, however, counterfactual thinking occurs in similar situations and ways: It is much more common in response to negative events than positive; the alternate universe is more likely to be better than worse; the solutions are more likely to be plausible than implausible.[89]

Yet there are large individual differences in how much time we each spend engaging in counterfactual thinking.[90] For instance, people who are high in fantasy proneness engage in more counterfactual thinking. Although no one has specifically researched this possibility yet, I suspect that a propensity for thinking counterfactually is related to a specific preference for reading fiction, especially novels that focus on chance events and paths not taken. If thinking counterfactually is your idea of a good time, I suggest you read Paul Auster's masterpiece *4-3-2-1*, in which main character Archie Ferguson experiences four ultimately different lives based on tiny changes in his early childhood experiences.

One important exception to our tendency to imagine better rather than worse possible worlds occurs when we encounter a close call. When my beloved dog Tui raced across the street to chase a cat and narrowly missed being hit by a car, my first reaction was relief. But in the midst of my gratitude, I immediately went back to what had happened just before—the phone notification that distracted me enough to drop Tui's leash. As I briefly imagined the horrible event that could have unfolded, I sternly told myself not to get distracted by my phone near traffic, even for a moment.

Counterintuitively, these gloomy alternate realities appear to be adaptive and healthy. People who engage in more of this worse-case scenario thinking tend to be optimists and to have stronger self-esteem.[91] I suspect that worse-case scenario thinking also helps us to remember a close call and to use that memory to prevent negative events in the future. This "downward" counterfactual thinking creates a positive feeling of relief. Unfortunately, children with high-functioning autism are impaired in their ability to engage in worse-case counterfactual thinking and to experience the resulting emotion of relief.[92] In contrast, "upward" counterfactual thinking of better-case scenarios ("I think about how much better things could have been") creates feelings of disappointment and regret. Children with high-functioning autism are similar to typically developing children in their better-case counterfactual thinking. Regret can be adaptive and healthy if it helps us to change our future behavior in positive ways, as Daniel Pink argues in his book *The Power of Regret: How Thinking Backward Moves Us Forward*. However, consistently high levels of better-case counterfactual thinking are linked to depression, anxiety, and low self-esteem.[93]

We assessed counterfactual thinking with *Origins* participants at age 20.[94] Indeed, the young people who reported thinking more about better-case (upward) scenarios in reaction to a negative event also reported more symptoms of stress and depression. Those who reported thinking more about worse-case (downward) scenarios in reaction to a negative event were no more likely to be stressed or depressed. Instead, these young people told more coherent life stories about high points in their lives, a practice linked to well-being, and reported more empathy for others.[95]

My optimist's reaction to being diagnosed with cancer was to engage in these healthier worse-case scenarios. If I weren't as fit and healthy . . . if I didn't have health insurance . . . if I hadn't gone to my scheduled mammogram that enabled early detection . . . I would have had a much worse prognosis. It actually made me feel lucky rather than unlucky! Worse-case counterfactual thinking is especially healthy when events happen to us that we can't control or change. But when confronted with the same kind of uncontrollable event, a person with depression might get stuck thinking unproductively about an alternate life where the negative event simply hadn't happened. With severe depression, or with brain disorders such as Parkinson's and schizophrenia, counterfactual thinking full-stop becomes extremely difficult.[96]

Most adults, however, can boost their well-being by engaging in worse-case counterfactual thinking. In one lovely experiment, researchers asked participants either to write about an imagined life in which they had not met their romantic partner (the worse-case counterfactual condition) or to simply write about the events that led up to meeting their romantic partner (the factual condition). Termed the "George Bailey effect" from the movie *It's a Wonderful Life*, those in the counterfactual condition reported higher levels of relationship satisfaction after imagining this alternate reality.[97] The authors concluded that mentally subtracting positive events from our lives can lead to greater gratitude, appreciation, and well-being.

Worse-case counterfactual thinking can even promote a sense of meaning in life. An extreme worst-case version is to imagine the overwhelming odds of never having been born. When psychologist Samantha Heintzelman and colleagues asked young people to engage in this exercise (again, in comparison to a factual list of events that led up to one's birth), they reported a renewed sense of meaning, purpose, and satisfaction with their lives.[98]

On the whole, simulation—in the form of mental imagery of past, imagined, and future events—is linked to learning, creativity, and well-being.[99] One reason for these benefits is that mental imagery helps us to envision alternate futures and to consciously choose among them.

⌘

For all of us who have survived the pandemic and other world-changing events, it is a luxury to create a new future story that extends beyond more than a few weeks or months. We are all re-envisioning our stories of the future right now to a greater or lesser extent. Each and every one of us will need to marshal all of our powers of imagination if we are to create a positive future for ourselves and for the world. Which stories will help us the most?

CHAPTER 8

∾

The Story Delivery System

Shouldn't stories work towards something that we can't get anywhere else?
—Richard Flanagan, *The Living Sea of Waking Dreams*

In the story sweepstakes, books, video, and real life all have their unique advantages and disadvantages. Which will ultimately win out for empathy and theory of mind, learning and well-being? Up until now, I have skirted around comparisons of reading to watching to gaming to real life for the benefits and hazards of stories. All forms of stories have their upsides and downsides.

IS THE MEDIUM *REALLY* THE MESSAGE?

For decades, scholars across disciplines and the popular press have debated whether and why oral, print, visual, and now digital forms of stories create different psychological effects.[1] Of course, the debate about whether oral or written stories are healthier dates back to antiquity with Socrates' and Plato's admonitions about the dangers of the written word, and it has continued over the centuries with each new story technology.[2] This ancient debate has come full circle with discussions of the benefits of *embodied literacies*—the latest term in early childhood education for story forms told through physical means such as oratory, acting, and dance.[3]

Many contemporary psychologists believe that reading books will ultimately prove to be the most beneficial system for delivering stories, and the least dangerous, compared to viewing or gaming.[4] When I started writing

How Stories Change Us. Elaine Reese, Oxford University Press. © Oxford University Press 2024.
DOI: 10.1093/oso/9780197747902.003.0008

this book, I agreed, but thought that crafting real-life stories would ultimately trump reading books in a cost/benefit analysis because of its direct applicability to our real lives.

It is true that only from books do we have access to the inner workings of others to know *precisely* what someone is thinking and feeling (although literary fiction leaves more gaps for the reader than does popular fiction).[5] But these mental states are always imagined, both in the mind of the author and the reader. Stories from books (for adults, at least) rely on a single-channel—either visual or auditory—so they are limited by one's ability to generate vivid mental images.

In contrast, only from video can we *see* intentions and emotions play out on people's faces in real time and track their consequences. Stories from TV and movies are dual-channel—visual and auditory—so are less reliant on our imagination than are stories from books. But actors are always simulating mental states, so there may be subtle differences in the way we receive them compared to true emotions. However, neuroimaging studies show that the default network is activated similarly, and across languages, whether we are reading, hearing, or viewing a story.[6]

Stories from video games are interactive and immersive, sometimes drawing upon three channels—visual, auditory, and haptic—so are the least reliant on imagination. But the physical and cognitive demands of playing the game mean that our focused attention network is activated to a greater degree than is our default network.[7] Here I am not proposing that gaming is solely externally focused, but that of all the story forms currently available, it involves the greatest external demands.[8] We will not be able to connect a storyline from a video game as effectively to our real-life experiences unless we do so afterward.

Finally, only stories from real life play on *actual* mental states and their consequences—a huge advantage. Only real-life stories are fully embodied, with lessons learned that apply directly to . . . well, real life! However, in real life with no pauses or replays, it can be difficult to understand others' emotions and their consequences. So many factors are at work in the moment, and our memory for these real-life interactions is biased and ephemeral. Unlike a book, movie, or game, we cannot ever fully revisit a real-life past event to check our interpretations. Even watching a video of an event offers only a partial perspective, from the camera's point of view, with no record of our internal musings. And in retelling or writing about an event, we are simultaneously reshaping our memories of that event.

Another obvious difference is that most of us are on the receiving end of fictional stories from books, TV, and movies, whereas we are all authors of our real-life stories. Video games are somewhere in between, given their interactive nature with manufactured content. All fictional stories entail a building up of details to create a whole. In contrast, real-life stories (including documentaries and autobiographies) are always a paring down, a removal of extraneous details, then adding in connections to create a coherent storyline. These two processes are fundamentally different. Fictional stories are bottom-up, whereas real-life stories are top-down.

What does the evidence tell us about which story delivery system is best?

EXPERIMENTING WITH STORY DELIVERY SYSTEMS

The problem is that it's very hard to conduct these comparative studies across platforms. In a true experiment, we would need to hold all aspects of the content constant, varying only the method of delivery: reading versus viewing versus gaming versus a real-life story. In practice, it's nearly impossible to keep the content the same across platforms. The design of every experiment is a constant balancing act of experimental control and real-life value. Yet it *is* possible to do these studies, as when neuroscientist John Hutton compared children's responses to stories delivered via picture books versus TV and found that picture books hit the neural sweet spot for young children.[9]

But children differ from adults in their neural responses to stories.[10] So we can't necessarily extrapolate these findings with children to adolescents or adults; neuroscientists will need to do that research at different ages to know whether books are better than visual stories across the lifespan. And, to skip to the punchline, no research yet to my knowledge has compared stories delivered via a fictional book versus a personalized, real-life tale for psychological benefits at any age.

A few clues do suggest that books offer more benefits and fewer dangers than visual media.

For young children at least, books are more educational and prosocial than visual media, and they are slightly less fantastical.[11] No experimental study has yet compared visual media to books for effects on children's theory of mind, while controlling for the content, but Hutton's findings imply more effective neural activation of theory-of-mind regions of the brain with a picture book than with a TV version of the same story.[12] But not all watching is bad, even for children—recall from Chapter 3 that children who heard more books *and* children who watched more movies both had more advanced theory-of-mind skills compared to children who watched more TV.[13] The long-form narrative of movies may help young children to better understand others' thoughts and feelings than watching a briefer TV program, which has less character development and depth.

Likewise, for adults, those who prefer to get their stories via TV exhibit more aggressive tendencies and lower empathy, whereas those who prefer to get their stories via books or plays show higher empathy and prosocial behavior.[14] These findings are all correlational so far, not experimental, but they do suggest an advantage for books and plays and long-form visual media over traditional TV shows when it comes to fostering social understanding and prosocial behavior. Plays are an especially intriguing story form because they are more embodied for the audience, given their physical proximity to the actors, and thus closer to real life. Although plays, like movies, do involve simulated emotions, those simulations are occurring in real time without the possibility of retakes.[15] For those who like to be on the stage itself, drama-based therapies are proving to be as beneficial as other psychotherapies for mental health difficulties.[16]

In the early 2010s, many book lovers felt validated by social media posts that reading fiction for just 6 minutes reduced your stress levels by 68%. Over a decade later, UK newspapers are still lauding this finding by MindLab at the University of Sussex.[17] Yet I couldn't find the scientific publication of this study in any database I searched. So I wrote to Duncan Smith, the Managing Director of MindLab, to ask for details. He revealed that UK's GALAXY® chocolate commissioned MindLab to conduct the study as part of their Irresistible Reads book drive.[18] It was never published in a journal and was not peer reviewed. However, Smith sent through a press release that contained a bit more information.

It turns out that this widely reported finding is based on a mere 16 volunteers, with no details on how those people were recruited, just that they were reportedly "keen readers of genres ranging from Mills and Boon romances to espionage stories and true-life crime to historical fiction." The volunteers were subjected to a series of stressful tasks, ranging from a difficult IQ test to a game where they received a mild electric shock if they made a mistake. (I do hope the participants at least received some chocolate at the end of the study.) In between each of the stressors, these hardy volunteers engaged in a relaxing activity for 6-minute stretches: either reading their favorite book; taking a walk outside; having a cup of tea or coffee; listening to *Beatles* songs; or playing a video game. Their stress levels were measured throughout the experiment via heart rate and skin conductance, which is basically a sweat secretion test.

Reading a book did in fact lower participants' sweat secretion by 67% (misreported as 68% somewhere along the line), with listening to *The Beatles* a close second, producing 61% less sweat. Playing a video game was the least effective method of relaxation, but it still reduced sweat secretion by 21% compared to the electric shock game. The video game was not specified, nor does the press release report whether the participants typically gamed for relaxation.

Although this study is not ideal in many ways, it is important because it's one of the few to directly compare the benefits of reading fiction to other leisure activities, like video games, using objective measures. But the details of the experiment need to be scrutinized more closely and replicated with much larger and more diverse samples before we can conclude that reading fiction is the most effective method of stress reduction for everyone. For instance, what about 6 minutes of meditation? And what if gamers were allowed to bring in their favorite video game to play as a relaxer? I'd also love to see a comparison of reading versus listening to an audiobook for stress reduction. I foresee that audiobooks will win out against all other activities for relaxation. What could be more comforting and relaxing than hearing someone read you a story? I recommend journalist Meghan Cox Gurdon's charming book *The Enchanted Hour: The Miraculous Power of Reading Aloud in the Age of Distraction* if you'd like to read aloud more often to family members of all ages.

Once again, these studies comparing across media are very difficult to do—my former PhD student Abigail Pigden and I know this firsthand because we tried for several years, first with a TV-versus-book version of *Game of Thrones* and next with a TV-versus-book version of *True Blood/Dead Until Dark* (from *The Sookie Stackhouse* series). We compared reading versus watching violent passages for inciting undergraduates' aggression and decreasing their empathy and theory of mind. We also measured prosocial behavior with a helping task, in which the experimenter "accidentally" knocks a cup containing 30 pens off a table and the researcher counts how many of the pens the participant helps to pick up.[19]

In line with our predictions, people who read the passage scored better on the Mind in the Eyes test than those who watched the TV clip or had no media.[20] Thus, reading still produced advantages for theory of mind, even though the reading material contained highly violent content of a female protagonist beating a couple with a chain and threatening them with a knife in order to protect another character. We also found, as predicted, that those who watched the TV version were less prosocial: They picked up the fewest pens (10), whereas those who read the book passage picked up a few more (12), and those who didn't consume any violent media picked up the most pens (15). However, these differences in theory of mind and helping across media were certainly not earth-shattering.

Perhaps because some people are more transported by movies, and others by books, these individual differences are erasing the effects of the media delivery system. Or, perhaps these weak differences by media platform simply tell us once again that, in media researcher Daniel Anderson's words, "the medium is *not* the message—the message is." Certainly the boundaries across media have become blurrier than they were in Marshall McLuhan's time, especially with the advent of art TV, long-form TV, movie adaptations of books, and new interactive media such as virtual reality (VR) and hypertexts.[21]

But first, let's consider the lowest-tech option of all: audiobooks.

THE MAGIC OF AUDIOBOOKS

So books may or may not still be best for promoting psychological benefits. But does it matter how we experience a book? What if we don't actually read it but listen to it instead? As a child, one of my favorite story memories was listening to Golden Records with my brother and sister, stretched out on the living room floor in our afternoon rest time once we were too old for naps. *Gulliver's Travels* was the most memorable, including the album cover depicting a huge Gulliver stretched out on the ground with hundreds of Lilliputians tying him down.

"Talking books" have been with us in some form since the 1930s when they were first used as an alternative to Braille as a way to deliver books to the blind. Audiobooks offer a sensory and aesthetic experience that is distinctly different from silent reading, especially when the author or a talented reader records the book.[22]

As of 2023, audiobooks were a $5.3 billion industry projected to grow to $35 billion in 2030, outpacing e-books, and expanding to non-English markets.[23] Prior to the pandemic, many Americans were already listening to audiobooks;[24] during the pandemic, audiobook use soared as a way to combat isolation.[25] Audiobooks are especially popular among younger generations, with nearly half of all audiobook listeners under 35.[26] These days, audiobooks are growing exponentially in popularity with young and old alike because they can be listened to virtually anywhere—while driving/walking/running, at the gym, or while doing household tasks.[27] In fact, audiobooks are the only way besides VR to be fully active while consuming a fictional story.

In the course of writing this book, I've become an ardent audiobook consumer. One of my favorites so far is Haruki Murakami's *Norwegian Wood*, read by John Chancer. The musical transitions between chapters added an extra layer, almost like another character, to immerse me fully in the story. And an especially alluring feature of audiobook memoirs is that they're often read by the author, like Michelle Obama's stunning memoir *Becoming*. I'm certain that these author-read audiobooks can create and intensify parasocial relationships.

Psychological research on audiobooks shows that they benefit listeners in all sorts of ways. (Recall from Chapter 3, however, that preschool children do not benefit as much from simply hearing a story read aloud as from discussing a picture book with an adult reader.) Much of the audiobook research is with older children and teens who struggle with reading or who have dyslexia. These studies show that audiobooks, especially if children and teens read along while listening, help them to become more fluent readers and to engage more fully in classroom activities.[28]

As a 10-year-old struggling reader who participated in an audiobook club put it, "Last year I read tiny books and only about six. This year I've read ten books, bigger books that take longer and are better. I love to read now."[29] And one of the teachers in the study reported, "Audiobooks are awesome! They make reading exciting! They allow struggling readers to love reading and feel confident about their reading."

For teens, audiobooks offer a way to maintain their engagement with long-form stories that isn't as sedentary as reading or watching movies.[30] For those learning a second language, listening to an audiobook while reading along with the text helps reading, listening, and writing skills compared to traditional ESL instruction.[31] Anecdotally, my younger friends with new babies tell me that audiobooks are a way to stay awake and feel less lonely during those interminable night-time feeding sessions. Audiobooks also provide a screen-free way for parents to entertain children. My mother was onto this back in the 1960s.

For older adults who like to read, audiobooks circumvent any vision problems they might have. In one longitudinal study, older volunteers were able to choose from a selection of prize-winning fiction audiobooks, such as Jhumpa Lahiri's *Interpreter of Maladies*, or nonfiction books, such as Jo Marchant's *Cure: A Journey Into the Science of Mind Over Body*.[32] Whether assigned to fiction or nonfiction, those listeners who became absorbed in their book selection reported greater well-being and a sense of meaning in life compared to those who were less absorbed.

Yet another positive is that we can't skim an audiobook, and we tend not to skip over passages. So far, there are few downsides to audiobooks.

One is that audiobooks are not self-paced. While listening, we don't tend to hit pause and stare off into the distance to reflect on what just happened in the story, and what it means for our lives. Instead, our minds tend to wander in more off-topic ways when listening to an audiobook versus reading, probably because we are engaged in other activities, such as driving, that demand our attention.[33] (Fortunately, new studies show that it's safe to listen to audiobooks while driving.[34]) I am lucky to have only a 5-minute commute, so the main time I listen to audiobooks is while making dinner. I know that I sometimes miss critical details in the story when I need to consult a recipe, juggle pans, or turn on the extractor fan, but I can't be bothered with rewinding. Consequently, we do not remember as much of the story when we hear it on audio compared to when we read it.[35] On the other hand, the broader meaning that we derive from a story we've heard versus one we've read is represented in nearly identical ways in the cerebral cortex.[36]

No one has yet compared audiobooks to print books, however, for fostering empathy, theory of mind, altruism, and well-being. Even if audiobooks do turn out to be inferior in these respects, they are—hands down—a great way to boost one's book consumption and to engage young readers, older readers, struggling readers, busy readers, and second-language readers. Audiobooks even help calm down the family dog.[37] Researchers played an audiobook of C. S. Lewis' *The Lion, The Witch, and the Wardrobe* to 31 dogs in a rescue shelter compared to music or no sound-track. The audiobook resulted in more resting/sleeping behavior among the dogs and less "vigilant" sitting/standing behavior compared to classical music, pop music, specially designed "dog" music, or the control condition. Dog whisperer Cesar Millan is now promoting audiobooks for dogs who stay at home alone all day.

Whether you prefer to listen to audiobooks in the kitchen or in the car (with or without your dog), these stories are nearly as low-tech as a printed book. Although they require a smartphone or other device, after that it's simply a disembodied storyteller's voice saying every word of the story unless we choose to stop or skip ahead.

DOUBLE-DUTY STORIES

Those of us who love to read often end up watching movie versions of books. But which order is best? Should you make sure you read the book first, or is it okay to watch the movie first? My literary friends have strong opinions on this subject; they vastly prefer to read the book first. And there's a bevy of blogs promoting book-first, with just a few movie-first diehards.

But communications researcher Melanie Green and colleagues did the actual test: They had people either read an excerpt from John Grisham's novel *The Rainmaker* first and then watch the corresponding clip from the 1997 movie, or watch the movie first and then read the book.[38] It turns out that my friends and the bloggers are right: People who read the book first reported greater transportation later when watching the movie compared to people's transportation for the book when they had watched the movie first. But perhaps this effect holds only for certain movie adaptations that are faithful to the novel.

My own experience is that I notice more nuances in the movie version if I've read the book first, perhaps because I'm already familiar with the storyline. If it's a great story, well told, watching after reading enhances the depth of your understanding of the characters and their actions. For instance, the scene in the long-form TV version of Sally Rooney's *Normal People* where Connell decides to go back to Sligo for the summer instead of stay with Marianne in Dublin is wonderfully subtle; their facial expressions and gestures make the misunderstanding more comprehensible than in the book version. Because I read the book first, however, I may not have experienced this same depth of understanding if I had instead watched the show first. Of course, the danger of watching a movie version second is that it will rewrite the sketchier mental images created when first reading the book. Can anyone who's seen the BBC miniseries of *Pride and Prejudice* think of Mr. Darcy *without* seeing Colin Firth?

My position in this debate is if you truly love a story, you will get more out of it by watching the movie *and* reading the book, no matter the order. Reese Witherspoon is incredibly talented at converting books into movies—no doubt because she is a passionate reader—so we should have a plethora of fantastic options for reading and watching in years to come.

Watching a movie version of a book is a type of rereading, according to literary scholar Meyer.[39] What about reading the same books, over and over (and over) again? As Nabokov claimed, "One cannot read a book: One can only reread it."

Fiction lovers are divided on the joys of rereading. Many avid adult readers passionately reread their favorites, whereas the remaining, equally avid readers, think of rereading a book as about as fun as chewing old gum. My artist and writer friends Clive Humphreys and Caroline Lark are a case in point. Clive adores rereading his favorites, especially a tattered copy of Norman Mailer's *Ancient Evenings*. "Books are like paintings; the best are never over."[40] Caroline abhors the thought of rereading. Why, with so many great books out there, especially when you already know the plot?

A Reuters UK survey found that 77% of their respondents enjoyed rereading; nearly 20% were rabid rereaders, reading certain books five or more times.[41] The top three books they loved to reread? First prize went to the *Harry Potter* series, second to *The Lord of the Rings*, and third to *Pride and Prejudice*.

Meyer book *On Rereading* offers insights gleaned across a lifetime. "The most profound pleasure of such rereading . . . perhaps derives from the thrill of rediscovering a past self, a self that we may have thought lost."[42] Spacks devotes an entire chapter to the staying power of Jane Austen's books for over 200 years, and why people all over the world reread Austen's books, especially *Pride and Prejudice*. "We find books that we reread both familiar and forever new partly because they change as we change: a truth that applies not only to the rereading of children's books. The experience we bring alters what we see. It's not just that Austen teaches us about life—life teaches us about Austen."[43] As psychologist and award-winning novelist Keith Oatley claims, reading Jane Austen, with her finely drawn scenes of nuanced intentions conveyed through direct and indirect speech, also sharpens our theory of mind.[44]

As a memory scholar, it's no coincidence to me that the most popular books for rereading are those that the reader probably experienced for the first time during their "reminiscence bump" between late childhood and adulthood. Recall from Chapter 4 that events from those years are emblazoned into our memory in part because we were in the thick of discovering who we are. Books that we read during those times, along with TV shows and movies watched, and video games played, are part of that indelible shaping of our identities.[45] As Spacks puts it so beautifully, "Rereading brings us more sharply in contact with how we—like the books we reread—have both changed and remained the same. Books help to constitute our identity."[46]

What does psychological research tell us about the value of rereading, and why we reread books, across the lifespan?

Every parent I know has experienced their young child wanting to read a favorite book again—and again and again—and to rewatch their favorite shows. According to a parent survey, rewatching peaks among 2- to 4-year-olds and then steadily declines.[47] One 3-year-old in the study asked to watch a favorite *Blue's Clues* episode no fewer than 17 times across a 3-week period![48] I suspect that rereading follows the same arc, with a peak in early childhood and then a steady decline for most, with a possible bump near the final chapter of our reading lives when we revisit our touchstone books.

The research is abundantly clear on the benefits of rereading picture books for young children's vocabulary and story understanding: Repeating the same book helps children acquire new words, especially if adults discuss the new words *during* and *after* reading.[49] With repeated readings, young children ask more questions and at a higher level, which shows they are becoming more actively engaged in the story over time.[50]

Rewatching also helps children's story understanding and problem-solving skills. For instance, a high-quality study of *Blue's Clues* showed that preschool children learned much more educational content after rewatching the same episode five times compared to only once. And only after repeated viewings were children able to apply their newfound problem-solving skills to novel problems not depicted in the show.[51] When Ben was a preschooler in the late 90s, each episode of *Blue's Clues* was shown 5 times across the week. New Zealand TV programming was still extremely limited at that time, so I assumed it was for lack of funding. I now know that the repeated showings were an intentional, evidence-based practice. And I can testify that Ben happily watched each episode 5 times in a row. Whenever a young child asks for the same story ad infinitum, it's because they're still getting something new out of it.

We know less about rereading and rewatching with older children and adolescents. Many older children and teens love to read books in a series, with the same characters and similar plot lines, which is somewhat akin to rereading. Rewatching of shows and movies still happens, too, but less avidly than for young children.[52] The limited research available shows that older children and adolescents benefit from rereading and rewatching in similar ways to younger children in their story comprehension, especially in terms of understanding characters' intentions.[53] From a memory perspective, these benefits of rereading and rewatching are no surprise—a basic fact of memory is that it strengthens with spaced repetition of material, especially if we're actively engaged with that material.[54]

But once we leave school, what do we as adults get out of rereading books and rewatching shows and movies? Of course, literary and media scholars are the royalty of rereading and rewatching. For over 30 years, my colleague and media scholar Catherine Fowler has studied an obscure Belgian film called *Jeanne Dielman, 23, quai du Commerce, 1080 Bruxelles*.[55] She was obviously onto something, because in 2022 *Jeanne Dielman* claimed "Greatest Film of All Time" over *Citizen Kane*. Like children, do we rewatch and reread because we're still getting something new each time? Unlike nearly all children, however, some adults do not enjoy doubling down on their stories. Are adult rereaders and rewatchers different in some way from those who are singular readers and viewers?

I could find only one psychological study on the personality characteristics and tendencies of adults who love to reread books.[56] Rereaders, cover your eyes: Rereading was linked to thwarted belonging, low self-esteem, insecure attachment, neuroticism, and higher levels of personal distress rather than true empathy. However, these negative associations were all weak; the strongest characteristic of a preference for rereading was instead a more developed ability to become transported into a book. (In an intriguing footnote, the authors note that these tendencies are very different for those who love to rewatch shows and movies, but they don't reveal any details, and that research has not yet been published.)

Rereaders are thus a select breed who are easily transported into fiction. Some of them are certainly rereading for comfort and familiarity, and to deepen parasocial relationships with the characters (as I discussed in Chapter 7), as well as to experience especially deep and aesthetic readings. Rereading helps children and adults alike to learn and to remember, and perhaps even to shape our identities. But in my view, the phenomenon of rereading (and rewatching) is still a bit of an intriguing mystery. It could have different functions and benefits across individuals, and across the lifespan.

HIGH-TECH STORIES

At the other extreme from the low-tech of audiobooks and rereading is storytelling through VR. VR headsets now allow us to fully enter the story world and to act, react, and make choices in the story. How does VR affect our experience of a story, and in particular, how does it affect our empathy?

Filmmaker Chris Milk called VR the "ultimate empathy machine" because these devices allow us to enter another's world to see through their eyes and to experience their lives.[57] "Through this machine we become more compassionate, we become more empathetic, and we become more connected. And ultimately, we become more human." For instance, *The New York Times* created an 11-minute segment called *The Displaced* that, when viewed through a VR headset, allows the viewer to interact with three refugee children from South Sudan, Ukraine, and Lebanon as they tell their stories. The effect is indeed powerful.

VR is undoubtedly a more interactive, embodied way to experience a story, but is it truly the ultimate empathy machine?

A study by psychologist Fernanda Herrera and team suggests that, yes, VR is superior to other media at promoting empathy.[58] The researchers wrote a narrative about a San Franciscan who becomes homeless and begins to live out of their car, but then the police impound the car. In the final scene, the protagonist is traveling on a bus during the night to sleep and keep warm. In the reading condition, participants read the story in second person (*You look around the car for your toothbrush so you can brush your teeth*) and imagined the events as if happening to themselves. In the VR-headset condition, the story was the same but more interactive: The viewer actively searched the car for their toothbrush and tried to move away from a man sitting behind them on the bus because he might steal their backpack. A two-dimensional game condition allowed the participants to explore the environment on screen as if they were playing a video game, and a final control condition gave participants a packet of information with facts about the homeless in San Francisco.

All three story conditions (VR, reading, gaming) produced more compassionate attitudes toward the homeless up to 8 weeks later compared to the information-only control condition. But the VR condition was superior to all other conditions in terms of prompting participants to sign a petition supporting the homeless. VR is truly astounding at promoting empathy and prosocial acts through experiencing another's reality.

For teens and young adults who find reading difficult, clever new VR-assisted reading technology can enhance their enjoyment of the printed word. In the first study of VR effects on reading, young adults wore a VR headset to experience a static two-dimensional image of a wooded scene as they read the words of *Alice in Wonderland* on the page.[59] Compared to regular reading, even this minimal version of VR-assisted reading enhanced transportation into the story, which then increased readers' empathy with Alice's plight, as well as their intention to continue reading the rest of the book.

IS MENTAL IMAGERY THE KEY?

Unlike low-tech options of reading or listening to a story, which rely completely on the reader's ability to visualize and put themselves into the character's head, VR does the visualizing for us by putting us entirely into others' heads *and* bodies. An experiment that measured visual imagery skill, an aspect of mental simulation, helps us understand why this embodied reality is so helpful for changing one's perspective.[60]

Undergraduates first took a test of their visual imagery skill in which they were asked to imagine different scenes, such as the sun rising above the horizon into a hazy sky, and to rate the vividness of the image.[61] They also reported on how easily transported they were into movies or books, and about their sense of agency in coping with difficult life events. A week later, they either watched clips from three Disney films with strong protagonists (*Pocahontas, Merida, Beauty and the Beast*) or weak protagonists (*Cinderella, Snow White, Rapunzel*) *or* read passages from books tied to those films. Then they reported again on their degree of agency in their own lives.

In line with Green and Brock's Transportation-Imagery theory,[62] transportation into the films or books depended on visual imagery skills. People with higher imagery skills reported being equally transported by movie and book versions, but people with lower imagery skills said they felt more transported by the movies than by the books. The films provided the imagery that the low-imagery people lacked, allowing them to transport themselves more effectively into the story. People benefitted in their sense of agency from those movies or books portraying strong protagonists *only* when they were transported more fully into the stories. Not surprisingly, another study showed that people who have more difficulty mentalizing when reading a story score lower on the Mind in the Eyes test.[63] Movies provide ready-made images for people who have difficulty creating them on their own, and these vivid images help them get into the story and experience the value of the message. People with greater mental imagery skills, on the other hand, can benefit equally from books and movies because they are easily transported into both. I predict that VR could help those with less developed imagery skills become transported into stories even more effectively than can movies.

Individuals vary dramatically in their ability to create vivid mental images, with some people experiencing aphantasia, a complete inability to create any visual images in the mind.[64] At the other end of the extreme, those with hyperphantasia can create mental images that are as clear and vivid as real life. These extremes in mental imagery have long been recognized, but public interest skyrocketed in 2015 when renamed after the Aristotlean term *phantasia* for an image or mental representation.[65] Take the test at https://aphantasia.com/vviq/ if you would like to know where you sit on this continuum. Impaired mental imagery is linked to poorer reading comprehension and especially to less vivid autobiographical memories, as well as to being on the autism spectrum.[66] Not surprisingly, people with impaired mental imagery skills also experience less activation of the default network.[67]

How do these mental imagery skills develop over a lifetime? In adulthood, mental imagery is a difficult skill to improve.[68] But for children, mental imagery is much more malleable. Psychologists Sebastian Suggate and Phillipp Martzog tracked children's development of mental imagery skill in accord with their screen time over a 10-month period.[69] The children were from a semirural German setting and had less screen time than the average North American child, but still the heaviest users watched an estimated 1,400 hours of TV over that period. The findings were robust—greater screen time impeded children's mental imagery skills over time. The type of screen time, whether more passive or interactive, did not make a difference: Both types were linked to lower levels of mental imagery skill over time.

In contrast to screen time, Suggate and Martzog recommend reading as one important way that children and adolescents can improve their mental imagery.[70] I agree, and I propose that these improved mental imagery skills will then make reading even more enjoyable and immersive, leading to what developmental psychologists call a "virtuous cycle."[71]

Children who struggle with reading could instead enter a vicious cycle of increased screen time, lower mental imagery skills, and ever more screen time with its typically violent and harmful content. And, yes, although girls and women do score somewhat higher than boys and men on the vividness of their visual images, and are more likely to report hyperphantasia as adults, individual differences far outweigh these gender differences.[72]

Older adults, in turn, experience normal declines in their mental imagery,[73] in concert with declines in mental simulation for past and future events.[74] These changes reflect decrements in default network functioning; the default network shrinks and gets less efficient with age, and at the same time is harder to turn off when we need to focus on something in the outside world.[75] (Recall, however, from Chapter 6 that we do get better at some things with advancing age, such as expanding our vocabularies.[76])

I believe there are other ways besides reading to increase mental imagery skill and mental simulation from early childhood, especially through reminiscing and imaginative play. Older children and adolescents may also increase their mental imagery skill by performing in plays and writing stories. Any activity that helps children visualize remembered or imagined events—and to experience other people's emotions, thoughts, and intentions—will support mental imagery skills. Nor is reminiscing restricted to events from real life. For instance, discussing a movie together afterward—or even a video game—is a form of reminiscing that would support mental imagery skills through encouraging the child to bring to mind scenes from the movie or game and explore them in depth. Thus, mental imagery can be promoted across delivery systems when conversations are used intentionally for that purpose after the story or event is over.

Instead of immersing young children in screens with their ready-made images, let's immerse them in face-to-face interactions instead, including poring over picture books together. Real life is the ultimate story delivery system in terms of embodiment and connectedness, and it is available to us all at any time, for free. Reliving these interactions will help children's mental imagery skills, which in turn will help them to enjoy reading more and to become more proficient readers. These everyday interactions also help young people with autism to develop stronger oral language skills.[77]

Vivid mental imagery has other benefits, too, in terms of creativity and planning.[78] Once again, it is a double-edged sword, with extremely vivid mental imagery linked to psychopathology, such as hallucinations in schizophrenia, and to the involuntary reliving of traumatic events in posttraumatic stress disorder (PTSD). Yet for most of us, vivid mental imagery is a boon.

THE FINAL WORD ON STORY DELIVERY
SYSTEMS: WATCH THIS SPACE

Which stories—from books, movies, video games, VR, or real life—are best for encouraging learning, empathy, theory of mind, and altruism? The jury is still out. Yet I predict that video games and VR are going to be particularly useful for people with imagination difficulties. VR and the new VR-assisted reading technology will be especially helpful for increasing social understanding among those on the autism spectrum. But for people who already possess strong mental imagery skills—such as modern-day Jane Austen fans—books may still be best, or as good as other media, for promoting social understanding and prosocial behavior.

We know the least about the comparative advantages of real-life stories, especially for social benefits. Remember the effects of expressive writing about real-life events for boosting forgiveness of others? My prediction is that these real-life stories, particularly when written down to support high-quality, private reflection (*not* for public consumption over social media), may ultimately be better than any fictional stories for fostering compassion for others, and for oneself.

Across story forms, increasing the social element is likely to produce greater benefits. Remember the finding from Chapter 5 that teens who play video games cooperatively rather than competitively went on to be less aggressive, even if the games contained violent content? New research also shows that watching dramatic movies together increases our pain tolerance and group bonding, and that laughing together while watching comedies makes us feel good by increasing opioid levels.[79] For older adults, sharing picture books with young children boosts their sense of meaning in life,[80] and reminiscing with others sharpens their episodic memory skill and improves well-being.[81]

Because there's a downside to each and every story mode, however, the key is balance: between reading and watching and gaming; between activating the default network and focusing attentively on the present moment; between fiction and real life. Each one of us needs to find our own sweet spot for reaping the benefits of stories.

With my own overactive imagination, I've concluded that reading books is my best story delivery system. Reading books and talking about them with others at book club helps me to reflect upon rather than ruminate about real-life events. I'm also at my happiest when I'm reading fiction; reading transports me back to that child-like sense of wonder about the world that I experienced when my mother read to me or when we listened to story records. I used to worry about my addiction to fiction, but as a consequence of writing this book, I now embrace it. However, I am trying whenever possible to make my fictional experiences more social, such as watching TV and movies with others rather than alone on my laptop. Finally, I'm more open-minded about the potential of video games for increasing empathy and theory of mind—at least for other people. Although I've tried to play a few empathy games, like *Gone Home*, my lack of technical skill is off-putting. Instead, I'll follow film director Werner Herzog's advice to "read, read, read, read, read, read, read . . . and after that, watch a few movies."[82] Of course, real-life stories are ubiquitous, not optional, so I will continue to craft and tell them, but with greater care than I have in the past.

That's simply what works best for me at this point in my life. The optimal story delivery system is likely to be different for different people and at different ages.[83]

Ultimately the best story form for you is the one that is the most transporting, because it is immersion into a story that enables psychological benefits. For instance, in the audiobook study with older people, only the frequent fiction readers reported higher levels of immersion and derived more meaning from life after listening.[84] Reading or listening to an audiobook only makes you happy and fulfilled if you already like books. For those who do, reading is not a guilty pleasure; it is a way to understand the world and to create meaning about one's own life. But for other people with lower imagery skills, movies and TV may deliver the most immersive stories. And for those who experience a better sense of flow from a video game, or who just have a harder time sitting still, perhaps gaming or VR will be the story delivery system with the greatest benefits. Plus, immersion is fun![85]

My position in the age-old debate between oral and written language is to be inclusive: All story forms, including the written word, have merit; all also have limitations. As long as we are aware of the potential negative effects of certain types of content and excessive use, all forms of stories can teach us about ourselves, connect us to others, and even turn us into better people.

∽

I hope that knowing more about the causes and consequences of all kinds of stories will assist each of you to curate the healthiest, most enjoyable options for yourself, and for the younger and older people in your care. We will all need a rich array of stories in our stockpile to help us face the future.

Epilogue: The Stories in Our Future

Yes, life was hard and full of danger. Let it bring whatever it wants, he would learn somehow to bear all of it.
—Felix Salten, *Bambi, A Life in the Woods*

Just as stories can heal us, they can cut us to the core. When I started writing this book, my own story preferences were for novels and real-life stories. The benefits of these two story forms are clearly borne out in the research, and they remain my personal favorites. But working on this book has opened my eyes to other story forms—especially to video games, a powerful mode of stories to so many people today. I'm hopeful that video games can be harnessed more for good than evil in the future.

According to author Barbara Kingsolver, however, novels are anything but dead:[1]

I'm really devoted to literary fiction as a genre, because it really gets at the core of a lot of our troubles which have to do with a failure of empathy. I think the polarization we're experiencing, I think the callous nationalist behaviours that are rising up, and even war, emerge from a failure of empathy, a failure of understanding and caring for the theoretical stranger. And I think that literature is really good medicine for that disease, because when you read a novel, you put down yourself, you put yourself aside on the nightstand, and you pick up someone else's life, and you go into that life.... No other form of entertainment does this. Journalism doesn't do it. Only literature, only fiction puts you inside another person's head.

How Stories Change Us. Elaine Reese, Oxford University Press. © Oxford University Press 2024.
DOI: 10.1093/oso/9780197747902.003.0009

Although we can learn about the world and people through nonfiction, we can't get into the hearts and minds of other people except through imagining—through stories. Only stories encourage us to simulate others' thoughts and emotions, to put ourselves in their bodies. The new genre of climate fiction (cli-fi), such as Barbara Kingsolver's *Flight Behavior* and Richard Powers' *The Overstory*, even encourages us to empathize with the natural world.[2]

THE FUTURE OF STORIES

Oral stories have existed across human history and will continue to be vital in the future. Video technology now enables us to engage in oral story-telling with others in real time regardless of distance. In fact, people from indigenous cultures with strong oral storytelling traditions are embracing this new form of the ancient art.[3]

But video games, TV and movies, even novels are all relatively recent inventions on the evolutionary story stage. New forms of fiction are emerging all the time. For instance, Rupi Kaur is growing a generation of poetry lovers through her multimedia creations of poems and line drawings that fit on a phone screen.

Who knows what new story shapes are waiting in the wings? Is there a future genre that is an amalgam, such as a video game based on real-life interactions that allows you to be and interact with different characters, and experience consequences in real time, in an augmented virtual world?[4] Players would guess characters' intentions and mental states and then would be told (or read) their actual inner workings. Such a game might be inherently rewarding, like reading or viewing fiction, but might also be used as a serious game to teach children and teens and those with autism about empathy and theory of mind in an environment without social risks. There are already crude versions of such games on the market, and no doubt more in the works, but they may rapidly become more sophisticated and more effective. And, of course, there's the looming metaverse, and artificial intelligence (AI) storytelling apps are getting better by the day.

Will there someday be fiction-delivery implants in our brains? Oh wait, each of us already has one of those—our default network. But will new story technologies fundamentally change our brain's natural abilities to create fictional worlds and to imagine the future? We may confront these questions sooner than we expect.

How will these old and new stories help Anna, Charlie, Tia, Joe, and all of our children to confront the challenges to come in this world? How will we ingest and create stories in different ways as we confront global

EPILOGUE *(145)*

crises, such as future pandemics and severe weather events? Isolation lends itself to binge-watching and gaming, maybe even to binge-listening of audiobooks, but probably not to binge-reading—although we can hope. My impression is that we are treasuring real-life stories more than ever in the post-COVID-19 world now that we have reestablished our face-to-face connections with others.

Because not one of us can see the future with certainty, however, it is vital to train the next generation for creativity and innovation. Science, technology, engineering, and mathematics (STEM) education alone cannot do that. The growing science, technology, engineering, the arts, and mathematics (STEAM) movement in education aims to insure that young people have a sense of history, coupled with empathy, so that new technologies they create are ethical and socially responsible.[5] Non-Western countries like Korea are at the forefront of STEAM education reforms.[6]

Whatever the form of fiction, we will continue to need stories as long as humans exist. If fewer and fewer people are reading books, we will discover new ways of creating and experiencing stories in our everyday lives. Perhaps these newly embodied ways of experiencing fiction will be even better than the novel at promoting empathy and understanding.

THE END OF OUR STORIES

As adult children, we can also continue to connect to our own parents through stories. As our parents near the end of their journey, the assigned seating flips; they start to need us in more ways than we could ever have imagined when we were younger. In addition to the physical caregiving that must happen, I argue that they also need to continue to share stories with us. They need a patient and receptive audience for *their* story, with all its highs and lows and wrong and right turns. We can give them the gift of listening deeply and accepting whatever version of it they need to fashion.[7]

Throughout most of the writing of this book I was separated from my elderly mother by over 7000 km and then by the pandemic. I talked to her often on the phone and by email. Inspired by my book club, we started our own little book club in which we read the same books during the week and then talked about them in our Sunday calls. Sometimes we reread classics together, like Jane Austen's *Emma*, or books by contemporary writers we both love, such as Alexander McCall Smith and Anne Tyler. Our shared reading gave us a change of topic from the everyday routines of our lives. As a bonus, reading books in old age slows down cognitive decline.[8]

Through these chats, I discovered lovely details of my mother's reading past, such as when her favorite aunt gave her a copy of *Little Women* in

1944 for her 10th birthday. It became her favorite book. Book talk often meandered into family stories, and my mother shared little gems from her childhood that gave me insight into who she is and into my family's history. Prior to the pandemic, whenever I was able to get back to Texas, amid our family gatherings and shopping trips and church visits, I always made time to sit with her for an afternoon and go through old photos together. These photos brought up memories that otherwise wouldn't have resurfaced. In an article with the beguiling title of "The End: Death as Part of the Life Story," psychologist Susan Bluck argues that telling these stories may help the elderly to face their own certain future.[9]

After the pandemic, in two treasured and lengthy stays in Texas, I sat with her for hours on end. In the first trip in March, she had gone from reading books to listening to me read them to her. By the second trip in October, the only stories that still mattered to her were the real-life stories with which we all begin, and end.

Although not one of us gets to tell that ending ourselves, if we, their children, know what's come before, we can help to complete our parents' stories after they've gone in a way that stays true to their version. Maybe these stories help us to let go. Perhaps our parents' stories will even help us to imagine how we want to live the rest of *our* days.

⚘

After all, the point of remembering and imagining is to figure out who to be and how to act — as individuals and as a society—in the future. It is our very essence as humans to envision the future, and that capacity is potentially our salvation. Those with a rich sense of past will have a richer array of possibilities from which to choose.

We must nurture the best possible stories for ourselves and for each other from the earliest days until the end of life, in every way imaginable. For although stories can be a curse, they are also a cure. Only through stories can we imagine a brighter future.

ACKNOWLEDGMENTS

This book has been nearly 8 years in the making. I first had the idea in 2016 when I was recovering from cancer, but I didn't have a chance to work on it steadily until my sabbatical leave in 2018, with gratitude to the University of Otago and the Centre for the Study of Social Cohesion at the University of Oxford. But my biggest thanks go out to the children and families who have participated in my research for the past 30 years, especially to those very special young people and their parents who are playing the long game in my longitudinal *Origins of Memory* study. I hope that the scientific knowledge gleaned from your stories will help your children and grandchildren in the generations to come. The Marsden Fund of the Royal Society of New Zealand funded the early childhood phase of that study, and the Division of Sciences at the University of Otago funded the adolescent and young adult phases.

I am indebted in so many ways to literally dozens of former students and research assistants who, without complaint, collected hours and hours of longitudinal data and then spent countless other hours transcribing, coding, and analyzing that data, especially (in rough chronological order) Kate Farrant, Keryn Harley, Sandy Sullivan, Stephanie Read, Rhiannon Newcombe, Amy Bird, Rebecca Brookland, Meagan Stephenson, Sarah Stewart, Emily Cleveland, Gabriel Trionfi, Sarah-Jane Robertson, Tia Neha, Helena McAnally, Donna Anderson, Yan Chen, Ella Myftari, Fiona Jack, Bridget Forsyth, Debbie Nicholas, Lucy Macfarlane, Joanna Parry, Georgina de Brélaz, Claire Mitchell, Jessica Riordan, Shika Das, Amanda Clifford, Jane Carroll, Sarah Timperley, Isabelle Swearingen, Sean Marshall, and Azhad Alias. Isabelle and Sean, hats off to you for encouraging the final few *Origins* participants to take part in the thick of the pandemic.

A big, caffeine-fueled thanks to my Psychology Book Club members, Abigail Pigden, Tugce Bakir-Demir, Sean Marshall, Isabelle Swearingen, and Keren Segal, for your thoughtful comments and for your enthusiasm for this book—you all motivated me to keep going at a time when I wanted to scrap the whole project. Isabelle, thank you for your final proofreading of the whole book and for your suggestions.

I'd like to extend a special thanks to former students Hadar Hazan, Alison Sparks, and Sebastian Suggate for reading the first full draft all the way through and giving me many ideas for the revision. Thank you all for our wonderful conversations about stories over the years. Hadar suggested the story list and provided narrative examples from her research, and Alison helped me with a speech-language therapy perspective on the childhood chapter. Sebastian's new research on mental imagery turned out to be the linchpin of the entire book, as spelled out in Chapter 8. Tia Neha, I am especially grateful for your patient tutelage about the Māori concept of *poipoia*, and for your cultural advice and friendship since we started on this *mahi* over 15 years ago.

To Janet Kuebli, my former Psychology Reading Group member and friend, and to the graduate students in your "Storytime" seminar at St. Louis University—I appreciate your close reading and your excellent suggestions.

My colleagues at the University of Otago and at those other universities up the road (Victoria University of Wellington and the University of Auckland) are an ongoing source of information and illuminating conversations about the value of stories, especially Elizabeth Schaughency, Karen Salmon, Mele Taumoepeau, Stuart McNaughton, Amanda Clifford, Lou Moses, and Hitaua Arahanga-Doyle. I will be forever grateful to Richie Poulton, long-time director of the world-renowned Dunedin Longitudinal Study, for the invaluable advice he has given me about the best ways to protect and nurture a longitudinal study and its members. Richie, I wish you had stuck around long enough for me to give you a copy of this book, and for one last big hug.

Richie also founded my new longitudinal intervention called Kia Tīmata Pai (Best Start study) with Clair Edgeler and Natasha Maruariki at BestStart Educare and with Jimmy McLauchlan, Julia Errington-Scott, and Scarlet Mollan at Methodist Mission Southern. It is turning out to be a joyous way to learn about the realities of being an early childhood teacher. Some of that knowledge of how to help teachers share stories with young children has crept into these pages. I look forward to telling you more in a future book!

I'd also like to thank my editor, Hayley Singer, at Oxford University Press for putting me onto the right track in terms of balancing scholarly, professional, and lay audiences, and for supporting me steadfastly throughout the writing process. Hayley and Emily Benitez patiently answered all my questions near the end to steer this project to completion.

ACKNOWLEDGMENTS *(149)*

I'm grateful to fellow memory and narrative researchers James Pennebaker, Dan McAdams, Karen Salmon, Robyn Fivush, Raymond Mar, Maryanne Garry, Rachel Barr, and Ashley Hinten for their close reading and valuable feedback. Thanks also to Charles Fernyhough and Marjorie Taylor for our many conversations about imagination over the years. Robyn, you inspired me to become a developmental scientist, and you have inspired me in so many other ways as well. I cannot imagine a better PhD supervisor, lifelong mentor, and friend. Karen, I value our growing connections over the past 10 years. You are a truly deep thinker, and your musings shaped the final form of this book. Dan, thank you for your gracious words and for sharing your own book club experiences with me. Jamie, thank you for teaching me about the field of expressive writing amid our reminiscences of growing up in west Texas—what are the odds that two narrative psychologists would have lived two blocks apart and both attended Midland High School, yet never met until 30 years later?

My heartfelt thanks go to neuroscientists Donna Rose Addis and Elizabeth Franz for reading the entire book and providing feedback. You are amazing scholars, and I'm fortunate to learn from you both. I can't wait to hear more about the neuroscience of stories in the years to come.

To Elizabeth Jones, Jo Buchan, and Kate Irvine at the National Library of New Zealand, and Alex Woodley at the Southern Initiative, thank you for your excitement about this book and for introducing me to Margaret Merga's work. I'm looking forward to deepening our partnership in the coming years.

A huge shout-out to my book club friends Judith Holloway and Megan Vaughan for enthusiastically reading very rough drafts of the first few chapters and for their helpful suggestions, and to all my other book club friends (Janine, Susan, Jane, Amy, and Trinie) for patiently answering my questions over the years about their own and their family's reading and viewing habits. Most of all, thank you for filling my life with fiction. No matter how wonderful or terrible the book, talking about fiction with you all refreshes me each and every month.

Thank you to my dear friends David Green, Caroline Barnes, Clive Humphreys, Angela and Peter Stupples, Geoff White, and Liz Poole for our lively and insightful conversations over the years about books, TV, films, aesthetics, book clubs, and the value of rereading and rewatching. David, I treasure your insights on the dangers of fiction, especially given your vantage point from the world of Hollywood movies and advertising where the slickest narratives can hide so much. Someday, Clive, I promise to read the Norman Mailer book that you continue to revisit.

To my *whānau*: Whether nearby or far away, you are all so important to me. Dylan, Steve, and Sam—I appreciate you all listening to me babble on about this book for years and for helping me to understand the history readers' and video gamers' perspectives. Casey, thank you for being my co-parent in raising two sons who love stories of all types. Ben and Viktoria, thanks for being my live-in fellow fiction fanatics and for your support of my writing of this book in a multitude of ways, not least of which were delicious meals delivered to my door during a bout of Covid in 2022. I hope your enthusiasm for books is lifelong and is passed down to the next generation. (I'm pretty sure that is a given!) Lou, thank you for being my most encouraging reader, astute editor, scientific advisor, snack-bearer, social media manager, and soulmate. You somehow managed to make the final stages of writing this book fun. Jen, thank you for being my advisor and editor, travel companion through thick and thin, and lifelong best friend. Our shared childhood story worlds were the inspiration for this book. Finally, my deepest gratitude goes to my mother, for being there with stories from the beginning until nearly the end. You never got to read the final chapter, but I hope you would have liked it.

Elaine Reese
December 2, 2023
Dunedin, New Zealand

RECOMMENDED STORIES

Note: This list is in order of mention, with a few extras thrown in. If the same story exists in multiple forms, I took the liberty of choosing my favorite version. Thanks to Dr. April Salchert for empathy game recommendations.

STORIES FROM BOOKS

All of a Kind Family by Sydney Taylor
Little House on the Prairie by Laura Ingalls Wilder
Little Women by Louisa May Alcott
A Tale of Two Cities by Charles Dickens
The Scarlet Letter by Nathaniel Hawthorne
Hamlet by William Shakespeare
Much Ado About Nothing by William Shakespeare
The Help by Kathryn Stockett
The Burgess Boys by Elizabeth Strout
Through the Looking Glass by Lewis Carroll
If on a Winter's Night a Traveler by Italo Calvino
The Unbearable Lightness of Being by Milan Kundera
Good Country People by Flannery O'Connor
Becoming by Michelle Obama
The Little Paris Bookshop by Nina George
The Runner by Don DeLillo
Chameleon by Anton Chekhov
Space Jockey by Robert Heinlein
Gone Girl by Gillian Flynn
The Dutch House by Ann Patchett
The No. 1 Ladies' Detective Agency by Alexander McCall Smith
44 Scotland Street series by Alexander McCall Smith
Mrs. Dalloway by Virginia Woolf

(152) Recommended Stories

The Right Attitude to Rain by Alexander McCall Smith
The Naturals by Jennifer Lynn Barnes
Breakfast at Tiffany's by Truman Capote
Harry Potter and the Chamber of Secrets by J. K. Rowling
The Night Circus by Erin Morganstern
Good Fullas: A Guide to Kiwi Blokes by Marc Ellis
The Girl With the Dragon Tattoo by Stieg Larsson
Infinite Jest by David Foster Wallace
Hunger Games by Suzanne Collins
Don Quixote by Miguel de Cervantes
The Luminaries by Eleanor Catton
The Goldfinch by Donna Tartt
Elinor Oliphant Is Completely Fine by Gail Honeyman
Where the Crawdads Sing by Delia Owens
Olive, Again by Elizabeth Strout
Tropic of Cancer by Henry Miller
To Kill a Mockingbird by Harper Lee
The Cat in the Hat by Dr. Seuss
Caillou by Christine L'Heureux
Clifford the Big Red Dog by Norman Bridwell
Maisy series by Lucy Cousins
Max and Ruby series by Rosemary Wells
The Little Red Hen by Paul Galdone
Ferguson's Night Fright by Natalie Morrell
The Three Billy Goats Gruff by Paul Galdone
A Weekend with Wendell by Kevin Henkes
The Paper Bag Princess by Robert Munsch
The Little Engine That Could by Watty Piper
Captain Underpants series by Dav Pilkey
Dog Man series by Dav Pilkey
My Happy Life series by Rose Lagercrantz
Charlie Bone series by Jenny Nimmo
Horrible Histories series by Terry Deary
Emma by Jane Austen
The Diary of a Young Girl by Anne Frank
The Wildwood Chronicles by Colin Meloy
Precious Ramotswe by Alexander McCall Smith
Harsu and the Werestoat by Barbara Else
The Golden Compass series by Philip Pullman
1984 by George Orwell
Rosie Revere, Engineer by Andrea Beaty

Ada Twist, Scientist by Andrew Beaty
Girl, Woman, Other by Bernardine Evaristo
Finn and Puss by Robert Vescio
Where the Wild Things Are by Maurice Sendak
March by Geraldine Brooks
Year of Wonders by Geraldine Brooks
The Sound of Things Falling by Juan Gabriel Vásquez
The Choice by Edith Eger
The Cut Out Girl by Bart van Es
Calvin & Hobbes by Bill Watterson
Eragon by Christopher Paolini
Twilight Saga by Stephenie Meyer
I Am, I Am, I Am: Seventeen Brushes With Death by Maggie O'Farrell
Euphoria by Lily King
Gulliver's Travels by Jonathan Swift
Norwegian Wood by Haruki Murakami
Flight Behavior by Barbara Kingsolver
The Overstory by Richard Powers

STORIES FROM TV AND MOVIES

Julius Caesar
Escape to Witch Mountain
Little House on the Prairie
The Sound of Music
Orange Is the New Black
The Killing
The Bridge
Borgen
Broadchurch
Bonus Family
Rita
Mad Men
West Wing
The Good Wife
Lost
Stuart: A Life Backwards
Ever After: A Cinderella Story
Amazing Spiderman 2
Big Little Lies

(154) *Recommended Stories*

Normal People
Little Fires Everywhere
Nine Perfect Strangers
From Scratch
The Power of the Dog
Fargo
The Big Lebowski
Unorthodox
Shtisel
Sesame Street
Dora the Explorer
Blue's Clues
Mister Rogers' Neighborhood
Barney & Friends
Special Agent Oso
Bluey
Kiri and Lou
Little Einsteins
Little Bill
Phineas and Ferb
Martha Speaks
High School Musical
Over the Hedge
Gilmore Girls
Daddy Daycare
Paw Patrol
The Wiggles
Star Wars
House
House of Cards
Mad Max
Heavenly Creatures
Pocahontas
Merida
The Rainmaker

STORIES FROM VIDEO GAMES

Gone Home
The Sims

Depression Quest
Hunt for the Gay Planet
Firewatch
Oxenfree
What Remains of Edith Finch
Papers Please
That Dragon, Cancer
The Book of Distance
Dear Esther
All the Delicate Duplicates
Kentucky Route Zero
Everyone's Gone to the Rapture
Tell Me Why
Orwell's Animal Farm

BOOKS ABOUT STORIES

Why We Read Fiction by Lisa Zunshine
On the Origin of Stories: Evolution, Cognition, and Fiction by Brian Boyd
The Stories We Live By: Personal Myths and the Making of Self by Dan McAdams
The Art and Science of Personality Development by Dan McAdams
Life Is in the Transitions by Bruce Feiler
Opening Up by Writing It Down by James W. Pennebaker and Joshua M. Smyth
Expressive Writing: Words That Heal by James W. Pennebaker
The Secret Life of Pronouns by James W. Pennebaker
Flicker: Your Brain on Movies by Jeffrey M. Zacks
The Storytelling Animal: How Stories Make Us Human by Jonathan Gottschall
The Co-Authored Self: Family Stories and the Construction of Personal Identity by Kate McLean
Moral Combat: Why the War on Violent Video Games Is Wrong by Patrick M. Markey
The Myth of Repressed Memories: False Memories and Allegations of Sexual Abuse by Elizabeth F. Loftus
Family Narratives and the Development of an Autobiographical Self by Robyn Fivush
The House of Make-Believe: Children's Play and the Developing Imagination by Dorothy G. Singer and Jerome L. Singer

(*156*) *Recommended Stories*

The Boy Who Would Be a Helicopter by Vivian G. Paley
A Child's Work: The Importance of Fantasy Play by Vivan G. Paley
Play = Learning by Dorothy G. Singer, Roberta Michnick Golinkoff, and Kathy Hirsh-Pasek
Imaginary Friends and the Children Who Have Them by Marjorie Taylor
Inventing Imaginary Worlds: From Childhood Play to Adult Creativity Across the Arts and Sciences by Michèle Root-Bernstein
The Voices Within: The History and Science of How We Talk to Ourselves by Charles Fernyhough

NOTES

PREFACE

1. Strout, E. (2013). *The Burgess boys* (p. 246), Kindle edition. New York: Random House.
2. Obama, M. (2018). *Becoming* (p. xvii). New York: Crown.
3. Reese, E., Hayne, H., & MacDonald, S. (2008). Looking back to the future: Māori and Pakeha mother–child birth stories. *Child Development, 79*(1), 114–125.
4. American Psychological Association. (2015). Guidelines for psychological practice with transgender and gender non-conforming people. *American Psychologist, 70,* 832–864.
5. Graham, S. (2004). It's like one of those puzzles: Conceptualising gender among Bugis (p. 108). *Journal of Gender Studies, 13*(2), 107–116.
6. Cameron, J. J., & Stinson, D. A. (2019). Gender (mis) measurement: Guidelines for respecting gender diversity in psychological research. *Social and Personality Psychology Compass, 13*(11), e12506. I am guilty of this oversight myself. In *Origins*, we relied on mothers' reports of children's gender at the outset of the study, when children were toddlers, and did not ask the participants themselves to report on their own gender at age 20. In any future data waves on this study, and in my other research, I will ask participants to report gender using the current guidelines of the Association of Psychological Science, or the single open-ended question suggested by Cameron and Stinson: *I identify my gender as ___ (please specify).*
7. Brown, C. S., Biefeld, S. D., & Tam, M. J. (2020). Gender in childhood. In M. H. Bornstein (Ed.), *Elements in child development.* Cambridge: Cambridge University Press, 1–64.
8. Gottschall, J. (2012). *The storytelling animal: How stories make us human.* New York: Houghton Mifflin Harcourt.
9. Dubourg, E., & Baumard, N. (2022). Why imaginary worlds? The psychological foundations and cultural evolution of fictions with imaginary worlds. *Behavioral and Brain Sciences, 45*, e276.
10. Henrich, J., Heine, S. J., & Norenzayan, A. (2010). The weirdest people in the world? *Behavioral and Brain Sciences, 33*(2–3), 61–83.
11. Addis, D. R., Wong, A. T., & Schacter, D. L. (2007). Remembering the past and imagining the future: Common and distinct neural substrates during event construction and elaboration. *Neuropsychologia, 45*(7), 1363–1377.
12. Muindi, F. J., Ramachandran, L., & Tsai, J. W. (2020). Human narratives in science: The power of storytelling. *Trends in Molecular Medicine, 26*(3), 249–251.

CHAPTER 1

1. Dunbar, R. I. (2004). Gossip in evolutionary perspective. *Review of General Psychology, 8*(2), 100–110; Boyd, B. (2010). *On the origin of stories: Evolution, cognition, and fiction*. Cambridge, MA: Harvard University Press.

2. Tomasello, M., Kruger, A. C., & Ratner, H. H. (1993). Cultural learning. *Behavioral and Brain Sciences, 16*(3), 495–511.

3. Smith, D., Schlaepfer, P., Major, K., et al. (2017). Cooperation and the evolution of hunter-gatherer storytelling. *Nature Communications, 8*(1), 1–9.

4. Mar, R. A., Oatley, K., Hirsh, J., Dela Paz, J., & Peterson, J. B. (2006). Bookworms versus nerds: Exposure to fiction versus non-fiction, divergent associations with social ability, and the simulation of fictional social worlds. *Journal of Research in Personality, 40*(5), 694–712.

5. Scores on the Author Recognition Test (ART; Stanovich & West, 1989) correlate with real-life reading behavior and with daily diary studies of reading (Allen et al., 1992). ART scores also correlate positively with vocabulary knowledge and reading skills in one's dominant language (McCarron & Kuperman, 2021).
   Stanovich, K. E., & West, R. F. (1989). Exposure to print and orthographic processing. *Reading Research Quarterly, 24*(4), 402–433; Allen, L., Cipielewski, J., & Stanovich, K. E. (1992). Multiple indicators of children's reading habits and attitudes: Construct validity and cognitive correlates. *Journal of Educational Psychology, 84*(4), 489–503; McCarron, S. P., & Kuperman, V. (2021). Is the author recognition test a useful metric for native and non-native English speakers? An item response theory analysis. *Behavior Research Methods, 53*(5), 2226–2237.

6. Definitions of empathy vary. For instance, Baron-Cohen (2011, p. 27) defines empathy as composed of affective and cognitive components, with these two components overlapping. Baron-Cohen defines sympathy as a subtype of empathy that—in addition to feeling another's emotions and understanding them—also includes the desire to help that person. My definition is instead closer to Bloom's (2016, p. 22) that empathy is the coexperiencing of emotion, whereas theory of mind is the cognitive understanding of another person's mental states. Baron-Cohen, S. (2011). *The science of evil: Empathy and the origins of cruelty*. New York: Basic Books; Bloom, P. (2016). *Against empathy: The case for rational compassion*. New York: HarperCollins.

7. Although the Reading the Mind in the Eyes test (Baron-Cohen et al., 2001) has its critics, one advantage is that it is not subject to social desirability bias like self-report measures (Black et al., 2021). Baron-Cohen, S., Wheelwright, S., Hill, J., Raste, Y., & Plumb, I. (2001). The "Reading the Mind in the Eyes" Test revised version: A study with normal adults, and adults with Asperger syndrome or high-functioning autism. *The Journal of Child Psychology and Psychiatry and Allied Disciplines, 42*(2), 241–251; Black, J. E., Barnes, J. L., Oatley, K., et al. (2021). Stories and their role in social cognition. In D. Kuiken & A. M. Jacobs (Eds.), *Handbook of empirical literary studies* (pp. 229–251). Berlin: Walter De Gruyter GmbH.

8. Mar, R. A., Oatley, K., & Peterson, J. B. (2009). Exploring the link between reading fiction and empathy: Ruling out individual differences and examining outcomes. *Communications, 34*, 407–428.

9. Fong, K., Mullin, J. B., & Mar, R. A. (2013). What you read matters: The role of fiction genre in predicting interpersonal sensitivity. *Psychology of Aesthetics, Creativity, and the Arts, 7*(4), 370–376.

NOTES *(159)*

10. Kidd, D. C., & Castano, E. (2013). Reading literary fiction improves theory of mind. *Science*, *342*(6156), 377–380.

11. Dodell-Feder, D., & Tamir, D. I. (2018). Fiction reading has a small positive impact on social cognition: A meta-analysis. *Journal of Experimental Psychology: General*, *147*(11), 1713–1727. Most of these studies were with undergraduates, with the social cognition outcomes comprising a range of performance (e.g., Reading the Mind in the Eyes Test) and self-report measures.

12. A p-curve analysis showed that although this body of research has "evidential value," the effect is not robust, and many of the studies are underpowered (Quinlan et al., 2022). Some newer well-powered studies continue to produce mixed findings (e.g., van Kujik et al., 2018 versus Wimmer et al., 2021). Quinlan, J. A., Padgett, J. K., Khajehnassiri, A., & Mar, R. A. (2023). Does a brief exposure to literary fiction improve social ability? Assessing the evidential value of published studies with a p-curve. *Journal of Experimental Psychology: General*, *152*(3), 723–732; Van Kuijk, I., Verkoeijen, P., Dijkstra, K., & Zwaan, R. A. (2018). The effect of reading a short passage of literary fiction on theory of mind: A replication of Kidd and Castano (2013). *Collabra: Psychology*, *4*(1), Article 7; Wimmer, L., Currie, G., Friend, S., & Ferguson, H. J. (2021). The effects of reading narrative fiction on social and moral cognition: Two experiments following a multi-method approach. *Scientific Study of Literature*, *11*(2), 223–265.

13. Johnson, D. R., Jasper, D. M., Griffin, S., & Huffman, B. L. (2013). Reading narrative fiction reduces Arab-Muslim prejudice and offers a safe haven from intergroup anxiety. *Social Cognition*, *31*(5), 578–598; Johnson, D. R., Cushman, G. K., Borden, L. A., & McCune, M. S. (2013). Potentiating empathic growth: Generating imagery while reading fiction increases empathy and prosocial behavior. *Psychology of Aesthetics, Creativity, and the Arts*, *7*(3), 306–312.

14. Mar, R. A., & Oatley, K. (2008). The function of fiction is the abstraction and simulation of social experience. *Perspectives on Psychological Science*, *3*(3), 173–192; Oatley, K. (2016). Fiction: Simulation of social worlds. *Trends in Cognitive Sciences*, *20*(8), 618–628.

15. Mumper, M. L., & Gerrig, R. J. (2017). Leisure reading and social cognition: A meta-analysis. *Psychology of Aesthetics, Creativity, and the Arts*, *11*(1), 109–120. This meta-analysis of 30 correlational studies showed that the overall association between fiction reading on the Author Recognition Test and theory of mind (mostly measured with the Mind in the Eyes test) was aggregate $r = .21$, and between fiction reading and dispositional empathy on the Davis empathy scale was aggregate $r = .07$ (the average of the empathic concern and perspective-taking subscales). Nonfiction reading also predicted dispositional empathy but weakly (aggregate $r = .05$), and actually predicted lower scores on the personal distress dimension of the Davis (1983) empathy scale (aggregate $r = -.10$). A limitation of all of these fiction-reading studies, however, is that they are comprised almost solely of WEIRD participants (from Western, Educated, Industrialized, Rich, and Democratic countries).

16. Koopman, E. M. (2018). Does originality evoke understanding? The relation between literary reading and empathy. *Review of General Psychology*, *22*(2), 169–177.

17. Zunshine, L. (2006). *Why we read fiction: Theory of mind and the novel*. Columbus, OH: Ohio State University Press.

18. Altmann, U., Bohrn, I. C., Lubrich, O., Menninghaus, W., & Jacobs, A. M. (2014). Fact vs fiction—How paratextual information shapes our reading processes. *Social Cognitive and Affective Neuroscience*, *9*(1), 22–29.

19. Andrews-Hanna (2012) and Addis (2018) provide excellent overviews of the role of the default network (comprising medial temporal lobes, medial aspects of the frontal and parietal cortices, inferior lateral parietal cortex, and lateral temporal cortex) in supporting autobiographical memory, imagination, and processing of fictional stories. Andrews-Hanna, J. R. (2012). The brain's default network and its adaptive role in internal mentation. *The Neuroscientist, 18*(3), 251–270; Addis, D. R. (2018). Are episodic memories special? On the sameness of remembered and imagined event simulation. *Journal of the Royal Society of New Zealand, 48*(2–3), 64–88; see also Mar, R. A. (2011). The neural basis of social cognitive and story comprehension. *Annual Review of Psychology, 62*(1), 103–134.

20. Zunshine, L. (2006). *Why we read fiction: Theory of mind and the novel* (p. 32). Columbus, OH: Ohio State University Press.

21. Perner, J., & Wimmer, H. (1985). John *thinks* that Mary *thinks* that . . .": Attribution of second-order beliefs by 5 to 10 year old children. *Journal of Experimental Child Psychology, 39*(3), 437–471.

22. Dumontheil, I., Apperly, I. A., & Blakemore, S.-J. (2010). Online usage of theory of mind continues to develop in late adolescence. *Developmental Science, 13*(2), 331–338; Valle, A., Massaro, D., Castelli, I., & Marchetti, A. (2015). Theory of mind development in adolescence and early adulthood: The growing complexity of recursive thinking ability. *Europe's Journal of Psychology, 11*(1), 112–124.

23. Barnes, J. L. (2018). Imaginary engagement, real-world effects: Fiction, emotion, and social cognition. *Review of General Psychology, 22*(2), 125–134; see also Consoli, G. (2018). Preliminary steps towards a cognitive theory of fiction and its effects. *Journal of Cultural Cognitive Science, 2*(1–2), 85–100; Mar, R. A. (2018). Evaluating whether stories can promote social cognition: Introducing the Social Processes and Content Entrained by Narrative (SPaCEN) framework. *Discourse Processes, 5/6*, 454–479.

24. Bellana, B., Mahabal, A., & Honey, C. J. (2022). Narrative thinking lingers in spontaneous thought. *Nature Communications, 13*(1), 4585.

25. Bal, P. M., & Veltkamp, M. (2013). How does fiction reading influence empathy? An experimental investigation on the role of emotional transportation. *PLoS One, 8*(1), e55341; Johnson, D. R. (2012). Transportation into a story increases empathy, prosocial behavior, and perceptual bias toward fearful expressions. *Personality and Individual Differences, 52*(2), 150–155; Johnson, D. R., Cushman, G. K., Borden, L. A., & McCune, M. S. (2013). Potentiating empathic growth: Generating imagery while reading fiction increases empathy and prosocial behavior. *Psychology of Aesthetics, Creativity, and the Arts, 7*(3), 306–312; Schwerin, J., & Lenhart, J. (2022). The effects of literariness on social-cognitive skills: Examining narrative engagement, transportation, and identification as moderators. *Psychology of Aesthetics, Creativity, and the Arts.*

26. Pino, M. C., & Mazza, M. (2016). The use of "literary fiction" to promote mentalizing ability. *PLoS one, 11*(8), e0160254.

27. Thank you to Raymond Mar for this suggestion.

28. See Appendix of Johnson et al. (2013). Johnson, D. R., Cushman, G. K., Borden, L. A., & McCune, M. S. (2013). Potentiating empathic growth: Generating imagery while reading fiction increases empathy and prosocial behavior. *Psychology of Aesthetics, Creativity, and the Arts, 7*(3), 306–312.

29. Tamir, D. I., Bricker, A. B., Dodell-Feder, D., & Mitchell, J. P. (2016). Reading fiction and reading minds: The role of simulation in the default network. *Social Cognitive and Affective Neuroscience, 11*(2), 215–224.

NOTES *(161)*

30. Mar, R. A. (2018). Evaluating whether stories can promote social cognition: Introducing the Social Processes and Content Entrained by Narrative (SPaCEN) framework. *Discourse Processes*, *55*(5–6), 454–479; Mar, R. A. (2018). Stories and the promotion of social cognition. *Current Directions in Psychological Science*, *27*(4), 257–262.

31. Zacks, J. (2015). *Flicker: Your brain on movies*. New York: Oxford University Press.

32. Black, J., & Barnes, J. L. (2015). Fiction and social cognition: The effect of viewing award-winning television dramas on theory of mind. *Psychology of Aesthetics, Creativity, and the Arts*, *9*(4), 423–429.

33. Dunbar, R. I. M., Teasdale, B., Thompson, J., et al. (2016). Emotional arousal when watching drama increases pain threshold and social bonding. *Royal Society Open Science*, *3*, 160288.

34. Rathje, S., Hackel, L., & Zaki, J. (2021). Attending live theatre improves empathy, changes attitudes, and leads to pro-social behavior. *Journal of Experimental Social Psychology*, *95*, 104138.

35. Bormann, D., & Greitemeyer, T. (2015). Immersed in virtual worlds and minds: Effects of in-game storytelling on immersion, need satisfaction, and affective theory of mind. *Social Psychological and Personality Science*, *6*(6), 646–652.

36. For example, Tan et al. (2022) documented higher rates of self-reported STI testing among Singaporean men who watched an award-winning TV drama called *People Like Us* compared to a no-viewing control condition. Tan, R. K. J., Koh, W. L., Le, D., et al. (2022). Effect of a popular web drama video series on HIV and other sexually transmitted infection testing among gay, bisexual, and other men who have sex with men in Singapore: Community-based, pragmatic, randomized controlled trial. *Journal of Medical Internet Research*, *24*(5), e31401.

37. Murphy, S. T., Frank, L. B., Chatterjee, J. S., & Baezconde-Garbanati, L. (2013). Narrative versus nonnarrative: The role of identification, transportation, and emotion in reducing health disparities. *Journal of Communication*, *63*(1), 116–137; Frank, L. B., Murphy, S. T., Chatterjee, J. S., Moran, M. B., & Baezconde-Garbanati, L. (2015). Telling stories, saving lives: Creating narrative health messages. *Health Communication*, *30*(2), 154–163.

38. McAdams, D. P., & McLean, K. C. (2013). Narrative identity. *Current Directions in Psychological Science*, *22*(3), 233–238.

39. Dunlop, W. L., & Tracy, J. L. (2013). Sobering stories: Narratives of self-redemption predict behavioral change and improved health among recovering alcoholics. *Journal of Personality and Social Psychology*, *104*(3), 576–590.

40. Bauer, J. J., & McAdams, D. P. (2010). Eudaimonic growth: Narrative growth goals predict increases in ego development and subjective well-being 3 years later. *Developmental Psychology*, *46*(4), 761–772. The stories in this study were of future life goals, not past events, a difference I address in Chapter 4. Bauer, J. J., Graham, L. E., Lauber, E. A., & Lynch, B. P. (2019). What growth sounds like: Redemption, self-improvement, and eudaimonic growth across different life narratives in relation to well-being. *Journal of Personality*, *87*(3), 546–565.

41. McLean, K. C., Syed, M., Pasupathi, M., et al. (2020). The empirical structure of narrative identity: The initial Big Three. *Journal of Personality and Social Psychology*, *119*(4), 920–944.

42. Adler, J. M., Lodi-Smith, J., Philippe, F. L., & Houle, I. (2016). The incremental validity of narrative identity in predicting well-being: A review of the field and recommendations for the future. *Personality and Social Psychology Review*, *20*(2), 142–175.

43. Wang, Q. (2013). *The autobiographical self in time and culture*. New York: Oxford University Press.
44. Wang, Q., Hou, Y., Koh, J. B. K., Song, Q., & Yang, Y. (2018). Culturally motivated remembering: The moderating role of culture for the relation of episodic memory to well-being. *Clinical Psychological Science*, 6(6), 860–871.
45. Pennebaker, J. W., & Beall, S. K. (1986). Confronting a traumatic event: toward an understanding of inhibition and disease. *Journal of Abnormal Psychology*, 95(3), 274–281.
46. Gao, X. (2022). Research on expressive writing in psychology: A forty-year bibliometric analysis and visualization of current status and research trends. *Frontiers in Psychology*, 13, 825626.
47. Pennebaker, J. W. (2018). Expressive writing in psychological science. *Perspectives on Psychological Science*, 13(2), 226–229. The largest meta-analyses of expressive writing include the following: Frattaroli, J. (2006). Experimental disclosure and its moderators: A meta-analysis. *Psychological Bulletin*, 132(6), 823–865; Guo, L. (2023). The delayed, durable effect of expressive writing on depression, anxiety and stress: A meta-analytic review of studies with long-term follow-ups. *British Journal of Clinical Psychology*, 62, 272–297; Reinhold, M., Bürkner, P. C., & Holling, H. (2018). Effects of expressive writing on depressive symptoms—A meta-analysis. *Clinical Psychology: Science and Practice*, 25(1), e12224; Pavlacic, J. M., Buchanan, E. M., Maxwell, N. P., Hopke, T. G., & Schulenberg, S. E. (2019). A meta-analysis of expressive writing on posttraumatic stress, posttraumatic growth, and quality of life. *Review of General Psychology*, 23(2), 230–250.
48. Koschwanez, H. E., Kerse, N., Darragh, M., Jarrett, P., Booth, R. J., & Broadbent, E. (2013). Expressive writing and wound healing in older adults: A randomized controlled trial. *Psychosomatic Medicine*, 75(6), 581–590.
49. Pennebaker, J. W., & Evans, J. F. (2014). *Expressive writing: Words that heal*. Bedford, IN: Idyll Arbor; Pennebaker, J. W., & Smyth, J. M. (2016). *Opening up by writing it down: How expressive writing improves health and eases emotional pain* (3rd ed.). New York: The Guilford Press.
50. Smyth, J. M., & Pennebaker, J. W. (2008). Exploring the boundary conditions of expressive writing: In search of the right recipe. *British Journal of Health Psychology*, 13(1), 1–7.
51. Boyd, R. L., Ashokkumar, A., Seraj, S., & Pennebaker, J. W. (2022). *The development and psychometric properties of LIWC-22*. Austin, TX: University of Texas at Austin.
52. Pennebaker, J. W. (2011). *The secret life of pronouns: What our words say about us*. London: Bloomsbury Press.
53. Guo (2023) found that gaps of 1–3 days between expressive writing sessions produced the greatest benefits for lowering depression, stress, and anxiety with adult samples. Guo, L. (2023). The delayed, durable effect of expressive writing on depression, anxiety and stress: A meta-analytic review of studies with long-term follow-ups. *British Journal of Clinical Psychology*, 62, 272–297.
54. Andersson, M. A., & Conley, C. S. (2013). Optimizing the perceived benefits and health outcomes of writing about traumative life events. *Stress and Health*, 29, 40–49.
55. Romero, C. (2008). Writing wrongs: Promoting forgiveness through expressive writing. *Journal of Personality and Social Relationships*, 25(4), 625–642. The empathy scale in this study was adapted from Davis' (1980) perspective-taking

NOTES *(163)*

scale from the *Interpersonal Reactivity Index*. Davis, M. H. (1980). *Interpersonal Reactivity Index*. Washington, DC: APA PsycTests.

56. Johnson, E. A., & O'Brien, K. A. (2013). Self-compassion soothes the savage ego-threat system: Effects on negative affect, shame, rumination, and depressive symptoms. *Journal of Social and Clinical Psychology, 32*(9), 939–963.

57. Pennebaker, J. W. (2011). *The secret life of pronouns: What our words say about us.* London: Bloomsbury Press.

58. Gao, X. (2022). Research on expressive writing in psychology: A forty-year bibliometric analysis and visualization of current status and research trends. *Frontiers in Psychology, 13,* 825626. Eekhof et al. (2022) argue that similar untapped moderator effects are also evident in the research on effects of fiction reading on social understanding: Eekhof, L. S., Van Krieken, K., & Willems, R. M. (2022). Reading about minds: The social-cognitive potential of narratives. *Psychonomic Bulletin & Review, 29*(5), 1703–1718.

59. Lu, Q., Yeung, N. C., Tsai, W., & Kim, J. H. (2023). The effects of culturally adapted expressive writing interventions on depressive and anxiety symptoms among Chinese American breast cancer survivors: A randomized controlled trial. *Behaviour Research and Therapy, 161,* 104244.

60. Nicolson, M. N., & Flett, J. A. (2020). The mental wellbeing of New Zealanders during and post-lockdown. *The New Zealand Medical Journal (Online), 133*(1523), 110–112.

61. Arahanga-Doyle, H., Moradi, S., Brown, K., Neha, T., Hunter, J. A., & Scarf, D. (2019). Positive youth development in Māori and New Zealand European adolescents through an adventure education programme. *Kōtuitui: New Zealand Journal of Social Sciences Online, 14*(1), 38–51; McNatty, W., & Roa, T. (2002). Whanaungatanga: An illustration of the importance of cultural context. *He Puna Korero: Journal of Maori and Pacific Development, 3*(1), 88–96; Reese, E., Hayne, H., & MacDonald, S. (2008). Looking back to the future: Māori and Pakeha mother–child birth stories. *Child Development, 79*(1), 114–125.

62. Rude, S. S., & Haner, M. L. (2018). Individual differences matter: Commentary on "Effects of expressive writing on depressive symptoms—A meta-analysis." *Clinical Psychology: Science and Practice, 25*(1), e12230.

63. Warwicker, S., Sant, D., Richard, A., et al. (2023). A retrospective longitudinal analysis of mental health admissions: Measuring the fallout of the pandemic. *International Journal of Environmental Research and Public Health, 20*(2), 1194.

64. Merz, E. L., Fox, R. S., & Malcarne, V. L. (2014). Expressive writing interventions in cancer patients: A systematic review. *Health Psychology Review, 8*(3), 339–361; Weinman, J., Ebrecht, M., Scott, S., Walburn, J., & Dyson, M. (2008). Enhanced wound healing after emotional disclosure intervention. *British Journal of Health Psychology, 13*(1), 95–102. However, a meta-analysis (Zachariae & O'Toole, 2015) found that standard expressive writing didn't produce significant main effects on cancer patients' health or well-being. Instead, only patients who experienced low levels of social support at the outset benefitted from expressive writing. Because expressive writing is easy and free, the authors encourage future studies of expressive writing with cancer patients to identify other subgroups who may benefit. Zachariae, R., & O'Toole, M. S. (2015). The effect of expressive writing intervention on psychological and physical health outcomes in cancer patients—a systematic review and meta-analysis. *Psycho-Oncology, 24,* 1349–1359.

65. Pennebaker, J. W. (2006). Theories, therapies, and taxpayers: On the complexities of the expressive writing paradigm. *Clinical Psychology: Science and Practice, 11*(2),

138–142. Therapist-assisted expressive writing is also promising: Gerger, H., Werner, C. P., Gaab, J., & Cuijpers, P. (2021). Comparative efficacy and acceptability of expressive writing treatments compared with psychotherapy, other writing treatments, and waiting list control for adult trauma survivors: A systematic review and network meta-analysis. *Psychological Medicine*, *52*(15), 3484–3496.

66. Spreng, R. N., Mar, R. A., & Kim, A. S. (2009). The common neural basis of autobiographical memory, prospection, navigation, theory of mind, and the default mode: A quantitative meta-analysis. *Journal of Cognitive Neuroscience*, *21*(3), 489–510; Stawarczyk, D., Bezdek, M. A., & Zacks, J. M. (2021). Event representations and predictive processing: The role of the midline default network core. *Topics in Cognitive Science*, *13*(1), 164–186.

67. Anderson, D. R., & Davidson, M. C. (2019). Receptive versus interactive video screens: A role for the brain's default mode network in learning from media. *Computers in Human Behavior*, *99*, 168–180; Chen, S., Wang, M., Dong, H., et al. (2021). Internet gaming disorder impacts gray matter structural covariance organization in the default mode network. *Journal of Affective Disorders*, *288*, 23–30.

CHAPTER 2

1. Flynn, J. (2010). *The torchlight list: Around the world in 200 books*. Wellington, NZ: Awa Press;Flynn, J. (2017). *The new torchlight list*. Wellington, NZ: Awa Press.

2. For instance, Mar et al. (2009) found a moderate female advantage among young adults on the fiction subscale of their modified Author Recognition Test (ART; d = 0.54). With older adults, Wimmer and Ferguson (2023) documented a weaker (d = .25) but significant female advantage for the fiction subscale of an updated ART (Mar & Rain, 2015). Mar, R. A., Oatley, K., & Peterson, J. B. (2009). Exploring the link between reading fiction and empathy: Ruling out individual differences and examining outcomes. *Communications*, *34*(4), 407–428; Mar, R. A., & Rain, M. (2015). Narrative fiction and expository nonfiction differentially predict verbal ability. *Scientific Studies of Reading*, *19*(6), 419–433; Wimmer, L., & Ferguson, H. J. (2023). Testing the validity of a self-report scale, author recognition test, and book counting as measures of lifetime exposure to print fiction. *Behavior Research Methods*, *55*, 103–134.

3. Baron-Cohen, S. (2004). *The essential difference: The truth about the male and female brain*. London: Penguin. Baron-Cohen outlined the different dimensions of sex and gender as follows: genetic sex, gonadal sex, genital sex, brain type, and sex-typical behavior. Most existing psychological research instead focuses only on participants' self-stated gender as a dichotomy—male or female—which for most people would be based only on their genetic, gonadal, and genital sex. New psychological research is instead capturing gender in more nuanced ways (see Fivush & Grysman, 2021). Fivush, R., & Grysman, A. (2022). Narrative and gender as mutually constituted meaning-making systems. *Memory, Mind & Media*, *1*(e2), 1–14.

4. Weiner, E. (2007, September 5). Why women read more than men. *Npr.org*. Retrieved on October 27, 2023, from https://www.npr.org/templates/story/story.php?storyId=14175229

5. National Endowment of the Arts. (2018). *U.S. trends in art attendance and literary reading, 2002–2017: A first look at the results from the 2017 Survey of Public Participation in the Arts*. Washington, DC: NEA Office of Research and Analysis.

NOTES *(165)*

6. Reader Habit Survey. (2017). Why, what, and where we read. *Thriftbooks.com*. Retrieved November 11, 2023, from https://www.thriftbooks.com/b/2017reade rsurvey-why-what-where-we-read/

7. Thomas-Corr, J. (2021). How women conquered the world of fiction. *TheGuardian. com*. Retrieved November 11, 2023, from https://www.theguardian.com/books/ 2021/may/16/how-women-conquered-the-world-of-fiction

8. Peterson, H. E. (2015). Male writers continue to dominate literary criticism, Vida study finds. *TheGuardian.com*. Retrieved on May 8, 2024, from https://www.theg uardian.com/books/2015/apr/07/male-writers-continue-dominate-literary-criticism-vida-study-finds.

9. The gender gap in reading is reversed in Arab countries. Of the one third of Arabs who are illiterate, two thirds are women. Online book clubs are growing in popularity in Arab countries, but the gender of book club members is difficult to ascertain. Elsayed, A. M. (2010). Arab online book clubs: A survey. *IFLA Journal, 36*(3), 235–250.

10. B. Brown, personal communication via email, November 15, 2018.

11. Heller, N. (2011). Book clubs: Why do we love them so much? Is it the zucchini bread? *Slate.com*. Retrieved on November 11, 2023, from https://slate.com/ news-and-politics/2011/07/book-clubs-in-america-why-do-we-love-them-so-much.html

12. Ripley, G. (1863). *The New American Cyclopaedia, Vol. 4: A Popular dictionary of general knowledge*. London: Forgotten Books.

13. B. Brown, personal communication via email, November 15, 2018.

14. Winfrey, O. (2020). Oprah Winfrey talks about Toni Morrison on 50th anniversary of "The Bluest Eye." *Today.com*. Retrieved on November 11, 2023, from https://www.today.com/video/oprah-winfrey-talks-about-toni-morrison-on-50th-anniversary-of-the-bluest-eye-98148421640

15. Sedo, D. R. (2003). Readers in reading groups: An online survey of face-to-face and virtual book clubs. *Convergence, 9*(1), 66–90;Sedo, D. R. (2011). *Reading communities from salons to cyberspace*. New York: Springer.

16. Driscoll, B., & Rehberg Sedo, D. (2019). Faraway, so close: Seeing the intimacy in Goodreads reviews. *Qualitative Inquiry, 25*(3), 248–259.

17. Mar, R. A., Oatley, K., & Peterson, J. B. (2009). Exploring the link between reading fiction and empathy: Ruling out individual differences and examining outcomes. *Communications, 34* (4), 407–428. The engagement measure in this study was the fantasy subscale of Davis' (1983) Interpersonal Reactivity Index, which was created as a measure of empathy; however, almost all items on the fantasy subscale are about narrative transportation. Davis, M. H. (1983). Measuring individual differences in empathy: Evidence for a multidimensional approach. *Journal of Personality and Social Psychology, 44*(1), 113–126.

18. I use the term "mental simulation" to refer collectively to mental time travel (Michaelian, 2016; Suddendorf & Corballis, 2007; Tulving, 1985), episodic simulation (past, future, and counterfactual thinking; Schacter et al., 2008), and mentalizing (Mar, 2019); my usage is closest to Addis' (2021) autobiographical cognition. Addis, D. R. (2021). Mythopoetic cognition is a form of autobiographical simulation. *Evolutionary Studies in Imaginative Culture, 5*(2), 37–40; Mar, R. A. (2019). Evaluating whether stories can promote social cognition: Introducing the Social Processes and Content Entrained by Narrative (SPaCEN) framework. *Discourse Processes, 55*(5–6), 454–479; Michaelian, K. (2016). *Mental time travel: Episodic memory and our knowledge of the personal past*. Cambridge, MA: MIT

Press; Schacter, D. L., Addis, D. R., & Buckner, R. L. (2008). Episodic simulation of future events: Concepts, data, and applications. *Annals of the New York Academic of Sciences, 1124,* 39–60; Suddendorf, T., & Corballis, M. C. (2007). The evolution of foresight: What is mental time travel, and is it unique to humans? *Behavioral and Brain Sciences, 30*(3), 299–313; Tulving, E. (1985). Memory and consciousness. *Canadian Psychology/Psychologie Canadienne, 26*(1), 1–12.

19. Gottschall, J. (2013). *The storytelling animal: How stories make us human.* New York: Mariner Books. See also Bruner, J. (1991). The narrative construction of reality. *Critical Inquiry, 18,* 1–21.

20. Stoll, J. (2023). U.S. TV consumption: Average viewing time 2009–2022, by gender. *Statista.com.* Retrieved on November 11, 2023, from https://www.stati sta.com/statistics/411745/average-dialy-time-watching-tv-us-by-gender/

21. Rentfrow, P. J., Goldberg, L. R., & Zilca, R. (2011). Listening, watching, and reading: The structure and correlates of entertainment preferences. *Journal of Personality, 79*(2), 223–258.

22. Schmitt et al. (2008) reported gender differences in personality traits across 55 nations. Women in those 55 nations scored higher on neuroticism, extraversion, agreeableness, and conscientiousness. Schmitt, D. P., Realo, A., Voracek, M., & Allik, J. (2008). Why can't a man be more like a woman? Sex differences in Big Five personality traits across 55 cultures. *Journal of Personality and Social Psychology, 94*(1), 168–182.

23. D. McAdams, personal communication by email, November 13, 2023.

24. The following studies, among others, all find a female advantage for real-life stories:

    Bauer, P., Stennes, L., & Haight, J. (2003). Representation of the inner self in autobiography: Women's and men's use of internal states language in personal narratives. *Memory, 11*(1), 27–42; Berntsen, D., & Rubin, D. C. (2006). The centrality of event scale: A measure of integrating a trauma into one's identity and its relation to post-traumatic stress disorder symptoms. *Behaviour Research and Therapy, 44*(2), 219–231; Ely, R., & Ryan, E. (2008). Remembering talk: Individual and gender differences in reported speech. *Memory, 16*(4), 395–409; Grysman, A. (2017). Gender differences in episodic encoding of autobiographical memory. *Journal of Applied Research in Memory and Cognition, 6*(1), 51–59;Rice, C., & Pasupathi, M. (2010). Reflecting on self-relevant experiences: Adult age differences. *Developmental Psychology, 46*(2), 479–490.

25. Grysman, A., & Hudson, J. A. (2013). Gender differences in autobiographical memory: Developmental and methodological considerations. *Developmental Review, 33*(3), 239–272.

26. Grysman, A. (2017). Gender differences in episodic encoding of autobiographical memory. *Journal of Applied Research in Memory and Cognition, 6*(1), 51–59.

27. Grysman, A., Merrill, N., & Fivush, R. (2017). Emotion, gender, and gender typical identity in autobiographical memory. *Memory, 25*(3), 289–297.

28. There is a small but reliable female advantage on the Reading the Mind in the Eyes test:

    Baron-Cohen, S., Wheelwright, S., Hill, J., Raste, Y., & Plumb, I. (2001). The "Reading the Mind in the Eyes" Test revised version: A study with normal adults, and adults with Asperger syndrome or high-functioning autism. *The Journal of Child Psychology and Psychiatry and Allied Disciplines, 42*(2), 241–251.

29. Hyde, J. S. (2007). New directions in the study of gender similarities and differences. *Current Directions in Psychological Science, 16*(5), 259–263. Gender

NOTES *(167)*

scholar Janet Sibley Hyde argues that most gender differences in social and personality variables are small: Women smile and self-disclose more often, and men are more aggressive and have a more tolerant attitude toward casual sex. However, no one has yet published a meta-analysis of gender differences in reading, viewing, and remembering preferences, so we don't know how these differences compare.

30. Davis, M. H. (1983). Measuring individual differences in empathy: Evidence for a multidimensional approach. *Journal of Personality and Social Psychology*, *44*, 113–126; Wakabayashi, A., Baron-Cohen, S., & Wheelwright, S. (2006). Individual and gender differences in empathizing and systemizing: Measurement of individual differences by the Empathy Quotient (EQ) and the Systemizing Quotient (SQ). *Japanese Journal of Psychology*, *77*(3), 271–277.

31. Buckner, R. L., Andrews-Hanna, J. R., & Schacter, D. L. (2008). The brain's default network: Anatomy, function, and relevance to disease. *Annals of the NY Academy of Science*, *1124*, 1–38.

32. Gong, G., He, Y., & Evans, A. C. (2011). Brain connectivity: Gender makes a difference. *The Neuroscientist*, *17*(5), 575–591; Tomasi, D., & Volkow, N. D. (2012). Gender differences in brain functional connectivity density. *Human Brain Mapping*, *33*(4), 849–860; Zhang, C., Dougherty, C. C., Baum, S. A., White, T., & Michael, A. M. (2018). Functional connectivity predicts gender: Evidence for gender differences in resting brain connectivity. *Human Brain Mapping*, *39*(4), 1765–1776.

33. D. R. Addis, personal communication via email, May 28, 2023.

34. Tomasi, D., & Volkow, N. D. (2012). Gender differences in brain functional connectivity density. *Human Brain Mapping*, *33*(4), 858.

35. Derntl, B., Finkelmeyer, A., Eickhoff, S., et al. (2010). Multidimensional assessment of empathic abilities: Neural correlates and gender differences. *Psychoneuroendocrinology*, *35*(1), 67–82; Bellucci, G., Camilleri, J. A., Eickhoff, S. B., & Krueger, F. (2020). Neural signatures of prosocial behaviors. *Neuroscience & Biobehavioral Reviews*, *118*, 186–195.

36. Singer, T., Seymour, B., O'Doherty, J., et al. (2006). Empathic neural responses are modulated by the perceived fairness of others. *Nature*, *439*(7075), 466–469.

37. Dodell-Feder, D., & Tamir, D. I. (2018). Fiction reading has a small positive impact on social cognition: A meta-analysis. *Journal of Experimental Psychology: General*, *147*(11), 1713–1727.

38. Klein, K. J., & Hodges, S. D. (2001). Gender differences, motivation, and empathic accuracy: When it pays to understand. *Personality and Social Psychology Bulletin*, *27*(6), 720–730.

39. Frattaroli, J. (2006). Experimental disclosure and its moderators: A meta-analysis. *Psychological Bulletin*, *132*(6), 823–865.

40. Baron-Cohen, S. (2002). The extreme male brain theory of autism. *Trends in Cognitive Sciences*, *6*(6), 248–254.

41. Buckner, R. L., Andrews-Hanna, J. R., & Schacter, D. L. (2008). The brain's default network: Anatomy, function, and relevance to disease. *Annals of the NY Academy of Science*, *1124*, 1–38; Padmanabhan, A., Lynch, C. J., Schaer, M., & Menon, V. (2017). The default mode network in autism. *Biological Psychiatry: Cognitive Neuroscience and Neuroimaging*, *2*(6), 476–486.

42. Tribble, E. B. (2011). *Cognition in the globe: Attention and memory in Shakespeare's theatre*. New York: Palgrave Macmillan.

43. Anderson, L. V. (2016). Feminists shouldn't roll our eyes at men-only book clubs. *Slate.com*. Retrieved on November 11, 2023, from https://slate.com/human-inter

(168) Notes

est/2016/05/men-only-books-clubs-are-not-as-worthy-of-eye-rolling-as-the-times-styles-section-would-have-you-believe.html

CHAPTER 3

1. DeCasper and Fifer (1980) was the original Dr. Seuss study showing that newborns already preferred the sound of their mother's voice to another woman's voice reading Dr. Seuss' *To Think That I Heard It on Mulberry Street*. But the first study with prenatal learning was DeCasper and Spence (1986), as described in the text. DeCasper, A. J., & Fifer, W. P. (1980). Of human bonding: Newborns prefer their mothers' voices. *Science, 208*(4448), 1174–1176; DeCasper, A. J., & Spence, M. J. (1986). Prenatal maternal speech influences newborns' perception of speech sounds. *Infant Behavior and Development, 9*(2), 133–150.
2. Morton, S. M. B., Atatoa Carr, P. E., Grant, C. C., et al. 2012. *Growing Up in New Zealand: A longitudinal study of New Zealand children and their families. Report 2: Now we are born*. Auckland: Growing Up in New Zealand.
3. Meissel, K., Reese, E., & Turnbull, S. (2019). *Factors of the early learning environment that promote early learning outcomes in Aotearoa/New Zealand*. Wellington, NZ: Ministry of Social Development.
4. Using the Infant Behavior Questionnaire-Revised (Putnam et al., 2014), the infant temperament dimensions identified in the *Growing Up in New Zealand* study of over 5,600 babies were as follows: positive affect/surgency, negative emotionality, fear, affiliation/regulation, and orienting tendencies (Peterson et al., 2017). Peterson, E. R., Mohal, J., Waldie, K. E., et al. (2017). A cross-cultural analysis of the Infant Behavior Questionnaire Very Short Form: An item response theory analysis of infant temperament in New Zealand. *Journal of Personality Assessment, 99*(6), 574–584; Putnam, S. P., Helbig, A. L., Gartstein, M. A., Rothbart, M. K., & Leerkes, E. (2014). Development and assessment of short and very short forms of the Infant Behavior Questionnaire–Revised. *Journal of Personality Assessment, 96*, 445–458.
5. Connellan, J., Baron-Cohen, S., Wheelwright, S., Batki, A., & Ahluwalia, J. (2000). Sex differences in human neonatal social perception. *Infant Behavior and Development, 23*(1), 113–118.
6. Lutchmaya, S., Baron-Cohen, S., & Raggatt, P. (2002). Foetal testosterone and eye contact in 12-month-old human infants. *Infant Behavior and Development, 25*(3), 327–335.
7. Moore, C., & Dunham, P. J. (Eds.) (1995/2014). *Joint attention: Its origins and role in development*. New York: Psychology Press; Rossmanith, N., Costall, A., Reichelt, A., Lopez, B., & Reddy, V. (2014). Jointly structuring shared spaces of meaning and action around objects in early infancy: The case of book sharing. *Frontiers in Psychology: Cognitive Science, 5*, Article 1390.
8. McClure, E. B. (2000). A meta-analytic review of sex differences in facial expression processing and their development in infants, children, and adolescents. *Psychological Bulletin, 126*, 424–453; Mundy, P., Block, J., Delgado, C., Pomares, Y., Van Hecke, A. V., & Parlade, M. V. (2007). Individual differences and the development of joint attention in infancy. *Child Development, 78*(3), 938–954; Olafsen, K. S., Rønning, J. A., Kaaresen, P. I., Ulvund, S. E., Handegård, B. H., & Dahl, L. B. (2006). Joint attention in term and preterm infants at 12 months corrected age: The significance of gender and intervention based on a randomized controlled trial. *Infant Behavior and Development, 29*(4), 554–563.

NOTES *(169)*

9. Else-Quest, N. M., Hyde, J. S., Goldsmith, H. H., & Van Hulle, C. A. (2006). Gender differences in temperament: A meta-analysis. *Psychological Bulletin, 132*(1), 33–72.

10. Eggebrecht, A. T., Elison, J. T., Feczko, E., et al. (2017). Joint attention and brain functional connectivity in infants and toddlers. *Cerebral Cortex, 27*(3), 1709–1720.

11. Farrant, B. M., & Zubrick, S. R. (2012). Early vocabulary development: The importance of joint attention and parent-child book reading. *First Language, 32*(3), 343–364; Farrant, B. M., & Zubrick, S. R. (2013). Parent–child book reading across early childhood and child vocabulary in the early school years: Findings from the Longitudinal Study of Australian Children. *First Language, 33*(3), 280–293.

12. Dunn, J., & Plomin, R. (1990). *Separate lives: Why siblings are so different.* New York: Basic Books.

13. Kucirkova, N., Dale, P. S., & Sylva, K. (2018). Parents reading with their 10-month-old babies: Key predictors for high-quality reading styles. *Early Child Development and Care, 188*(2), 195–207; van den Berg, H., & Bus, A. G. (2014). Beneficial effects of BookStart in temperamentally highly reactive infants. *Learning and Individual Differences, 36*, 69–75.

14. Hoff, E. (2013). *Language development.* Sydney: Cengage Learning.

15. This phenomenon, called child-directed speech (or serve-and-return), varies dramatically across cultures and social class (Cristia et al., 2019; Hoff, 2003). Even in higher-socioeconomic status cultures, parents engage in less child-directed speech in times of financial hardship (Ellwood-Lowe et al., 2020). Although child-directed speech is not a necessary ingredient for children's language development, when adults expand upon children's utterances and ask for more information, children's language development proceeds at a faster rate (Rowe, 2012). Cristia, A., Dupoux, E., Gurven, M., & Stieglitz, J. (2019). Child-directed speech is infrequent in a forager-farmer population: A time allocation study. *Child Development, 90*(3), 759–773; Ellwood-Lowe, M. E., Foushee, R., & Srinivasan, M. (2022). What causes the word gap? Financial concerns may systematically suppress child-directed speech. *Developmental Science, 25*(1), e13151; Hoff, E. (2003). The specificity of environmental influence: Socioeconomic status affects early vocabulary development via maternal speech. *Child Development, 74*(5), 1368–1378; Rowe, M. L. (2012). A longitudinal investigation of the role of quantity and quality of child-directed speech vocabulary development. *Child Development, 83*(5), 1762–1774.

16. Erard, M. (2019, April 30). The mystery of babies' first words. *TheAtlantic.com.* Retrieved on November 15, 2023, from https://www.theatlantic.com/family/arch ive/2019/04/babies-first-words-babbling-or-actual-language/588289/

17. Cultures vary dramatically too in how often they provide and read books with young children (Raikes et al., 2006). Raikes, H., Alexander Pan, B., Luze, G., et al. (2006). Mother–child bookreading in low-income families: Correlates and outcomes during the first three years of life. *Child Development, 77*(4), 924–953.

18. Nelson, K., & Ross, G. (1980). The generalities and specifics of long-term memory in infants and young children. *New Directions for Child and Adolescent Development, 1980*(10), 87–101; Reese, E. (1999). What children say when they talk about the past. *Narrative Inquiry, 9*(2), 215–241.

19. Fenson, L., Dale, P. S., Reznick, J. S., et al. (1994). Variability in early communicative development. *Monographs of the Society for Research in Child Development, 59*(5), i–185.

20. Marrus, N., Eggebrecht, A. T., Todorov, A., et al. (2018). Walking, gross motor development, and brain functional connectivity in infants and toddlers. *Cerebral Cortex, 28*(2), 750–763.

21. Dinstein, I., Pierce, K., Eyler, L., et al. (2011). Disrupted neural synchronization in toddlers with autism. *Neuron, 70*(6), 1218–1225. These differences are not straightforward, however. Children with autism spectrum disorder may initially display *hyperconnectivity* or overactivation within and between hubs of the default network, and then later as adolescents and adults display *hypoconnectivity* or underactivation within the default network, and between the default network and other crucial brain networks, especially the salience network and the central executive network (Padmanabhan et al., 2017). Padmanabhan, A., Lynch, C. J., Schaer, M., & Menon, V. (2017). The default mode network in autism. *Biological Psychiatry: Cognitive Neuroscience and Neuroimaging, 2*(6), 476–486.

22. Gilkerson, J., Richards, J. A., Warren, S. F., Oller, D. K., Russo, R., & Vohr, B. (2018). Language experience in the second year of life and language outcomes in late childhood. *Pediatrics, 142*(4), e20174276.

23. Romeo, R. R., Leonard, J. A., Robinson, S. T., et al. (2018). Beyond the 30-million-word gap: Children's conversational exposure is associated with language-related brain function. *Psychological Science, 29*(5), 700–710.

24. Carpenter, M., Nagell, K., Tomasello, M., Butterworth, G., & Moore, C. (1998). Social cognition, joint attention, and communicative competence from 9 to 15 months of age. *Monographs of the Society for Research in Child Development, 63*(4), i–174.

25. Gilkerson, J., Richards, J. A., Warren, S. F., Oller, D. K., Russo, R., & Vohr, B. (2018). Language experience in the second year of life and language outcomes in late childhood. *Pediatrics, 142*(4), e20174276.

26. Reese, E., & Newcombe, R. (2007). Training mothers in elaborative reminiscing enhances children's autobiographical memory and narrative. *Child Development, 78*(4), 1153–1170.

27. Reese, E., Keegan, P., McNaughton, S., et al. (2018). Te Reo Māori: Indigenous language acquisition in the context of New Zealand English. *Journal of Child Language, 45*(2), 340–367.

28. Singer, T. (2006). The neuronal basis and ontogeny of empathy and mind reading: Review of literature and implications for future research. *Neuroscience & Biobehavioral Reviews, 30*(6), 855–863; Mahy, C. E., Moses, L. J., & Pfeifer, J. H. (2014). How and where: Theory-of-mind in the brain. *Developmental Cognitive Neuroscience, 9*, 68–81.

29. Knafo, A., Zahn-Waxler, C., Van Hulle, C., Robinson, J. L., & Rhee, S. H. (2008). The developmental origins of a disposition toward empathy: Genetic and environmental contributions. *Emotion, 8*(6), 737–752; Bird, A. L., Reese, E., Taumoepeau, M., et al. (2016). "You are our eyes and ears": A new tool for observing parent-child interactions in large samples. *Longitudinal and Life Course Studies, 7*(4), 386–408.

30. Hines, M. (2006). Prenatal testosterone and gender-related behaviour. *European Journal of Endocrinology, 155*(Suppl. 1), S115–S121; Todd, B. K., Fischer, R. A., Di Costa, S., et al. (2018). Sex differences in children's toy preferences: A systematic review, meta-regression, and meta-analysis. *Infant and Child Development, 27*(2), e2064.

31. Auyeung, B., Baron-Cohen, S., Ashwin, E., et al. (2009). Fetal testosterone predicts sexually differentiated childhood behavior in girls and in boys. *Psychological Science, 20*(2), 144–148; Lamminmäki, A., Hines, M., Kuiri-Hänninen, T., Kilpeläinen, L., Dunkel, L., & Sankilampi, U. (2012). Testosterone measured in infancy predicts subsequent sex-typed behavior in boys and in girls. *Hormones and Behavior, 61*(4), 611–616.

NOTES *(171)*

32. Golombok, S., Fivush, R., & Fivush, G. (1994). *Gender development*. Cambridge: Cambridge University Press.

33. Rhodes, M. (2017, February 16). Combatting stereotypes: How to talk to your children. *Theconversation.com*. Retrieved November 15, 2023, from https://thec onversation.com/combatting-stereotypes-how-to-talk-to-your-children-71929

34. Johnson, K. E., Alexander, J. M., Spencer, S., Leibham, M. E., & Neitzel, C. (2004). Factors associated with the early emergence of intense interests within conceptual domains. *Cognitive Development*, *19*(3), 325–343.

35. Knickmeyer, R., Baron-Cohen, S., Raggatt, P., & Taylor, K. (2005). Foetal testosterone, social relationships, and restricted interests in children. *Journal of Child Psychology and Psychiatry*, *46*(2), 198–210. Fetal testosterone is also linked to children's tendency to systemize: Auyeung, B., Baron-Cohen, S., Chapman, E., Knickmeyer, R., Taylor, K., & Hackett, G. (2006). Foetal testosterone and the child systemizing quotient. *European Journal of Endocrinology*, *155*(Suppl. 1), S123–S130.

36. Merga, M. (2017). Do males really prefer non-fiction, and why does it matter? *English in Australia*, *52*(1), 27–35.

37. Baker, M., & Milligan, K. (2016). Boy-girl differences in parental time investments: Evidence from three countries. *Journal of Human Capital*, *10*(4), 399–441.

38. Breen, K. (2019, June 6). 13 Reese Witherspoon-approved books to read this summer. *Today.com*. Retrieved November 15, 2023, from https://www.today. com/shop/reese-witherspoon-talks-book-clubs-summer-reads-t155475

39. Adrián, J. E., Clemente, R. A., & Villanueva, L. (2007). Mothers' use of cognitive state verbs in picture-book reading and the development of children's understanding of mind: A longitudinal study. *Child Development*, *78*(4), 1052–1067; Dowdall, N., Melendez-Torres, G. J., Murray, L., Gardner, F., Hartford, L., & Cooper, P. J. (2020). Shared picture book reading interventions for child language development: A systematic review and meta-analysis. *Child Development*, *91*(2), e383–e399; Rose, E., Lehrl, S., Ebert, S., & Weinert, S. (2018). Long-term relations between children's language, the home literacy environment, and socioemotional development from ages 3 to 8. *Early Education and Development*, *29*(3), 342–356; Taumoepeau, M., & Ruffman, T. (2008). Stepping stones to others' minds: Maternal talk relates to child mental state language and emotion understanding at 15, 24, and 33 months. *Child Development*, *79*(2), 284–302; Taumoepeau, M., Sadeghi, S., & Nobilo, A. (2019). Cross-cultural differences in children's theory of mind in Iran and New Zealand: The role of caregiver mental state talk. *Cognitive Development*, *51*, 32–45.

40. Hindman, A. H., Skibbe, L. E., & Foster, T. D. (2014). Exploring the variety of parental talk during shared book reading and its contributions to preschool language and literacy: Evidence from the Early Childhood Longitudinal Study-Birth Cohort. *Reading and Writing*, *27*(2), 287–313.

41. Gaudreau, C., King, Y. A., Dore, R. A., et al. (2020). Preschoolers benefit equally from video chat, pseudo-contingent video, and live book reading: Implications for storytime during the coronavirus pandemic and beyond. *Frontiers in Psychology*, *11*, 2158; Reich, S. M., Yau, J. C., & Warschauer, M. (2016). Tablet-based ebooks for young children: What does the research say? *Journal of Developmental & Behavioral Pediatrics*, *37*(7), 585–591; Strouse, G. A., Troseth, G. L., & Stuckelman, Z. D. (2023). Page and screen: Storybook features that promote parent-child talk during shared reading. *Journal of Applied Developmental Psychology*, *86*, 101522.

42. Barr, R. (2010). Transfer of learning between 2D and 3D sources during infancy: Informing theory and practice. *Developmental Review, 30*(2), 128–154; Munzer, T. G., Miller, A. L., Weeks, H. M., Kaciroti, N., & Radesky, J. (2019). Differences in parent-toddler interactions with electronic versus print books. *Pediatrics, 143*(4).

43. Kuebli, J., Butler, S., & Fivush, R. (1995). Mother-child talk about past emotions: Relations of maternal language and child gender over time. *Cognition & Emotion, 9*(2–3), 265–283; Reese, E., & Newcombe, R. (2007). Training mothers in elaborative reminiscing enhances children's autobiographical memory and narrative. *Child Development, 78*(4), 1153–1170; Taumoepeau, M., & Reese, E. (2013). Maternal reminiscing, elaborative talk, and children's theory of mind: An intervention study. *First Language, 33*(4), 388–410.

44. Van Bergen, P., Salmon, K., Dadds, M. R., & Allen, J. (2009). The effects of mother training in emotion-rich, elaborative reminiscing on children's shared recall and emotion knowledge. *Journal of Cognition and Development, 10*(3), 162–187; Van Bergen, P., Salmon, K., & Dadds, M. R. (2018). Coaching mothers of typical and conduct problem children in elaborative parent-child reminiscing: Influences of a randomized controlled trial on reminiscing behaviour and everyday talk preferences. *Behaviour Research and Therapy, 111*, 9–18.

45. Fivush, R. (2001). Owning experience: Developing subjective perspective in autobiographical narratives. In C. Moore & K. Lemmon (Eds.), *The self in time: Developmental perspectives* (pp. 35–52). Mahwah, NJ: Lawrence Erlbaum.

46. Salmon, K., & Reese, E. (2016). The benefits of reminiscing with young children. *Current Directions in Psychological Science, 25*(4), 233–238.

47. The *whakatauki* "E tipu e rea" is credited to Sir Apirana Ngata in 1949. Keelan, J. (2014). *Nga reanga youth development: Māori styles*. Auckland, NZ: Unitec Institute of Technology.

48. Another module of *Tender Shoots* with the same books called *Strengthening Sound Sensitivity*, created by Elizabeth Schaughency, encouraged parents to instead have conversations with children about the sounds of words. This module helped children's early literacy skills, such as recognizing letters, and with beginning reading (Schaughency et al., 2023). Riordan, J., Reese, E., Das, S., Carroll, J., & Schaughency, E. (2021). *Tender Shoots*: A randomized controlled trial of two shared-reading approaches for enhancing parent-child interactions and children's oral language and literacy skills. *Scientific Studies of Reading, 26*(3), 183–203; Schaughency, E., Linney, K., Carroll, J., Das, S., Riordan, J., & Reese, E. (2023). Tender Shoots: A randomized controlled trial with preschool children benefits beginning reading one year later. *Reading Research Quarterly, 58*(3), 450–470. Note that others have developed story enrichment programs with similar benefits for children's oral language, such as Vibeke Grover's EXTEND technique and Ageliki Nicolopolou's storytelling/story-acting technique: Grøver, V., Rydland, V., Gustafsson, J. E., & Snow, C. E. (2020). Shared book reading in preschool supports bilingual children's second-language learning: A cluster-randomized trial. *Child Development, 91*(6), 2192–2210; Nicolopoulou, A., Cortina, K. S., Ilgaz, H., Cates, C. B., & de Sá, A. B. (2015). Using a narrative-and play-based activity to promote low-income preschoolers' oral language, emergent literacy, and social competence. *Early Childhood Research Quarterly, 31*, 147–162.

49. Das, S. A. (2018). *Rich reading and reminiscing: Benefits of parent-preschooler interactions for children's developing language, behavioral regulation, and*

socio-emotional competences. Unpublished PhD thesis, University of Otago, Dunedin, New Zealand.

50. Clifford, A. E., Schaughency, E., Das, S., Riordan, J., Carroll, J. L., & Reese, E. (2024). Tender Shoots: Effects of a preschool shared reading and reminiscing initiative on parent-child interactions and for socio-emotional and self-regulation outcomes after school entry. *Learning and Individual Differences, 112,* 102443.

51. Reese, E., Barrett-Young, A., Gilkison, L., et al. (2022). Tender Shoots: A parent book-reading and reminiscing program to enhance children's oral narrative skills. *Reading and Writing, 36,* 541–561.

52. Reese, E., Suggate, S., Long, J., & Schaughency, E. (2010). Children's oral narrative and reading skills in the first 3 years of reading instruction. *Reading and Writing, 23*(6), 627–644.

53. Raikes, H., Alexander Pan, B., Luze, G., et al. (2006). Mother–child bookreading in low-income families: Correlates and outcomes during the first three years of life. *Child Development, 77*(4), 924–953; Wang, Q. (2021). Cultural pathways and outcomes of autobiographical memory development. *Child Development Perspectives, 15*(3), 196–202.

54. Reese, E., Taumoepeau, M., & Neha, T. (2014). Remember drawing on the cupboard? New Zealand Maori, European, and Pasifika parents' conversations about children's transgressions. In C. Wainryb & H. E. Recchia (Eds.), *Talking about right and wrong: Parent-child conversations as contexts for moral development* (pp. 44–70). Cambridge: Cambridge University Press.

55. Raikes, H., Alexander Pan, B., Luze, G., et al. (2006). Mother–child bookreading in low-income families: Correlates and outcomes during the first three years of life. *Child Development, 77*(4), 924–953; Araújo, L., & Costa, P. (2015). Home book reading and reading achievement in EU countries: The progress in international reading literacy study 2011 (PIRLS). *Educational Research and Evaluation, 21*(5-6), 422–438; Neha, T., Reese, E., Schaughency, E., & Taumoepeau, M. (2020). The role of whānau (New Zealand Māori families) for Māori children's early learning. *Developmental Psychology, 56*(8), 1518–1531; Garnett, M., Reese, E., Swearingen, I., et al. (2023). Maternal reminiscing and children's socioemotional development: Evidence from a large pre-birth longitudinal cohort study, Growing Up in New Zealand. *Journal of Cognition and Development, 24*(5), 678–703; Wang, Q. (2021). Cultural pathways and outcomes of autobiographical memory development. *Child Development Perspectives, 15*(3), 196–202.

56. Russell, J., Grant, C. C., Morton, S., Denny, S., & Paine, S. J. (2023). Prevalence and predictors of developmental health difficulties within New Zealand preschool-aged children: A latent profile analysis. *Journal of the Royal Society of New Zealand, 53*(5), 587–614. See also: Woodley, A. (2017). *The first 1000 days in the Southern Initiative. Risk, resilience and opportunities for change: A collaboration between Growing Up in New Zealand, The Southern Initiative, the Co-Design Lab and Point and Associates.* Dunedin, NZ: The Southern Initiative.

57. My working definition of social understanding is broad to encompass the diverse cognitive, emotional, and social skills necessary for children to function in different cultures. For instance, in Pacific societies such as Tonga, children are advanced in understanding how others' emotions can change their behavior, a skill that is essential for group belonging, relative to their understanding of others' beliefs (Taumoepeau et al., 2022). Taumoepeau, M., Kata, U. F., Veikune, A. H., Lotulelei, S., Vea, P. T. I., & Fonua, I. (2022). Could, would, should: Theory of mind and deontic reasoning in Tongan children. *Child Development, 93*(5), 1511–1526.

58. Tsunemi, K., Tamura, A., Ogawa, S., Isomura, T., & Masataka, N. (2014). Intensive exposure to narrative in story books as a possibly effective treatment of social perspective-taking in schoolchildren with autism. *Frontiers in Psychology*, 5, Article 2.

59. Strouse, G. A., O'Doherty, K., & Troseth, G. L. (2013). Effective co-viewing: Preschoolers' learning from video after a dialogic questioning intervention. *Developmental Psychology*, 49(12), 2368–2382.

60. Parents co-view TV shows or movies with their preschoolers only about half the time (Acevedo et al., 2007). Acevedo-Polakovich, I. D., Lorch, E. P., & Milich, R. (2007). Comparing television use and reading in children with ADHD and non-referred children across two age groups. *Media Psychology*, 9(2), 447–472.

61. Mar, R. A., Tackett, J. L., & Moore, C. (2010). Exposure to media and theory-of-mind development in preschoolers. *Cognitive Development*, 25(1), 69–78.

62. Linebarger, D. L., & Walker, D. (2005). Infants' and toddlers' television viewing and language outcomes. *American Behavioral Scientist*, 48(5), 624–645; Mares, M. L., & Pan, Z. (2013). Effects of Sesame Street: A meta-analysis of children's learning in 15 countries. *Journal of Applied Developmental Psychology*, 34(3), 140–151.

63. Taggart, J., Eisen, S., & Lillard, A. S. (2019). The current landscape of US children's television: Violent, prosocial, educational, and fantastical content. *Journal of Children and Media*, 13(3), 276–294; Mares, M. L., & Woodard, E. (2005). Positive effects of television on children's social interactions: A meta-analysis. *Media Psychology*, 7(3), 301–322.

64. Rasmussen, E. E., Shafer, A., Colwell, M. J., et al. (2016). Relation between active mediation, exposure to Daniel Tiger's Neighborhood, and US preschoolers' social and emotional development. *Journal of Children and Media*, 10(4), 443–461.

65. Madigan, S., McArthur, B. A., Anhorn, C., Eirich, R., & Christakis, D. A. (2020). Associations between screen use and child language skills: A systematic review and meta-analysis. *JAMA Pediatrics*, 174(7), 665–675.

66. Anderson, D. R., Huston, A. C., Schmitt, K. L., Linebarger, D. L., Wright, J. C., & Larson, R. (2001). Early childhood television viewing and adolescent behavior: The recontact study. *Monographs of the Society for Research in Child Development*, 66(1), i–154.

67. These results were especially impressive because they were consistent across Western, Eastern European, and East Asian countries, even after controlling for age, gender, total screen use, and violent media use (Prot et al., 2014). So far, the effects of prosocial digital games on prosocial behaviors are mixed to date, but promising (Saleme et al., 2020). Prot, S., Gentile, D. A., Anderson, C. A., et al. (2014). Long-term relations among prosocial-media use, empathy, and prosocial behavior. *Psychological Science*, 25(2), 358–368; Saleme, P., Pang, B., Dietrich, T., & Parkinson, J. (2020). Prosocial digital games for youth: A systematic review of interventions. *Computers in Human Behavior Reports*, 2, 100039.

68. Greitemeyer, T., & Mügge, D. O. (2014). Video games do affect social outcomes: A meta-analytic review of the effects of violent and prosocial video game play. *Personality and Social Psychology Bulletin*, 40(5), 578–589.

69. Hutton, J. S., Dudley, J., Horowitz-Kraus, T., DeWitt, T., & Holland, S. K. (2020). Differences in functional brain network connectivity during stories presented in audio, illustrated, and animated format in preschool-age children. *Brain Imaging and Behavior*, 14(1), 130–141.

NOTES *(175)*

70. Hutton, J. S., Phelan, K., Horowitz-Kraus, T., et al. (2017). Shared reading quality and brain activation during story listening in preschool-age children. *The Journal of Pediatrics, 191*, 204–211. See also Romeo, R. R., Segaran, J., Leonard, J. A., et al. (2018). Language exposure relates to structural neural connectivity in childhood. *Journal of Neuroscience, 38*(36), 7870–7877.

71. Rutter, M., Caspi, A., Fergusson, D., et al. (2004). Sex differences in developmental reading disability: New findings from 4 epidemiological studies. *JAMA, 291*(16), 2007–2012.

72. August, G. J., & Garfinkel, B. D. (1990). Comorbidity of ADHD and reading disability among clinic-referred children. *Journal of Abnormal Child Psychology, 18*(1), 29–45; Mayes, S. D., Calhoun, S. L., & Crowell, E. W. (2000). Learning disabilities and ADHD: Overlapping spectrum disorders. *Journal of Learning Disabilities, 33*(5), 417–424.

73. National Library of New Zealand. Retrieved on November 15, 2023, from https://natlib.govt.nz/schools/reading-engagement

74. Dutro, E. (2001). "But that's a girls' book!" Exploring gender boundaries in children's reading practices. *The Reading Teacher, 55*(4), 376–384.

75. Brown, C. S., Biefeld, S. D., & Tam, M. J. (2020). *Gender in childhood.* Cambridge: Cambridge University Press.

76. Robertson, S. J. L., & Reese, E. (2017). The very hungry caterpillar turned into a butterfly: Children's and parents' enjoyment of different book genres. *Journal of Early Childhood Literacy, 17*(1), 3–25.

77. Clark, C., & Teravainen-Goff, A. (2020). *Children and young people's reading in 2019: Findings from our Annual Literacy Survey.* London: National Literacy Trust.

78. Scholastic.com. (2018). *Kids' and Family Reading Report* (6th ed.). You.Gov.

79. Suggate, S. P., Lenhard, W., Neudecker, E., & Schneider, W. (2013). Incidental vocabulary acquisition from stories: Second and fourth graders learn more from listening than reading. *First Language, 33*(6), 551–571.

80. Mullis, I. V. S., von Davier, M., Foy, P., Fishbein, B., Reynolds, K.A., & Wry, E. (2023). *PIRLS 2021 international results in reading.* Boston: Boston College, TIMSS & PIRLS International Study Center.

81. Hulme, C., Snowling, M. J., West, G., Lervåg, A., & Melby-Lervåg, M. (2020). Children's language skills can be improved: Lessons from psychological science for educational policy. *Current Directions in Psychological Science, 29*(4), 372–377; Snowling, M. J., & Hulme, C. (2021). Annual research review: Reading disorders revisited—The critical importance of oral language. *Journal of Child Psychology and Psychiatry, 62*(5), 635–653.

82. Gottfried, A. W., Schlackman, J., Gottfried, A. E., & Boutin-Martinez, A. S. (2015). Parental provision of early literacy environment as related to reading and educational outcomes across the academic lifespan. *Parenting, 15*(1), 24–38. This 28-year Fullerton Longitudinal Study found that the quantity of shared book reading in toddlerhood predicted children's later reading achievement and intrinsic motivation to read, which in turn predicted reading achievement and motivation to read in adolescence, which then predicted educational attainment by age 29 (see Figure 1 in Gottfried et al., 2015). Once these variables were taken into account, gender didn't add significantly to the model.

CHAPTER 4

1. Murakami, H. (2022). *Novelist as a vocation* (p. 144). New York: Harvill Secker.

(176) *Notes*

2. Rideout, V., and Robb, M. B. (2019). *The Common Sense census: Media use by tweens and teens, 2019*. San Francisco, CA: Common Sense Media.
3. Chall, J. S., Jacobs, V. A., & Baldwin, L. E. (1990). *The reading crisis: Why poor children fall behind*. Cambridge, MA: Harvard University Press.
4. Nagy, W., & Scott, J. (2000). Vocabulary processes. In M. L. Kamil, P. B. Mosenthal, P. D. Pearson, & R. Barr, R. (Eds.), *Handbook of reading research*, vol. 3, (pp. 269–284). Mahwah, NJ: Lawrence Erlbaum.
5. Bottomley, D. M., Truscott, D. M., Marinak, B. A., Henk, W. A., & Melnick, S. A. (1998). An affective comparison of whole language, literature-based, and basal reader literacy instruction. *Literacy Research and Instruction, 38*(2), 115–129.
6. Gillon, G., McNeill, B., Scott, A., Arrow, A., Gath, M., & Macfarlane, A. (2023). A better start literacy approach: Effectiveness of Tier 1 and Tier 2 support within a response to teaching framework. *Reading and Writing, 36*(3), 565–598.
7. Suggate, S., Schaughency, E., McAnally, H., & Reese, E. (2018). From infancy to adolescence: The longitudinal links between vocabulary, early literacy skills, oral narrative, and reading comprehension. *Cognitive Development, 47*, 82–95.
8. Lecce, S., Bianco, F., & Hughes, C. (2021). Reading minds and reading texts: Evidence for independent and specific associations. *Cognitive Development, 57*, 101010. In this study, children's reading comprehension also supported their later theory-of-mind skills, providing further evidence for the importance of reading for theory of mind.
9. Eekhof, L. S., Van Krieken, K., & Willems, R. M. (2022). Reading about minds: The social-cognitive potential of narratives. *Psychonomic Bulletin & Review, 29*(5), 1703–1718.
10. Rideout, V., and Robb, M. B. (2019). *The Common Sense census: Media use by tweens and teens, 2019*. San Francisco, CA: Common Sense Media.
11. Scholastic. (2019). *Kids & family reading report* (7th ed.). https://www.scholastic.com/content/dam/scholastic/site/KFRR/KFRR_7th%20Edtidion.pdf
12. UK Literacy Trust. (2021, June 14). Children and young people's reading in 2019. *LiteracyTrust.org.uk*. Retrieved on November 17, 2023, from https://literacytrust.org.uk/research-services/research-reports/children-and-young-peoples-reading-in-2019/
13. Twenge, J. M., Martin, G. N., & Spitzberg, B. H. (2019). Trends in US adolescents' media use, 1976–2016: The rise of digital media, the decline of TV, and the (near) demise of print. *Psychology of Popular Media Culture, 8*(4), 329–345.
14. D'Addario, D., Nathan, G., & Rayman, N. (2015, January 8). The 100-best young adult books of all time. *Time.com*. Retrieved on November 17, 2023, from https://time.com/100-best-young-adult-books/embed/
15. Rideout, V., Peebles, A., Mann, S., & Robb, M. B. (2022). *Common Sense census: Media use by tweens and teens, 2021*. San Francisco, CA: Common Sense.
16. Rideout, V., and Robb, M. B. (2019). *The Common Sense census: Media use by tweens and teens, 2019*. San Francisco, CA: Common Sense Media.
17. Arnett, J. J. (2006). G. Stanley Hall's *Adolescence:* Brilliance and nonsense. *History of Psychology, 9*, 186–197.
18. Clark, C., & Picton, I. (2020). *Children's reading in 2020 before and during the COVID-19 lockdown*. London: National Literacy Trust.
19. Rideout, V., Peebles, A., Mann, S., & Robb, M. B. (2022). *Common Sense census: Media use by tweens and teens, 2021*. San Francisco, CA: Common Sense.
20. Duncan, L. G., McGeown, S. P., Griffiths, Y. M., Stothard, S. E., & Dobai, A. (2016). Adolescent reading skill and engagement with digital and traditional literacies as

predictors of reading comprehension. *British Journal of Psychology, 107*, 209–238. Other studies with teens and young adults around the world have found similar patterns (Jerrim & Moss, 2019; Mar & Rain, 2015; Mar et al., 2021; Pfost et al., 2013): Jerrim, J., & Moss, G. (2019). The link between fiction and teenagers' reading skills: International evidence from the OECD PISA study. *British Educational Research Journal, 45*(1), 181–200; Pfost, M., Dörfler, T., & Artelt, C. (2013). Students' extracurricular reading behavior and the development of vocabulary and reading comprehension. *Learning and Individual Differences, 26*, 89–102; Mar, R. A., & Rain, M. (2015). Narrative fiction and expository nonfiction differentially predict verbal ability. *Scientific Studies of Reading, 19*(6), 419–433; Mar, R. A., Li, J., Nguyen, A. T., & Ta, C. P. (2021). Memory and comprehension of narrative versus expository texts: A meta-analysis. *Psychonomic Bulletin & Review, 28*, 732–749.

21. Grimshaw, S., Dungworth, N., McKnight, C., & Morris, A. (2007). Electronic books: Children's reading and comprehension. *British Journal of Educational Technology, 38*, 583–599; Zucker, T. A., Moody, A. K., & McKenna, M. C. (2009). The effects of electronic books on pre-kindergarten-to-grade 5 students' literacy and language outcomes: A research synthesis. *Journal of Educational Computing Research, 40*(1), 47–87; Schwabe, A., Lind, F., Kosch, L., & Boomgaarden, H. G. (2022). No negative effects of reading on screen on comprehension of narrative texts compared to print: A meta-analysis. *Media Psychology, 25*(6), 779–796.

22. Schneps, M. H., Thomson, J. M., Chen, C., Sonnert, G., & Pomplun, M. (2013). E-Readers are more effective than paper for some with dyslexia. *PLoS ONE, 8*(9), e75634.

23. Mak, H. W., & Fancourt, D. (2020). Longitudinal associations between reading for pleasure and child maladjustment: Results from a propensity score matching analysis. *Social Science & Medicine, 253*, 112971. This study used a sophisticated analysis called Propensity Score Matching that compares groups of children who are nearly identical on all measures except for the key predictor: in this case, the frequency of reading for pleasure at age 7. However, the reading for pleasure variable didn't specify fiction versus nonfiction.

24. Vezzali, L., Stathi, S., Giovannini, D., Capozza, D., & Trifiletti, E. (2015). The greatest magic of Harry Potter: Reducing prejudice. *Journal of Applied Social Psychology, 45*(2), 105–121.

25. Clark, C., & Teravainen-Goff, A. (2018). *Mental wellbeing, reading and writing: How children and young people's mental wellbeing is related to their reading and writing experiences.* London: National Literacy Trust.

26. Twenge, J. M., Joiner, T. E., Rogers, M. L., & Martin, G. N. (2018). Increases in depressive symptoms, suicide-related outcomes, and suicide rates among US adolescents after 2010 and links to increased new media screen time. *Clinical Psychological Science, 6*(1), 3–17.

27. Scholastic. (2022). Reading's impact on kids' mental health. *Scholastic.com.* Retrieved on November 17, 2023, from https://www.scholastic.com/content/corp-home/kids-and-family-reading-report.html

28. Clark, C., & Teravainen-Goff, A. (2018). *Mental wellbeing, reading and writing: How children and young people's mental wellbeing is related to their reading and writing experiences.* London: National Literacy Trust.

29. Montgomery, P., & Maunders, K. (2015). The effectiveness of creative bibliotherapy for internalizing, externalizing, and prosocial behaviors in children: A systematic review. *Children and Youth Services Review, 55*, 37–47.

30. Schleicher, A. (2019). *PISA 2018: Insights and Interpretations*. Paris: OECD; OECD. (2019). *PISA 2018 results (Volume II): Where all students can succeed*. Paris: OECD; Mullis, I. V. S., von Davier, M., Foy, P., Fishbein, B., Reynolds, K.A., & Wry, E. (2023). *PIRLS 2021 International Results in Reading*. Boston: Boston College TIMSS & PIRLS International Study Center.

31. OECD. (2019). *Do Boys and Girls Differ in Their Attitudes Towards School and Learning?*, (pp. 156–175). Paris: OECD.

32. Clark, C., & Picton, I. (2020). *Children's reading in 2020 before and during the COVID-19 lockdown*. London: National Literacy Trust.

33. O'Brien, C. (2017, December 5). How did Irish schoolchildren become the best readers in Europe? Retrieved on November 17, 2023, from https://www.irishti mes.com/news/education/how-did-irish-schoolchildren-become-the-best-read ers-in-europe-1.3316259

34. Stoet, G., & Geary, D. C. (2020). Gender differences in the pathways to higher education. *Proceedings of the National Academy of Sciences, 117*(25), 14073–14076.

35. Rideout, V., and Robb, M. B. (2019). *The Common Sense census: Media use by tweens and teens, 2019*. San Francisco, CA: Common Sense Media.

36. OECD. (2019). *PISA 2018 results (Volume II): Where all students can succeed*. Paris: OECD.

37. Greitemeyer, T., & Mügge, D. O. (2014). Video games do affect social outcomes: A meta-analytic review of the effects of violent and prosocial video game play. *Personality and Social Psychology Bulletin, 40*(5), 578–589.

38. Greitemeyer, T., & Osswald, S. (2011). Playing prosocial video games increases the accessibility of prosocial thoughts. *The Journal of Social Psychology, 151*(2), 121–128.

39. Entertainment Software Association (2022, June). 2022 Essential facts about the video game industry. *TheESA.com*. Retrieved on November 17, 2023, from https://www.theesa.com/resource/2022-essential-facts-about-the-video-game-industry/

40. OECD. (2019). *PISA 2018 results (Volume II): Where all students can succeed*. Paris: OECD.

41. Elphinstone, B., & Conway, S. (2020, April 8). Time well spent, not wasted: Video games are boosting well-being during the coronavirus lockdown. *Theconversation.com*. Retrieved on November 17, 2023, from https://theconversation.com/time-well-spent-not-wasted-video-games-are-boosting-well-being-during-the-coro navirus-lockdown-135642

42. Merga, M. (2022, August 1). Turning boys of all ages into life-long readers. *TheEducationHub.org.nz*. Retrieved on November 17, 2023, from https://theeduca tionhub.org.nz/turning-boys-of-all-ages-into-life-long-readers/

43. Picton, I. (2014). *The impact of ebooks on the reading motivation and reading skills of children and young people: A rapid literature review*. London: National Literacy Trust.

44. Grimshaw, S., Dungworth, N., McKnight, C., & Morris, A. (2007). Electronic books: Children's reading and comprehension. *British Journal of Educational Technology, 38*(4), 583–599.

45. Pianzola, F. (2021). *Digital social reading: Sharing fiction in the 21st century*. Cambridge, MA: MIT Press.

46. Clark, C., & Picton, I. (2020). *Children's reading in 2020 before and during the COVID-19 lockdown*. London: National Literacy Trust.

47. However, there are neuroimaging studies comparing adolescents with dyslexia to typically developing readers (e.g., Pugh et al., 2008). Pugh, K. R., Frost, S. J.,

NOTES *(179)*

Sandak, R., et al. (2008). Effects of stimulus difficulty and repetition on printed word identification: An fMRI comparison of nonimpaired and reading-disabled adolescent cohorts. *Journal of Cognitive Neuroscience, 20*(7), 1146–1160.

48. Hutton, J. S., Dudley, J., Horowitz-Kraus, T., DeWitt, T., & Holland, S. K. (2020). Differences in functional brain network connectivity during stories presented in audio, illustrated, and animated format in preschool-age children. *Brain Imaging and Behavior, 14*(1), 130–141.

49. Scholastic. (2019). *Kids & Family Reading Report* (7th ed.).

50. Grose, J. (2022, May 11). This perfect mother-daughter read holds a powerful lesson for fighting antisemitism. *NYTimes.com*. Retrieved on November 17, 2023, from https://www.nytimes.com/2022/11/05/opinion/number-the-stars.html

51. National Library of New Zealand. (2022). Librarians' role in creating readers. *Natlib.govt.nz*. Retrieved on November 17, 2023, from https://natlib.govt.nz/schools/reading-engagement/libraries-supporting-readers/librarians-role-in-creating-readers.

52. McDowall, S. (2022). Teachers as readers: Listening to, reading, and talking about stories—for pleasure. *New Zealand Council for Educational Research Journal, 2*, 22–28.

53. Mullan, K. (2010). Families that read: A time-diary analysis of young people's and parents' reading. *Journal of Research in Reading, 33*(4), 414–430; Wollscheid, S. (2013). Parents' cultural resources, gender and young people's reading habits: Findings from a secondary analysis with time-survey data in two-parent families. *International Journal About Parents in Education, 7*(1), 69–83.

54. Clark, C. (2009). *Why fathers matter to their children's literacy*. London: National Literacy Trust.

55. Kou, X., Konrath, S., & Goldstein, T. R. (2020). The relationship among different types of arts engagement, empathy, and prosocial behavior. *Psychology of Aesthetics, Creativity, and the Arts, 14*(4), 481–492.

56. Pruitt, J. (2016). Common queer readers band together on YouTube. *The Popular Culture Studies Journal, 4*, 56–82.

57. Merga, M. K. (2018). *Reading engagement for tweens and teens*. London: Bloomsbury; Merga, M. K. (2022). *School libraries supporting literacy and wellbeing*. London: Facet Publishing; Merga, M. K. (2021). How can Booktok on TikTok inform readers' advisory services for young people? *Library & Information Science Research, 43*(2), 101091.

58. Rideout, V., & Robb, M. B. (2018). *Social media, social life: Teens reveal their experiences*. San Francisco, CA: Common Sense Media.

59. Blakemore, S. J. (2012). Development of the social brain in adolescence. *Journal of the Royal Society of Medicine, 105*(3), 111–116.

60. Kral, T. R., Solis, E., Mumford, J. A., et al. (2017). Neural correlates of empathic accuracy in adolescence. *Social Cognitive and Affective Neuroscience, 12*(11), 1701–1710; Singer, T. (2006). The neuronal basis and ontogeny of empathy and mind reading: Review of literature and implications for future research. *Neuroscience & Biobehavioral Reviews, 30*(6), 855–863.

61. Jann, K., Hernandez, L. M., Beck-Pancer, D., et al. (2015). Altered resting perfusion and functional connectivity of default mode network in youth with autism spectrum disorder. *Brain and Behavior, 5*(9), e00358; Sebastian, C. L., Fontaine, N. M., Bird, G., et al. (2012). Neural processing associated with cognitive and affective theory of mind in adolescents and adults. *Social Cognitive and Affective Neuroscience, 7*(1), 53–63.

62. Habermas, T., & Reese, E. (2015). Getting a life takes time: The development of the life story in adolescence, its precursors and consequences. *Human Development*, *58*(3), 172–201.

63. Giedd, J. N. (2015). The amazing teen brain. *Scientific American*, *312*(6), 32–37.

64. Habermas, T. (2011). Autobiographical reasoning: Arguing and narrating from a biographical perspective. *New Directions for Child and Adolescent Development*, *2011*(131), 1–17.

65. Habermas, T., & Bluck, S. (2000). Getting a life: The emergence of the life story in adolescence. *Psychological Bulletin*, *126*(5), 748–769.

66. Reese, E., Myftari, E., McAnally, H. M., et al. (2017). Telling the tale and living well: Adolescent narrative identity, personality traits, and well-being across cultures. *Child Development*, *88*(2), 612–628.

67. Although Anna's reasoning here is more mature than Charlie's at the same age, note that researchers do not typically find any differences between teenage boys and girls in their autobiographical reasoning. However, teenage girls do include more mental states in their real-life narratives than do teenage boys. Fivush, R., Bohanek, J. G., Zaman, W., & Grapin, S. (2012). Gender differences in adolescents' autobiographical narratives. *Journal of Cognition and Development*, *13*(3), 295–319; McLean, K. C., & Breen, A. V. (2009). Processes and content of narrative identity development in adolescence: Gender and well-being. *Developmental Psychology*, *45*(3), 702–710; Mitchell, C., Reese, E., Salmon, K., & Jose, P. (2020). Narrative coherence, psychopathology, and wellbeing: Concurrent and longitudinal findings in a mid-adolescent sample. *Journal of Adolescence*, *79*, 16–25.

68. Jones, B. K., Destin, M., & McAdams, D. P. (2018). Telling better stories: Competence-building narrative themes increase adolescent persistence and academic achievement. *Journal of Experimental Social Psychology*, *76*, 76–80.

69. McLean, K. (2015). *The co-authored self: Family stories and the construction of personal identity*. New York: Oxford University Press.

70. Theories abound for the reasons for this plethora of memories. Two of the most compelling are that this period is one of dramatic changes in identity, and a period in which many expected milestones in a life occur (e.g., education, occupation, relationships, having children). Both of these factors could lead to stronger memories. Munawar, K., Kuhn, S. K., & Haque, S. (2018). Understanding the reminiscence bump: A systematic review. *PLoS ONE*, *13*(12), e0208595; Rubin, D. C., Wetzler, S. E., & Nebes, R. D. (1986). Autobiographical memory across the lifespan. In D. C. Rubin (Ed.), *Autobiographical memory* (pp. 202–221). Cambridge: Cambridge University Press.

71. Merrill, N., & Fivush, R. (2016). Intergenerational narratives and identity across development. *Developmental Review*, *40*, 72–92; Reese, E., Fivush, R., Merrill, N., Wang, Q., & McAnally, H. (2017). Adolescents' intergenerational narratives across cultures. *Developmental Psychology*, *53*(6), 1142–1153.

72. Chen, Y., Cullen, E., Fivush, R., Wang, Q., & Reese, E. (2021). Mother, father, and I: A cross-cultural investigation of adolescents' intergenerational narratives and well-being. *Journal of Applied Research in Memory and Cognition*, *10*(1), 55–64.

73. Suggate, S., Schaughency, E., McAnally, H., & Reese, E. (2018). From infancy to adolescence: The longitudinal links between vocabulary, early literacy skills, oral narrative, and reading comprehension. *Cognitive Development*, *47*, 82–95.

74. Reese, E., Barrett-Young, A., Gilkison, L., et al. (2022). *Tender Shoots*: A parent book-reading and reminiscing program to enhance children's oral narrative skills. *Reading and Writing*, *36*(3), 541–564.

NOTES *(181)*

75. Hutton, J. S., Phelan, K., Horowitz-Kraus, T., et al. (2017). Shared reading quality and brain activation during story listening in preschool-age children. *The Journal of Pediatrics*, *191*, 204–211.
76. Reese, E. (2013). *Tell me a story: Sharing stories to enrich your child's life.* New York: Oxford University Press.
77. Reese, E., Macfarlane, L., McAnally, H., Robertson, S. J., & Taumoepeau, M. (2020). Coaching in maternal reminiscing with preschoolers leads to elaborative and coherent personal narratives in early adolescence. *Journal of Experimental Child Psychology*, *189*, 104707.
78. Mitchell, C., & Reese, E. (2022). Growing Memories: Coaching mothers in elaborative reminiscing with toddlers benefits adolescents' turning-point narratives and wellbeing. *Journal of Personality, 90*(6), 887–901.
79. Marshall, S., & Reese, E. (2022). Growing Memories: Benefits of an early childhood maternal reminiscing intervention for emerging adults' turning point narratives and well-being. *Journal of Research in Personality, 99*, 104262.
80. Travagin, G., Margola, D., & Revenson, T. A. (2015). How effective are expressive writing interventions for adolescents? A meta-analytic review. *Clinical Psychology Review*, *36*, 42–55.
81. Fivush, R., Marin, K., Crawford, M., Reynolds, M., & Brewin, C. R. (2007). Children's narratives and well-being. *Cognition and Emotion, 21*(7), 1414–1434.
82. Rideout, V., and Robb, M. B. (2019). *The Common Sense census: Media use by tweens and teens, 2019.* San Francisco, CA: Common Sense Media.
83. Rideout, V., Peebles, A., Mann, S., & Robb, M. B. (2022). *Common Sense census: Media use by tweens and teens, 2021.* San Francisco, CA: Common Sense.

CHAPTER 5

1. Anderson, D. R., Huston, A. C., Schmitt, K. L., Linebarger, D. L., Wright, J. C., & Larson, R. (2001). Early childhood television viewing and adolescent behavior: The recontact study. *Monographs of the Society for Research in Child Development*, *66*(1), viii.
2. Larrick, N. (1965, September 11). The all-white world of children's books. *Saturday Review*, 63–65, 84–85; Cooperative Children's Book Center (CCBC). (2021). Publishing statistics on children's books about people of color and First/Native Nations and by people of color and First/Native Nations authors and illustrators. Retrieved May 26, 2022, from ⟨https://ccbc.education.wisc.edu/books/pcst ats.asp⟩.
3. Ishizuka, K. (2019). The cat is out of the bag: Orientalism, anti-blackness, and white supremacy in Dr. Seuss' children's books. *Research on Diversity in Youth Literature*, *1*(2), 4–50.
4. Aronson, K. M., Callahan, B. D., & O'Brien, A. S. (2018). Messages matter: Investigating the thematic content of picture books portraying underrepresented racial and cultural groups. *Sociological Forum*, *33*(1), 165–185.
5. Anderson, D. A., Hamilton, M. C., Gilkison, G. M., & Palmer, S. K. (2021). Gender socialization, family leadership, and the invisible father in children's literature. *Journal of Family Issues, 44*(5), 1343–1357; Berry, T., & Wilkins, J. (2017). The gendered portrayal of inanimate characters in children's books. *Journal of Children's Literature*, *43*(2), 4–15; Hamilton, M. C., Anderson, D., Broaddus, M., & Young, K. (2006). Gender stereotyping and under-representation of female characters in 200 popular children's picture books: A twenty-first century update. *Sex Roles*, *55*(11), 757–765; Lewis, M., Cooper Borkenhagen, M., Converse, E., Lupyan, G.,

& Seidenberg, M. S. (2022). What might books be teaching young children about gender? *Psychological Science*, *33*(1), 33–47; McCabe, J., Fairchild, E., Grauerholz, L., Pescosolido, B. A., & Tope, D. (2011). Gender in twentieth-century children's books: Patterns of disparity in titles and central characters. *Gender & Society*, *25*(2), 197–226.

6. Abad, C., & Pruden, S. M. (2013). Do storybooks really break children's gender stereotypes? *Frontiers in Psychology*, *4*, 986.

7. Schulz, D., & Bahník, Š. (2019). Gender associations in the twentieth-century English-language literature. *Journal of Research in Personality*, *81*, 88–97.

8. Legare, C. H., Lane, J. D., & Evans, E. M. (2013). Anthropomorphizing science: How does it affect the development of evolutionary concepts? *Merrill-Palmer Quarterly*, *59*(2), 168–197; Li, H., Eisen, S., & Lillard, A. S. (2019). Anthropomorphic media exposure and preschoolers' anthropomorphic thinking in China. *Journal of Children and Media*, *13*(2), 149–162. Curiously, the children in this study who watched videos of *Thomas the Tank Engine* did not report increased anthropomorphism for real trains; the effect was restricted to those in the picture book condition. Strouse, G. A., Nyhout, A., & Ganea, P. A. (2018). The role of book features in young children's transfer of information from picture books to real-world contexts. *Frontiers in Psychology*, *9*, 50.

9. Larsen, N. E., Lee, K., & Ganea, P. A. (2018). Do storybooks with anthropomorphized animal characters promote prosocial behaviors in young children? *Developmental Science*, *21*(3), e12590.

10. Barnes, J. L., Bernstein, E., & Bloom, P. (2015). Fact or fiction? Children's preferences for real versus make-believe stories. *Imagination, Cognition and Personality*, *34*(3), 243–258. This effect was especially pronounced for young children. The older children in the study and the adults were more positive about fantasy themes and fantastical characters.

11. Strouse, G. A., Nyhout, A., & Ganea, P. A. (2018). The role of book features in young children's transfer of information from picture books to real-world contexts. *Frontiers in Psychology*, *9*, 50.

12. Nikolajeva, M. (2016). Recent trends in children's literature research: Return to the body. *International Research in Children's Literature*, *9*(2), 132–145.

13. Tod, M. K. (2014, January 10). 2013 Historical Fiction survey results. *AWriterofHistory.com*. Retrieved on November 22, 2023, from https://awriterof history.com/2014/01/10/2013-historical-fiction-survey-results/

14. Marsh, E. J., Meade, M. L., & Roediger III, H. L. (2003). Learning facts from fiction. *Journal of Memory and Language*, *49*(4), 519–536.

15. Fazio, L. K., Barber, S. J., Rajaram, S., et al. (2013). Creating illusions of knowledge: Learning errors that contradict prior knowledge. *Journal of Experimental Psychology: General*, *142*(1), 1–5.

16. Appel, M., & Richter, T. (2007). Persuasive effects of fictional narratives increase over time. *Media Psychology*, *10*(1), 113–134.

17. Marsh, E. J., & Fazio, L. K. (2006). Learning errors from fiction: Difficulties in reducing reliance on fictional stories. *Memory & Cognition*, *34*(5), 1140–1149; Eslick, A. N., Fazio, L. K., & Marsh, E. J. (2011). Ironic effects of drawing attention to story errors. *Memory*, *19*(2), 184–191.

18. Marsh, E. J., Meade, M. L., & Roediger III, H. L. (2003). Learning facts from fiction. *Journal of Memory and Language*, *49*(4), 534.

NOTES *(183)*

19. Grub, D. (2014, June 8). Colombia PCVs damaged by Juan Gabriel Vasquez novel, "The Sound of Things". *PeaceCorpsWorldwide.org*. Retrieved on November 22, 2023, from https://peacecorpsworldwide.org/colombia-pcvs/

20. Fazio, L. K., & Marsh, E. J. (2008). Older, not younger, children learn more false facts from stories. *Cognition, 106*(2), 1081–1089; Marsh, E. J., Balota, D. A., & Roediger III, H. L. (2005). Learning facts from fiction: Effects of healthy aging and early-stage dementia of the Alzheimer type. *Neuropsychology, 19*(1), 115–129.

21. Hinze, S. R., Slaten, D. G., Horton, W. S., Jenkins, R., & Rapp, D. N. (2014). Pilgrims sailing the Titanic: Plausibility effects on memory for misinformation. *Memory & Cognition, 42*(2), 305–324.

22. Rapp, D. N., Hinze, S. R., Slaten, D. G., & Horton, W. S. (2014). Amazing stories: Acquiring and avoiding inaccurate information from fiction. *Discourse Processes, 51*(1–2), 50–74.

23. Riddle, K., & Martins, N. (2022). A content analysis of American primetime television: A 20-year update of the National Television Violence Studies. *Journal of Communication, 72*(1), 33–58. Note that this analysis from 2016/2017 did not include content that aired only on streaming platforms, in order to be consistent with the prior 1996/1996 analysis of violent content.

24. Bandura, A., Ross, D., & Ross, S. A. (1963). Imitation of film-mediated aggressive models. *The Journal of Abnormal and Social Psychology, 66*(1), 3–11.

25. Zimmerman, B. J., & Schunk, D. H. (2003). Albert Bandura: The scholar and his contributions to educational psychology. In B. J. Zimmerman & D. H. Schunk (Eds.), *Educational psychology: A century of contributions* (pp. 431–457). Mahwah, NJ: Lawrence Erlbaum.

26. Huesmann, L. R., Moise-Titus, J., Podolski, C. L., & Eron, L. D. (2003). Longitudinal relations between children's exposure to TV violence and their aggressive and violent behavior in young adulthood: 1977–1992. *Developmental Psychology, 39*(2), 201–221; Sharif, I., Wills, T. A., & Sargent, J. D. (2010). Effect of visual media use on school performance: A prospective study. *Journal of Adolescent Health, 46*(1), 52–61.

27. Anderson, C. A., & Bushman, B. J. (2002). Human aggression. *Annual Review of Psychology, 53*, 27–51. The General Aggression model (GAM) is complex, integrating individual, environmental, and societal factors: Allen, J. J., Anderson, C. A., & Bushman, B. J. (2018). The general aggression model. *Current Opinion in Psychology, 19*, 75–80.

28. Dillon, K. P., & Bushman, B. J. (2017). Effects of exposure to gun violence in movies on children's interest in real guns. *JAMA Pediatrics, 171*(11), 1057–1062.

29. Taggart, J., Eisen, S., & Lillard, A. S. (2019). The current landscape of US children's television: Violent, prosocial, educational, and fantastical content. *Journal of Children and Media, 13*(3), 276–294.

30. Taggart, J., Eisen, S., & Lillard, A. S. (2019). The current landscape of US children's television: Violent, prosocial, educational, and fantastical content. *Journal of Children and Media, 13*(3), 276–294.

31. Lillard, A. S., Drell, M. B., Richey, E. M., Boguszewski, K., & Smith, E. D. (2015). Further examination of the immediate impact of television on children's executive function. *Developmental Psychology, 51*(6), 792–805; Rhodes, S. M., Stewart, T. M., & Kanevski, M. (2020). Immediate impact of fantastical television content on children's executive functions. *British Journal of Developmental Psychology, 38*(2), 268–288. Note, however, that other studies are showing this effect of fantastical

TV content on children's executive function to be extremely small or to fail to replicate entirely.

32. White, R. E., & Carlson, S. M. (2021). Pretending with realistic and fantastical stories facilitates executive function in 3-year-old children. *Journal of Experimental Child Psychology*, *207*, 105090.

33. Moffitt, T. E., Arseneault, L., Belsky, D., et al. (2011). A gradient of childhood self-control predicts health, wealth, and public safety. *Proceedings of the National Academy of Sciences*, *108*(7), 2693–2698; Moffitt, T. E., Poulton, R., & Caspi, A. (2013). Lifelong impact of early self-control. *American Scientist*, *101*(5), 352–359; Robson, D. A., Allen, M. S., & Howard, S. J. (2020). Self-regulation in childhood as a predictor of future outcomes: A meta-analytic review. *Psychological Bulletin*, *146*(4), 324–354.

34. Li, H., Hsueh, Y., Yu, H., & Kitzmann, K. M. (2020). Viewing fantastical events in animated television shows: Immediate effects on Chinese preschoolers' executive function. *Frontiers in Psychology*, *11*, Article 583174. This study used a technique called functional near-infrared spectroscopy (fNIRS) via a specially fitted cap to measure children's brain activation. The advantages over fMRI are that children can sit in a chair during the task rather than enter a claustrophobic tunnel, and it's completely silent.

35. Thank you to neuroscientist Donna Rose Addis for pointing out that this pattern fits with the ideas in her 2020 paper that if the stimulus is too novel (or fantastical), it requires frontoparietal control network involvement, with less default network involvement as a result. Addis, D. R. (2020). Mental time travel? A neurocognitive model of event simulation. *Review of Philosophy and Psychology*, *11*, 233–259.

36. Barr, R., Lauricella, A., Zack, E., & Calvert, S. L. (2010). Infant and early childhood exposure to adult-directed and child-directed television programming: Relations with cognitive skills at age four. *Merrill-Palmer Quarterly*, *56*(1), 21–48; Kostyrka-Allchorne, K., Cooper, N. R., & Simpson, A. (2017). The relationship between television exposure and children's cognition and behaviour: A systematic review. *Developmental Review*, *44*, 19–58; Madigan, S., McArthur, B. A., Anhorn, C., Eirich, R., & Christakis, D. A. (2020). Associations between screen use and child language skills: A systematic review and meta-analysis. *JAMA Pediatrics*, *174*(7), 665–675.

37. Hinten, A. E., Wolsey, K., Henderson, A. M., & Scarf, D. (2023). A survey of screen media access and use in primary school children's households. *Children*, *10*(1), 28.

38. Radesky, J. S., Silverstein, M., Zuckerman, B., & Christakis, D. A. (2014). Infant self-regulation and early childhood media exposure. *Pediatrics*, *133*(5), e1172–e1178.

39. Certain, L. K., & Kahn, R. S. (2002). Prevalence, correlates, and trajectory of television viewing among infants and toddlers. *Pediatrics*, *109*(4), 634–642.

40. Reid Chassiakos, Y., Radesky, J., Christakis, D., Moreno, M. A., & Cross, C. (2016). Children and adolescents and digital media. *Pediatrics*, *138*(5), Article e20162593; McClure, E., Chentsova-Dutton, Y., Holochwost, S., Parrott, W. G., & Barr, R. (2020). Infant emotional engagement in face-to-face and video chat interactions with their mothers. *Enfance*, *3*(3), 353–374; Myers, L. J., LeWitt, R. B., Gallo, R. E., & Maselli, N. M. (2017). Baby FaceTime: Can toddlers learn from online video chat?. *Developmental Science*, *20*(4), e12430.

41. Barr, R. (2010). Transfer of learning between 2D and 3D sources during infancy: Informing theory and practice. *Developmental Review*, *30*(2), 128–154;

NOTES *(185)*

Barr, R. (2019). Growing up in the digital age: Early learning and family media ecology. *Current Directions in Psychological Science, 28*(4), 341–346. This difficulty transferring knowledge from media to real life is similar to older children's difficulties learning from animal characters in books; they have difficulty mapping knowledge from the story world to real life.

42. Corkin, M. T., Peterson, E. R., Henderson, A. M., Waldie, K. E., Reese, E., & Morton, S. M. (2021). Preschool screen media exposure, executive functions and symptoms of inattention/hyperactivity. *Journal of Applied Developmental Psychology, 73*, 101237; Dore, R. A., & Zimmermann, L. (2020). Coviewing, scaffolding, and children's media comprehension. In Jan Van den Bulck, David Ewoldsen, Marie-Louise Mares, and Erica Scharrer (Eds.), *The International Encyclopedia of Media Psychology*, (pp. 1–8). John Wiley & Sons, Inc.

43. Kirkorian, H. L., Pempek, T. A., Murphy, L. A., Schmidt, M. E., & Anderson, D. R. (2009). The impact of background television on parent–child interaction. *Child Development, 80*(5), 1350–1359; Kostyrka-Allchorne, K., Cooper, N. R., & Simpson, A. (2017). The relationship between television exposure and children's cognition and behaviour: A systematic review. *Developmental Review, 44*, 19–58.

44. Gueron-Sela, N., Shalev, I., Gordon-Hacker, A., Egotubov, A., & Barr, R. (2023). Screen media exposure and behavioral adjustment in early childhood during and after COVID-19 home lockdown periods. *Computers in Human Behavior, 140*, 107572.

45. Rogers, O., Mastro, D., Robb, M. B., & Peebles, A. (2021). *The inclusion imperative: Why media representation matters for kids' ethnic-racial development.* San Francisco, CA: Common Sense; Ward, L. M., & Grower, P. (2020). Media and the development of gender role stereotypes. *Annual Review of Developmental Psychology, 2*, 177–199.

46. Corkin, M. T., Peterson, E. R., Henderson, A. M., et al. (2021). The predictors of screen time at two years in a large nationally diverse cohort. *Journal of Child and Family Studies, 30*(8), 2076–2096; Corkin, M. T., Peterson, E. R., Henderson, A. M., Waldie, K. E., Reese, E., & Morton, S. M. (2021). Preschool screen media exposure, executive functions and symptoms of inattention/hyperactivity. *Journal of Applied Developmental Psychology, 73*, 101237; Rogers, O., Mastro, D., Robb, M. B., & Peebles, A. (2021). *The inclusion imperative: Why media representation matters for kids' ethnic-racial development.* San Francisco, CA: Common Sense.

47. Digital Spy. (2018, August 30). Racist stereotypes in TV and film that White people don't see. *DigitalSpy*. Retrieved on November 22, 2023, from https://www.youtube.com/watch?v=EKAAtHARb4M.

48. Ward, L. M., & Grower, P. (2020). Media and the development of gender role stereotypes. *Annual Review of Developmental Psychology, 2*, 177–199.

49. Martins, N., & Harrison, K. (2012). Racial and gender differences in the relationship between children's television use and self-esteem: A longitudinal panel study. *Communication Research, 39*(3), 338–357.

50. Bond, B. J. (2016). Fairy godmothers' robots: The influence of televised gender stereotypes and counter-stereotypes on girls' perceptions of STEM. *Bulletin of Science, Technology & Society, 36*(2), 91–97.

51. Trekels, J., & Eggermont, S. (2017). Beauty is good: The appearance culture, the internalization of appearance ideals, and dysfunctional appearance beliefs among tweens. *Human Communication Research, 43*(2), 173–192.

52. Stice, E., Spangler, D., & Agras, W. S. (2001). Exposure to media-portrayed thin-ideal images adversely affects vulnerable girls: A longitudinal experiment. *Journal of Social and Clinical Psychology, 20*(3), 270–288.

53. Driesmans, K., Vandenbosch, L., & Eggermont, S. (2016). True love lasts forever: The influence of a popular teenage movie on Belgian girls' romantic beliefs. *Journal of Children and Media, 10*(3), 304–320.

54. Calvin, R. (2008). *The politics of Gilmore Girls: Essays on family and feminism in the television series.* London: McFarland & Company.

55. Butler, A. C., Zaromb, F. M., Lyle, K. B., & Roediger III, H. L. (2009). Using popular films to enhance classroom learning: The good, the bad, and the interesting. *Psychological Science, 20*(9), 1161–1168.

56. Nathan, J. R. (2017). Movies and suggestibility: This is your brain on movies. In W. B. Russell & S. Waters (Eds.), *Cinematic social studies: A resource for teaching and learning social studies with film* (pp. 37–54). Charlotte, NC: Information Age Publishing.

57. Surrey, M. (2020, May 29). A marine biologist talks about what Hollywood gets wrong about the ocean. *TheRinger.com.* Retrieved on November 22, 2023, from https://www.theringer.com/movies/2020/5/29/21273288/a-marine-biologist-talks-about-what-hollywood-gets-wrong-about-the-ocean

58. Barriga, C. A., Shapiro, M. A., & Fernandez, M. L. (2010). Science information in fictional movies: Effects of context and gender. *Science Communication, 32*(1), 3–24.

59. Zacks, J. (2015). *Flicker: Your brain on movies.* New York: Oxford University Press.

60. Rideout, V., Peebles, A., Mann, S., & Robb, M. B. (2022). *Common Sense census: Media use by tweens and teens, 2021.* San Francisco, CA: Common Sense.

61. Boyle, E. A., Hainey, T., Connolly, T. M., et al. (2016). An update to the systematic literature review of empirical evidence of the impacts and outcomes of computer games and serious games. *Computers & Education, 94*, 178–192.

62. Merry, S. N., Stasiak, K., Shepherd, M., Frampton, C., Fleming, T., & Lucassen, M. F. (2012). The effectiveness of SPARX, a computerised self-help intervention for adolescents seeking help for depression: Randomised controlled non-inferiority trial. *British Medical Journal, 344*, e2598.

63. Most of these meta-analyses also suffer from methodological issues, such as publication bias. For instance, when Hilgard et al. (2017) reanalyzed an early meta-analysis using contemporary techniques, the new results suggested that the effects of violent video games on aggressive affect and behavior were overestimated, but the stated effects on aggressive thoughts were relatively accurate. Hilgard, J., Engelhardt, C. R., & Rouder, J. N. (2017). Overstated evidence for short-term effects of violent games on affect and behavior: A reanalysis of Anderson et al. (2010). *Psychological Bulletin, 143*(7), 757–774.

64. Greitemeyer, T., & Mügge, D. O. (2014). Video games do affect social outcomes: A meta-analytic review of the effects of violent and prosocial video game play. *Personality and Social Psychology Bulletin, 40*(5), 578–589.

65. Prescott, A. T., Sargent, J. D., & Hull, J. G. (2018). Meta-analysis of the relationship between violent video game play and physical aggression over time. *Proceedings of the National Academy of Sciences, 115*(40), 9882–9888; Mathur, M. B., & VanderWeele, T. J. (2019). Finding common ground in meta-analysis "wars" on violent video games. *Perspectives on Psychological Science, 14*(4), 705–708.

66. Burkhardt, J., & Lenhard, W. (2022). A meta-analysis on the longitudinal, age-dependent effects of violent video games on aggression. *Media Psychology, 25*(3),

499–512. See also Willoughby, T., Adachi, P. J., & Good, M. (2012). A longitudinal study of the association between violent video game play and aggression among adolescents. *Developmental Psychology*, 48(4), 1044. In contrast, Coyne and Stockdale (2021) followed 500 young people from early adolescence to young adulthood, tracking their self-reported violent video game play over 10 years via a person-centered approach rather than group analysis. Moderate yet consistent playing over time of violent video games like *Grand Theft Auto* was associated with higher aggression in young adulthood compared to playing high amounts of violent video games in early adolescence (associated concurrently with depression) and then desisting in middle adolescence, or consistently low use of violent video games over time. This study instead suggests a cumulative effect of violent video games on aggression, not a critical-period effect. Coyne, S. M., & Stockdale, L. (2021). Growing up with Grand Theft Auto: A 10-year study of longitudinal growth of violent video game play in adolescents. *Cyberpsychology, Behavior, and Social Networking*, 24(1), 11–16. A rare intervention study did not find long-term effects of playing *Grand Theft Auto V* (compared to *The Sims*) for 8 weeks on adult players' empathy, mind-reading, or aggression (Kühn et al., 2019); however, participants were young adults and over half were women, both of which could have reduced the effect, and *Grand Theft Auto V* is a third-person shooter, not first-person game. Given the risks of playing violent video games, such an experimental design would not be ethical with adolescents. Kühn, S., Kugler, D. T., & Schmalen, K. (2019). Does playing violent video games cause aggression? A longitudinal intervention study. *Molecular Psychiatry*, 24(8), 1220–1234.

67. Greitemeyer, T. (2019). The contagious impact of playing violent video games on aggression: Longitudinal evidence. *Aggressive Behavior*, 45(6), 635–642.

68. Hummer, T. A., Kronenberger, W. G., Wang, Y., & Mathews, V. P. (2019). Decreased prefrontal activity during a cognitive inhibition task following violent video game play: A multi-week randomized trial. *Psychology of Popular Media Culture*, 8(1), 63–75. Another limitation of this study is the lack of a nonviolent video game control group. Thus, these changes in prefrontal cortex activity may not be solely due to the violent content of the game.

69. Brockmyer, J. F. (2022). Desensitization and violent video games: mechanisms and evidence. *Child and Adolescent Psychiatric Clinics*, 31(1), 121–132; Gentile, D. A., Swing, E. L., Anderson, C. A., Rinker, D., & Thomas, K. M. (2016). Differential neural recruitment during violent video game play in violent-and nonviolent-game players. *Psychology of Popular Media Culture*, 5(1), 39–51.

70. Chou, Y. H., Yang, B. H., Hsu, J. W., et al. (2013). Effects of video game playing on cerebral blood flow in young adults: A SPECT study. *Psychiatry Research: Neuroimaging*, 212(1), 65–72. The nonviolent control game in this experiment was *Super Mario 64*.

71. Palaus, M., Marron, E. M., Viejo-Sobera, R., & Redolar-Ripoll, D. (2017). Neural basis of video gaming: A systematic review. *Frontiers in Human Neuroscience*, 11, 248.

72. Hummer, T. A. (2015). Media violence effects on brain development: What neuroimaging has revealed and what lies ahead. *American Behavioral Scientist*, 59(14), 1790–1806.

73. Beck, V. S., Boys, S., Rose, C., & Beck, E. (2012). Violence against women in video games: A prequel or sequel to rape myth acceptance?. *Journal of Interpersonal Violence*, 27(15), 3016–3031.

74. Driesmans, K., Vandenbosch, L., & Eggermont, S. (2015). Playing a videogame with a sexualized female character increases adolescents' rape myth acceptance and tolerance toward sexual harassment. *Games for Health Journal*, *4*(2), 91–94.

75. Velez, J. A., Greitemeyer, T., Whitaker, J. L., Ewoldsen, D. R., & Bushman, B. J. (2016). Violent video games and reciprocity: The attenuating effects of cooperative game play on subsequent aggression. *Communication Research*, *43*(4), 447–467. Note, however, that the measure of aggressive behavior in this study was of delivering white noise blasts to a fellow participant, a controversial measure of aggression.

76. Gitter, S. A., Ewell, P. J., Guadagno, R. E., Stillman, T. F., & Baumeister, R. F. (2013). Virtually justifiable homicide: The effects of prosocial contexts on the link between violent video games, aggression, and prosocial and hostile cognition. *Aggressive Behavior*, *39*(5), 346–354.

77. Ferguson, C. J., Ivory, J. D., & Beaver, K. M. (2013). Genetic, maternal, school, intelligence, and media use predictors of adult criminality: A longitudinal test of the catalyst model in adolescence through early adulthood. *Journal of Aggression, Maltreatment & Trauma*, *22*(5), 447–460; Greitemeyer, T. (2022). The dark and bright side of video game consumption: effects of violent and prosocial video games. *Current Opinion in Psychology*, 101326.

78. Bavelier, D., Green, C. S., Han, D. H., Renshaw, P. F., Merzenich, M. M., & Gentile, D. A. (2011). Brains on video games. *Nature Reviews Neuroscience*, *12*(12), 765.

79. American Psychiatric Association. (2013). *Diagnostic and statistical manual of mental disorders* (5th ed., text rev.). Washington, DC: American Psychiatric Association.

80. Kamenetz, A. (2019, May 28). Is gaming disorder an illness? WHO says yes, adding it to its list of diseases. *NPR.com*. Retrieved on November 22, 2023, from https://www.npr.org/2019/05/28/727585904/is-gaming-disorder-an-illness-the-who-says-yes-adding-it-to-its-list-of-diseases

81. Vadlin, S., Åslund, C., Hellström, C., & Nilsson, K. W. (2016). Associations between problematic gaming and psychiatric symptoms among adolescents in two samples. *Addictive Behaviors*, *61*, 8–15; Kim, N. R., Hwang, S. S. H., Choi, J. S., et al. (2016). Characteristics and psychiatric symptoms of internet gaming disorder among adults using self-reported DSM-5 criteria. *Psychiatry Investigation*, *13*(1), 58; Király, O., Griffiths, M. D., King, D. L., et al. (2018). Policy responses to problematic video game use: A systematic review of current measures and future possibilities. *Journal of Behavioral Addictions*, *61*, 8–15.

82. Lopez-Fernandez, O., Williams, A. J., & Kuss, D. J. (2019). Measuring female gaming: Gamer profile, predictors, prevalence, and characteristics from psychological and gender perspectives. *Frontiers in Psychology*, *10*, 898.

83. Rehbein, F., King, D. L., Staudt, A., Hayer, T., & Rumpf, H. J. (2021). Contribution of game genre and structural game characteristics to the risk of problem gaming and gaming disorder: A systematic review. *Current Addiction Reports*, *8*(2), 263–281.

84. Radesky, J., & Hiniker, A. (2022). From moral panic to systemic change: Making child-centered design the default. *International Journal of Child-Computer Interaction*, *31*, 100351.

85. Johannes, N., Vuorre, M., Magnusson, K., & Przybylski, A. K. (2022). Time spent playing two online shooters has no measurable effect on aggressive affect. *Collabra: Psychology*, *8*(1), 34606.

NOTES *(189)*

86. Ort, A., Wirz, D. S., & Fahr, A. (2021). Is binge-watching addictive? Effects of motives for TV series use on the relationship between excessive media consumption and problematic viewing habits. *Addictive Behaviors Reports, 13,* 100325.

87. Flayelle, M., Maurage, P., Di Lorenzo, K. R., Vögele, C., Gainsbury, S. M., & Billieux, J. (2020). Binge-watching: What do we know so far? A first systematic review of the evidence. *Current Addiction Reports, 7*(1), 44–60.

88. Troles, H. (2019). *Binge-watching and its influence on psychological well-being and important daily life duties: An Experience Sampling Study.* Bachelor's thesis, University of Twente. Although this study is as yet unpublished, it is one of the few examples using high-quality measures of experience sampling.

89. Ort, A., Wirz, D. S., & Fahr, A. (2021). Is binge-watching addictive? Effects of motives for TV series use on the relationship between excessive media consumption and problematic viewing habits. *Addictive Behaviors Reports, 13,* 100325.

90. Erickson, S. E., Dal Cin, S., & Byl, H. (2019). An experimental examination of binge watching and narrative engagement. *Social Sciences, 8*(1), 19.

91. Exelmans, L., & Van den Bulck, J. (2017). Binge viewing, sleep, and the role of pre-sleep arousal. *Journal of Clinical Sleep Medicine, 13,* 1001–8; Ort, A., Wirz, D. S., & Fahr, A. (2021). Is binge-watching addictive? Effects of motives for TV series use on the relationship between excessive media consumption and problematic viewing habits. *Addictive Behaviors Reports, 13,* 100325.

92. Keadle, S. K., Arem, H., Moore, S. C., Sampson, J. N., & Matthews, C. E. (2015). Impact of changes in television viewing time and physical activity on longevity: A prospective cohort study. *International Journal of Behavioral Nutrition and Physical Activity, 12*(1), 1–11.

93. Sisson, S. B., Shay, C. M., Broyles, S. T., & Leyva, M. (2012). Television-viewing time and dietary quality among US children and adults. *American Journal of Preventive Medicine, 43*(2), 196–200.

94. Da Cunha Goncalves, K. V. (2020). *How good or bad is Netflix for its users? The relationship between binge-watching and self-regulation of eating behaviour.* Unpublished bachelor's thesis, University of Twente.

95. Flayelle, M., Maurage, P., Di Lorenzo, K. R., Vögele, C., Gainsbury, S. M., & Billieux, J. (2020). Binge-watching: What do we know so far? A first systematic review of the evidence. *Current Addiction Reports, 7*(1), 44–60.

CHAPTER 6

1. Gottschall, J. (2012). *The storytelling animal: How stories make us human.* New York: Houghton Mifflin Harcourt; Miller, P. J., Potts, R., Fung, H., Hoogstra, L., & Mintz, J. (1990). Narrative practices and the social construction of self in childhood. *American Ethnologist, 17*(2), 292–311; Mullen, M. K., & Yi, S. (1995). The cultural context of talk about the past: Implications for the development of autobiographical memory. *Cognitive Development, 10*(3), 407–419.

2. Bohanek, J. G., Fivush, R., Zaman, W., Lepore, C. E., Merchant, S., & Duke, M. P. (2009). Narrative interaction in family dinnertime conversations. *Merrill-Palmer Quarterly, 55*(4), 488–515.

3. Devitt, A. L., Monk-Fromont, E., Schacter, D. L., & Addis, D. R. (2016). Factors that influence the generation of autobiographical memory conjunction errors. *Memory, 24*(2), 204–222.

4. Loftus, E. F. (2005). Planting misinformation in the human mind: A 30-year investigation of the malleability of memory. *Learning & Memory, 12*(4), 361–366.

5. Loftus, E. F. (1975). Leading questions and the eyewitness report. *Cognitive Psychology, 7*, 560–572.
6. Loftus, E. F. (2005). Planting misinformation in the human mind: A 30-year investigation of the malleability of memory. *Learning & Memory, 12*(4), 361–366.
7. Zhu, B., Chen, C., Loftus, E. F., et al. (2010). Individual differences in false memory from misinformation: Personality characteristics and their interactions with cognitive abilities. *Personality and Individual Differences, 48*(8), 889–894.
8. Loftus, E. F., & Pickrell, J. E. (1995). The formation of false memories. *Psychiatric Annals, 25*(12), 720–725.
9. Braun, K. A., Ellis, R., & Loftus, E.F. (2002). Make my memory: How advertising can change our memories of the past. *Psychology & Marketing, 19*, 1–23.
10. Garry, M., & Polaschek, D. L. (2000). Imagination and memory. *Current Directions in Psychological Science, 9*(1), 6–10.
11. Edelson, M., Sharot, T., Dolan, R. J., & Dudai, Y. (2011). Following the crowd: Brain substrates of longterm memory conformity. *Science, 333*, 108–111.
12. Lawson, M., Rodriguez-Steen, L., & London, K. (2018). A systematic review of the reliability of children's event reports after discussing experiences with a naïve, knowledgeable, or misled parent. *Developmental Review, 49*, 62–79; Principe, G. F., DiPuppo, J., & Gammel, J. (2013). Effects of mothers' conversation style and receipt of misinformation on children's event reports. *Cognitive Development, 28*(3), 260–271.
13. Cleveland, E. S., & Reese, E. (2005). Maternal structure and autonomy support in conversations about the past: contributions to children's autobiographical memory. *Developmental Psychology, 41*(2), 376–388.
14. Principe, G. F., & London, K. (2022). How parents can shape what children remember: Implications for the testimony of young witnesses. *Journal of Applied Research in Memory and Cognition, 11*(3), 289.
15. Frontline (1997, May). Innocence lost the plea. *PBS.org*. Retrieved on November 25, 2023, from https://www.pbs.org/wgbh/pages/frontline/shows/innocence/etc/sum.html
16. Paz-Alonso, P. M., & Goodman, G. S. (2016). Developmental differences across middle childhood in memory and suggestibility for negative and positive events. *Behavioral Sciences & The Law, 34*(1), 30–54; Zajac, R., & Hayne, H. (2006). The negative effect of cross-examination style questioning on children's accuracy: older children are not immune. *Applied Cognitive Psychology, 20*(1), 3–16.
17. Loftus, E., & Ketcham, K. (1994). *The myth of repressed memory: False memories and allegations of sexual abuse*. New York: St. Martin's Press.
18. Otgaar, H., Howe, M. L., Patihis, L., et al. (2019). The return of the repressed: The persistent and problematic claims of long-forgotten trauma. *Perspectives on Psychological Science, 14*(6), 1072–1095.
19. Goodman, G. S., Gonzalves, L., & Wolpe, S. (2019). False memory and true memory of childhood trauma: Balancing the risks. *Clinical Psychological Science, 7*, 29–31.
20. Schacter, D. L., Guerin, S. A., & Jacques, P. L. S. (2011). Memory distortion: An adaptive perspective. *Trends in Cognitive Sciences, 15*(10), 467–474.
21. Jacoby, L. L., Bishara, A. J., Hessels, S., & Toth, J. P. (2005). Aging, subjective experience, and cognitive control: Dramatic false remembering by older adults. *Journal of Experimental Psychology: General, 134*(2), 131–148; Sutherland, R., & Hayne, H. (2001). Age-related changes in the misinformation effect. *Journal of Experimental Child Psychology, 79*(4), 388–404.

NOTES *(191)*

22. Tulving, E. (1972). Episodic and semantic memory. In E. Tulving & W. Donaldson (Eds.), *Organization of memory* (pp. 381–403). New York: Academic Press; Tulving, E. (2002). Episodic memory: From mind to brain. *Annual Review of Psychology*, *53*(1), 1–25.

23. Binder, J. R., & Desai, R. H. (2011). The neurobiology of semantic memory. *Trends in Cognitive Sciences*, *15*(11), 527–536; Duff, M. C., Covington, N. V., Hilverman, C., & Cohen, N. J. (2020). Semantic memory and the hippocampus: Revisiting, reaffirming, and extending the reach of their critical relationship. *Frontiers in Human Neuroscience*, *13*, 471.

24. Fazio, L. K., & Marsh, E. J. (2008). Older, not younger, children learn more false facts from stories. *Cognition*, *106*(2), 1081–1089.

25. Marsh, E. J., Balota, D. A., & Roediger III, H. L. (2005). Learning facts from fiction: Effects of healthy aging and early-stage dementia of the Alzheimer type. *Neuropsychology*, *19*(1), 115–129.

26. Fazio, L. K., & Marsh, E. J. (2008). Older, not younger, children learn more false facts from stories. *Cognition*, *106*(2), 1081–1089; Jarjat, G., Ward, G., Hot, P., Portrat, S., & Loaiza, V. M. (2021). Distinguishing the impact of age on semantic and nonsemantic associations in episodic memory. *The Journals of Gerontology: Series B*, *76*(4), 722–731.

27. Frenda, S. J., Nichols, R. M., & Loftus, E. F. (2011). Current issues and advances in misinformation research. *Current Directions in Psychological Science*, *20*(1), 20–23. Under certain conditions, however, we can be motivated to resist misinformation (Clifasefi et al., 2007). When undergraduates were given a baking soda placebo solution that experimenters told them was a memory aid, they resisted incorporating misinformation into their memories more than participants in a control condition.

   Clifasefi, S., Garry, M., Harper, D., Sharman, S. J., & Sutherland, R. (2007). Psychotropic placebos create resistance to the misinformation effect. *Psychonomic Bulletin & Review*, *12*, 112–117.

28. McAdams, D. P., Reynolds, J., Lewis, M., Patten, A. H., & Bowman, P. J. (2001). When bad things turn good and good things turn bad: Sequences of redemption and contamination in life narrative and their relation to psychosocial adaptation in midlife adults and in students. *Personality and Social Psychology Bulletin*, *27*(4), 474–485.

29. Adler, J. M., & Poulin, M. J. (2009). The political is personal: Narrating 9/11 and psychological well-being. *Journal of Personality*, *77*(4), 903–932 (p. 915).

30. Adler, J. M., Kissel, E. C., & McAdams, D. P. (2006). Emerging from the CAVE: Attributional style and the narrative study of identity in midlife adults. *Cognitive Therapy and Research*, *30*, 39–51.

31. Dunlop, W. L., Guo, J., & McAdams, D. P. (2016). The autobiographical author through time: Examining the degree of stability and change in redemptive and contaminated personal narratives. *Social Psychological and Personality Science*, *7*(5), 428–436.

32. Eger, E. (2018). *The choice: A true story of hope*. Auckland, NZ: Penguin Books (p. 348).

33. Reese, E., Myftari, E., McAnally, H. M., Chen, Y., Neha, T., Wang, Q., Jack, F., & Robertson, S. J. (2017). Telling the tale and living well: Adolescent narrative identity, personality traits, and well-being across cultures. *Child Development*, *88*(2), 612–628.

34. Banks, M. V., & Salmon, K. (2013). Reasoning about the self in positive and negative ways: Relationship to psychological functioning in young adulthood. *Memory*, *21*(1), 10–26.

35. In one longitudinal study with teens (Mitchell et al., 2020), we found that earlier self-event connections predicted *lower* levels of depression 1 year later, but we did not code separately for positive and negative self-event connections. Not surprisingly, the link with depression appears to be specific to negative self-event connections. Mitchell, C., Reese, E., Salmon, K., & Jose, P. (2020). Narrative coherence, psychopathology, and wellbeing: Concurrent and longitudinal findings in a mid-adolescent sample. *Journal of Adolescence*, *79*, 16–25. For one of the few experimental studies of autobiographical reasoning, see Jones, B. K., Destin, M., & McAdams, D. P. (2018). Telling better stories: Competence-building narrative themes increase adolescent persistence and academic achievement. *Journal of Experimental Social Psychology*, *76*, 76–80.

36. Breslau et al., 1998; Breslau, N., Kessler, R. C., Chilcoat, H. D., Schultz, L. R., Davis, G.C., & Andreski, P. (1998). Trauma and posttraumatic stress disorder in the community: The 1996 Detroit area survey of trauma. *Archives of General Psychiatry*, *55*, 626–632; Darves-Bornoz, J., Alonso, J., Girolamo, G., et al. (2008). Main traumatic events in Europe: PTSD in the European study of the epidemiology of mental disorders survey. *Journal of Traumatic Stress*, *21*, 455–462; Kessler, R. C., Sonnega, A., Bromet, E., Hughes, M., & Nelson, C. B. (1995). Posttraumatic stress disorder in the National Comorbidity Survey. *Archives of General Psychiatry*, *52*, 1048–1060.

37. U.S. Department of Veterans Affairs (2023, August 31). PTSD Basics. *PTSD. VA.gov*. Retrieved on November 25, 2023, from https://www.ptsd.va.gov/underst and/what/ptsd_basics.asp

38. Salmon, K., & Reese, E. (2015). Talking (or not talking) about the past: The influence of parent–child conversation about negative experiences on children's memories. *Applied Cognitive Psychology*, *29*(6), 791–801; Fivush, R. (2019). *Family narratives and the development of an autobiographical self: Social and cultural perspectives on autobiographical memory*. New York: Routledge.

39. Dalgleish et al. (2008) states that this lack of integration means the memory is less consciously accessible, so emerges more often involuntarily in dreams and during the day; however, Fitzgerald et al. (2016) argue that PTSD symptoms increase as memories become *more* accessible. Dalgleish, T., Hauer, B., & Kuyken, W. (2008). The mental regulation of autobiographical recollection in the aftermath of trauma. *Current Directions in Psychological Science*, *17*(4), 259–263; Fitzgerald, J. M., Berntsen, D., & Broadbridge, C. L. (2016). The influences of event centrality in memory models of PTSD. *Applied Cognitive Psychology*, *30*(1), 10–21; Rubin, D. C., Dennis, M. F., & Beckham, J. C. (2011). Autobiographical memory for stressful events: The role of autobiographical memory in posttraumatic stress disorder. *Consciousness and Cognition*, *20*(3), 840–856.

40. Berntsen, D., & Rubin, D. C. (2007). When a trauma becomes a key to identity: Enhanced integration of trauma memories predicts posttraumatic stress disorder symptoms. *Applied Cognitive Psychology*, *21*(4), 417–431.

41. Banks, M. V., & Salmon, K. (2013). Reasoning about the self in positive and negative ways: Relationship to psychological functioning in young adulthood. *Memory*, *21*(1), 10–26. See also Gehrt, T. B., Berntsen, D., Hoyle, R. H., & Rubin, D. C. (2018). Psychological and clinical correlates of the Centrality of Event Scale: A systematic review. *Clinical Psychology Review*, *65*, 57–80; Pillemer, D. (1998). *Momentous*

NOTES *(193)*

events, vivid memories: How unforgettable moments help us understand the meaning of our lives. Cambridge, MA: Harvard University Press.

42. Fitzgerald, J. M., Berntsen, D., & Broadbridge, C. L. (2016). The influences of event centrality in memory models of PTSD. *Applied Cognitive Psychology, 30*(1), 10–21. Rubin et al.'s (2011) "cube" encapsulates the three most important memory features that lead to PTSD symptoms after trauma: an emotionally intense event, more rehearsal, and centrality of the event to the life story. Rubin's cube also delineates the type of people most likely to experience PTSD: those with intense emotions, who ruminate often, and who place greater importance on the meaning of life's events. Rubin, D. C., Dennis, M. F., & Beckham, J. C. (2011). Autobiographical memory for stressful events: The role of autobiographical memory in posttraumatic stress disorder. *Consciousness and Cognition, 20*(3), 840–856.

43. Cyniak-Cieciura, M., & Zawadzki, B. (2021). The relationship between temperament traits and post-traumatic stress disorder symptoms and its moderators: Meta-analysis and meta-regression. *Trauma, Violence, & Abuse, 22*(4), 702–716.

44. Fitzgerald, J. M., Berntsen, D., & Broadbridge, C. L. (2016). The influences of event centrality in memory models of PTSD. *Applied Cognitive Psychology, 30*(1), 10–21.

45. NICE Guidelines (2018, December 5). Post-traumatic stress disorder. *Nice.org. uk*. Retrieved on November 23, 2023, from https://www.nice.org.uk/guidance/ng116. Pearson, J., Naselaris, T., Holmes, E. A., & Kosslyn, S. M. (2015). Mental imagery: functional mechanisms and clinical applications. *Trends in Cognitive Sciences, 19*(10), 590–602.

46. Kongshøj, I. L. L., & Bohn, A. (2020). PTSD in youth from a developmental perspective. In S. Gülgöz & B. Sahin-Acar (Eds.), *Autobiographical memory development: Theoretical and methodological approaches*. New York: Routledge.

47. Reese, E., Myftari, E., McAnally, H. M., et al.(2017). Telling the tale and living well: Adolescent narrative identity, personality traits, and well-being across cultures. *Child Development, 88*(2), 612–628; McLean, K. C., Breen, A. V., & Fournier, M. A. (2010). Constructing the self in early, middle, and late adolescent boys: Narrative identity, individuation, and well-being. *Journal of Research on Adolescence, 20*(1), 166–187.

48. Habermas, T., & Reese, E. (2015). Getting a life takes time: The development of the life story in adolescence, its precursors and consequences. *Human Development, 58*(3), 172–201.

49. Chen, Y., Cullen, E., Fivush, R., Wang, Q., & Reese, E. (2021). Mother, Father, and I: A cross-cultural investigation of adolescents' intergenerational narratives and well-being. *Journal of Applied Research in Memory and Cognition, 10*(1), 55–64.

50. Goodman, G. S., Ogle, C. M., Block, S. D., et al. (2011). False memory for trauma-related Deese–Roediger–McDermott lists in adolescents and adults with histories of child sexual abuse. *Development and Psychopathology, 23*(2), 423–438; Moradi, A. R., Heydari, A. H., Abdollahi, M. H., Rahimi-Movaghar, V., Dalgleish, T., & Jobson, L. (2015). Visual false memories in posttraumatic stress disorder. *Journal of Abnormal Psychology, 124*(4), 905–917.

51. Ross, M. C., & Cisler, J. M. (2020). Altered large-scale functional brain organization in posttraumatic stress disorder: A comprehensive review of univariate and network-level neurocircuitry models of PTSD. *NeuroImage: Clinical, 27*, 102319.

52. Viard, A., Mutlu, J., Chanraud, S., et al. (2019). Altered default mode network connectivity in adolescents with post-traumatic stress disorder. *NeuroImage: Clinical,*

22, 101731; Akiki, T. J., Averill, C. L., Wrocklage, K. M., et al. (2018). Default mode network abnormalities in posttraumatic stress disorder: A novel network-restricted topology approach. *Neuroimage, 176,* 489–498.

53. Moulds, M. L., Bisby, M. A., Wild, J., & Bryant, R. A. (2020). Rumination in posttraumatic stress disorder: A systematic review. *Clinical Psychology Review, 82,* 101910.

54. Brooks, M., Graham-Kevan, N., Lowe, M., & Robinson, S. (2017). Rumination, event centrality, and perceived control as predictors of post-traumatic growth and distress: The Cognitive Growth and Stress model. *British Journal of Clinical Psychology, 56*(3), 286–302; Lilgendahl, J. P., McLean, K. C., & Mansfield, C. D. (2013). When is meaning making unhealthy for the self? The roles of neuroticism, implicit theories, and memory telling in trauma and transgression memories. *Memory, 21*(1), 79–96.

55. Aldao, A., Gee, D. G., De Los Reyes, A., & Seager, I. (2016). Emotion regulation as a transdiagnostic factor in the development of internalizing and externalizing psychopathology: Current and future directions. *Development and Psychopathology, 28*(4pt1), 927–946; Schweizer, S., Gotlib, I. H., & Blakemore, S. J. (2020). The role of affective control in emotion regulation during adolescence. *Emotion, 20*(1), 80–86.

56. D. P. McAdams, & Jones, B.,K. (2017). Making meaning in the wake of trauma: Resilience and redemption. In E. M. Altmeier (Ed.), *Reconstructing meaning after trauma: Theory, research, and practice* (pp. 3–16). London: Academic Press.

57. Brooks, M., Graham-Kevan, N., Lowe, M., & Robinson, S. (2017). Rumination, event centrality, and perceived control as predictors of post-traumatic growth and distress: The Cognitive Growth and Stress model. *British Journal of Clinical Psychology, 56*(3), 286–302.

58. Frattaroli, J. (2006). Experimental disclosure and its moderators: A meta-analysis. *Psychological Bulletin, 132*(6), 823.

59. Fivush, R., Marin, K., Crawford, M., Reynolds, M., & Brewin, C. R. (2007). Children's narratives and well-being. *Cognition and Emotion, 21*(7), 1414–1434.

60. Travagin, G., Margola, D., & Revenson, T. A. (2015). How effective are expressive writing interventions for adolescents? A meta-analytic review. *Clinical Psychology Review, 36,* 42–55.

61. Gerger, H., Werner, C. P., Gaab, J., & Cuijpers, P. (2022). Comparative efficacy and acceptability of expressive writing treatments compared with psychotherapy, other writing treatments, and waiting list control for adult trauma survivors: A systematic review and network meta-analysis. *Psychological Medicine, 52,* 3484–3496.

62. Chen, Y., Cullen, E., Fivush, R., Wang, Q., & Reese, E. (2021). Mother, father, and I: A cross-cultural investigation of adolescents' intergenerational narratives and well-being. *Journal of Applied Research in Memory and Cognition, 10*(1), 55–64.

63. Fivush, R. (2019). *Family narratives and the development of an autobiographical self: Social and cultural perspectives on autobiographical memory.* New York: Routledge.

64. Van Es, B. (2018). *The cut out girl: A story of war and family, lost and found.* New York: Penguin Random House.

65. Baron-Cohen, S. (2011). *The science of evil: On empathy and the origins of cruelty.* New York: Basic Books.

66. Eger, E. (2017). *The choice: Embrace the possible.* New York: Penguin Books.

NOTES *(195)*

67. Aslam, S. (2023, March 3). 80 + Facebook statistics you need to know in 2023. *OmnicoreAgency.com*. Retrieved on November 25, 2023, from https://www.omn icoreagency.com/facebook-statistics/

68. Avila, R., Freuler, J. O., & Fagan, C. (2018, April). The invisible curation of content: Facebook's news feed and our information diets. *WebFoundation.org*. Retrieved on November 25, 2023, from http://webfoundation.org/docs/2018/04/WF_InvisibleCurationContent_Screen_AW.pdf

69. Appel, M., Marker, C., & Gnambs, T. (2020). Are social media ruining our lives? A review of meta-analytic evidence. *Review of General Psychology*, *24*(1), 60–74; Yoon, S., Kleinman, M., Mertz, J., & Brannick, M. (2019). Is social network site usage related to depression? A meta-analysis of Facebook–depression relations. *Journal of Affective Disorders*, *248*, 65–72.

70. Paus, T., Keshavan, M., & Giedd, J. N. (2008). Why do many psychiatric disorders emerge during adolescence? *Nature Reviews Neuroscience*, *9*(12), 947–957.

71. Rideout, V., & Robb, M. B. (2018). *Social media, social life: Teens reveal their experiences*. San Francisco, CA: Common Sense Media.

72. Common Sense Media (2022). *The Common Sense census: Media use by tweens and teens, 2021*. https://www.commonsensemedia.org/sites/default/files/research/report/2022-infographic-8-18-census-web-final-release_0.pdf

73. Bagot, K. S., Tomko, R. L., Marshall, A. T., et al. (2022). Youth screen use in the ABCD® study. *Developmental Cognitive Neuroscience*, 101150.

74. Orben, A., Przybylski, A. K., Blakemore, S. J., & Kievit, R. A. (2022). Windows of developmental sensitivity to social media. *Nature Communications*, *13*(1), 1–10. Another sensitive window for risks of social media for both boys and girls was at age 19; the authors speculate this window is due to social factors such as moving from home and changes in social networks. Across ages and gender, they also found that lower life satisfaction was linked to increased use of social media 1 year later, so the relationship is bidirectional. See also longitudinal analyses, meta-analyses, and umbrella reviews of those meta-analyses: Boer, M., Stevens, G. W., Finkenauer, C., & van den Eijnden, R. J. (2022). The complex association between social media use intensity and adolescent wellbeing: A longitudinal investigation of five factors that may affect the association. *Computers in Human Behavior*, *128*, 107084; Ivie, E. J., Pettitt, A., Moses, L. J., & Allen, N. B. (2020). A meta-analysis of the association between adolescent social media use and depressive symptoms. *Journal of Affective Disorders*, *275*, 165–174; Valkenburg, P. M., Meier, A., & Beyens, I. (2022). Social media use and its impact on adolescent mental health: An umbrella review of the evidence. *Current Opinion in Psychology*, *44*, 58–68.

75. Haidt, J. (2021, November 21). The dangerous experiment on teenage girls. *TheAtlantic.com*. Retrieved on November 25, 2023, from https://www.theatlan tic.com/ideas/archive/2021/11/facebooks-dangerous-experiment-teen-girls/620767/

76. Ghai, S., Magis-Weinberg, L., Stoilova, M., Livingstone, S., & Orben, A. (2022). Social media and adolescent well-being in the Global South. *Current Opinion in Psychology*, *46*, 101318.

77. Yoon, S., Kleinman, M., Mertz, J., & Brannick, M. (2019). Is social network site usage related to depression? A meta-analysis of Facebook–depression relations. *Journal of Affective Disorders*, *248*, 65–72.

78. Feinstein, B. A., Hershenberg, R., Bhatia, V., Latack, J. A., Meuwly, N., & Davila, J. (2013). Negative social comparison on Facebook and depressive

symptoms: Rumination as a mechanism. *Psychology of Popular Media Culture*, *2*(3), 161–170.

79. Jang, W. E., Bucy, E. P., & Cho, J. (2018). Self-esteem moderates the influence of self-presentation style on Facebook users' sense of subjective well-being. *Computers in Human Behavior*, *85*, 190–199.

80. Wright, E. J., White, K. M., & Obst, P. L. (2018). Facebook false self-presentation behaviors and negative mental health. *Cyberpsychology, Behavior, and Social Networking*, *21*(1), 40–49.

81. Seabrook, E. M., Kern, M. L., & Rickard, N. S. (2016). Social networking sites, depression, and anxiety: A systematic review. *JMIR Mental Health*, *3*(4), e5842.

82. Rosenthal, S. R., Buka, S. L., Marshall, B. D., Carey, K. B., & Clark, M. A. (2016). Negative experiences on Facebook and depressive symptoms among young adults. *Journal of Adolescent Health*, *59*(5), 510–516.

83. Seabrook, E. M., Kern, M. L., & Rickard, N. S. (2016). Social networking sites, depression, and anxiety: A systematic review. *JMIR Mental Health*, *3*(4), e5842.

84. Vogel, E. A., & Rose, J. P. (2016). Self-reflection and interpersonal connection: Making the most of self-presentation on social media. *Translational Issues in Psychological Science*, *2*(3), 294.

85. Lambert, J., Barnstable, G., Minter, E., Cooper, J., & McEwan, D. (2022). Taking a one-week break from social media improves well-being, depression, and anxiety: A randomized controlled trial. *Cyberpsychology, Behavior, and Social Networking*, *25*(5), 287–293.

86. Tromholt, M. (2016). The Facebook experiment: Quitting Facebook leads to higher levels of well-being. *Cyberpsychology, Behavior, and Social Networking*, *19*(11), 661–666. See also Allcott, H., Braghieri, L., Eichmeyer, S., & Gentzkow, M. (2020). The welfare effects of social media. *American Economic Review*, *110*(3), 629–76.

87. Sagioglou, C., & Greitemeyer, T. (2014). Facebook's emotional consequences: Why Facebook causes a decrease in mood and why people still use it. *Computers in Human Behavior*, *35*, 359–363.

88. Monge Roffarello, A., & De Russis, L. (2022, April). Towards understanding the dark patterns that steal our attention. In *CHI Conference on Human Factors in Computing Systems Extended Abstracts* (pp. 1–7). New Orleans, LA: CHI conference.

89. Bago, B., Rand, D. G., & Pennycook, G. (2020). Fake news, fast and slow: Deliberation reduces belief in false (but not true) news headlines. *Journal of Experimental Psychology: General*, *149*(8), 1608–1613; Pennycook, G., Cannon, T. D., & Rand, D. G. (2018). Prior exposure increases perceived accuracy of fake news. *Journal of Experimental Psychology: General*, *147*(12), 1865–1880; Pennycook, G., & Rand, D. G. (2021). The psychology of fake news. *Trends in Cognitive Sciences*, *25*(5), 388–402; Martel, C., Pennycook, G., & Rand, D. G. (2020). Reliance on emotion promotes belief in fake news. *Cognitive Research: Principles and Implications*, *5*(1), 1–20. The effect of emotionality on belief in fake news held whether the emotion experienced was positive or negative, and experienced naturally or induced experimentally.

90. Kahneman, D. (2011). *Thinking, fast and slow*. New York: Penguin Books.

91. Bago, B., Rand, D. G., & Pennycook, G. (2020). Fake news, fast and slow: Deliberation reduces belief in false (but not true) news headlines. *Journal of Experimental Psychology: General*, *149*(8), 1608–1613.

92. Maass, A. (1999). Linguistic intergroup bias: Stereotype perpetuation through language. In *Advances in Experimental Social Psychology* (Vol. 31, pp. 79–121). New York: Academic Press.

NOTES *(197)*

93. Lazer, D. M., Baum, M. A., Benkler, Y., et al. (2018). The science of fake news. *Science, 359*(6380), 1094–1096.

94. Vosoughi, S., Roy, D., & Aral, S. (2018). The spread of true and false news online. *Science, 359*(6380), 1146–1151; Arun, C. (2019). On WhatsApp, rumours, lynchings, and the Indian Government. *Economic & Political Weekly, 54*(6); Hills, T. T. (2019). The dark side of information proliferation. *Perspectives on Psychological Science, 14*(3), 323–330.

95. Walter, N., & Tukachinsky, R. (2020). A meta-analytic examination of the continued influence of misinformation in the face of correction: How powerful is it, why does it happen, and how to stop it?. *Communication Research, 47*(2), 155–177.

96. Lewandowsky, S., & Van Der Linden, S. (2021). Countering misinformation and fake news through inoculation and prebunking. *European Review of Social Psychology, 32*(2), 348–384; Roozenbeek, J.,& van der Linden, S. (2019b). Fake news game confers psychological resistance against online misinformation. *Palgrave Communications, 5*(1), Article 65.

97. Brashier, N. M., & Schacter, D. L. (2020). Aging in an era of fake news. *Current Directions in Psychological Science, 29*(3), 316–323;
    Ruffman, T., Murray, J., Halberstadt, J., & Vater, T. (2012). Age-related differences in deception. *Psychology and Aging, 27*(3), 543–549.

98. Lewandowsky, S., Ecker, U. K., & Cook, J. (2017). Beyond misinformation: Understanding and coping with the "post-truth" era. *Journal of Applied Research in Memory and Cognition, 6*(4), 353–369; van der Linden, S., Roozenbeek, J., Maertens, R., Basol, M., Kácha, O., Rathje, S., & Traberg, C. S. (2021). How can psychological science help counter the spread of fake news? *The Spanish Journal of Psychology, 24*, e25.

CHAPTER 7

1. Harris, P. L. (2000). *The work of the imagination.* Oxford: Blackwell; Taylor, M. (Ed.) (2013). *The Oxford handbook of the development of imagination.* New York: Oxford University Press.

2. Note that my definition of parasocial interactions and relationships to include childhood role-play is broader than that of some other theorists (e.g., Gleason et al., 2019). Gleason, T. R., Theran, S. A., & Newberg, E. M. (2020). Connections between adolescents' parasocial interactions and recollections of childhood imaginative activities. *Imagination, Cognition and Personality, 39*(3), 241–260.

3. Bretherton, I. (1984). Representing the social world in symbolic play: Reality and fantasy. In I. Bretherton's (Ed.), *Symbolic play: The Development of Social Understanding* (pp. 3–41). New York: Academic Press; Sachet, A. B., & Mottweiler, C. M. (2013). The distinction between role-play and object substitution in pretend play. In M. Taylor's (Ed.), *The Oxford handbook of the development of imagination* (pp. 175–185). New York: Oxford University Press.

4. Scott, F. J. (2013). The development of imagination in children with autism. In M. Taylor's (Ed.), *The Oxford handbook of the development of imagination* (pp. 499–515). New York: Oxford University Press.

5. Buckner, R. L., & Carroll, D. C. (2007). Self-projection and the brain. *Trends in Cognitive Sciences, 11*, 49–57; Gleason, T. R. (2013). Imaginary relationships. In M. Taylor's (Ed.), *The Oxford handbook of the development of imagination* (pp. 251–271). New York: Oxford University Press; Carroll, J. (2020). Imagination, the brain's default mode network, and imaginative verbal artifacts. In J. Carroll, M.

Clasen, & E. Jonsson (Eds.), *Evolutionary perspectives on imaginative culture* (pp. 31–52). Cham, Switzerland: Springer Nature.

6. Gaskins, S. (2013). Pretend play as culturally constructed activity. In M. Taylor (Ed.), *The Oxford handbook of the development of imagination* (pp. 224–247). New York: Oxford University Press.

7. Nicolopoulou, A., Ilgaz, H., & Shiro, M. (2022). "And they had a big, big, very long fight:" The development of evaluative language in preschoolers' oral fictional stories told in a peer-group context. *Journal of Child Language*, *49*(3), 522–551; Brown, C. S., Biefeld, S. D., & Tam, M. J. (2020). *Gender in childhood*. Cambridge: Cambridge University Press.

8. Singer, D. G., & Singer, J. L. (1990). *The house of make-believe* (p. 64). Cambridge, MA: Harvard University Press.

9. Paley, V. (1990). *The boy who would be a helicopter: The uses of storytelling in the classroom*. Cambridge, MA: Harvard University Press; Paley, V. (2009). *The child's work: The importance of fantasy play*. Chicago: University of Chicago Press.

10. Lillard, A. S., Lerner, M. D., Hopkins, E. J., Dore, R. A., Smith, E. D., & Palmquist, C. M. (2013). The impact of pretend play on children's development: A review of the evidence. *Psychological Bulletin*, *139*(1), 1–34.

11. Weisberg, D. S., Ilgaz, H., Hirsh-Pasek, K., Golinkoff, R., Nicolopoulou, A., & Dickinson, D. K. (2015). Shovels and swords: How realistic and fantastical themes affect children's word learning. *Cognitive Development*, *35*, 1–14. See also Nicolopoulou, A., Cortina, K. S., Ilgaz, H., Cates, C. B., & de Sá, A. B. (2015). Using a narrative-and play-based activity to promote low-income preschoolers' oral language, emergent literacy, and social competence. *Early Childhood Research Quarterly*, *31*, 147–162. Note, however, that both of these interventions involved structured storytelling, so the unique contribution of role-play to children's language development is still unclear.

12. Singer, D. G., Golinkoff, R. M., & Hirsh-Pasek, K. (2006). *Play = Learning: How play motivates and enhances children's cognitive and social-emotional growth*. New York: Oxford University Press.

13. Lillard, A. S., Lerner, M. D., Hopkins, E. J., Dore, R. A., Smith, E. D., & Palmquist, C. M. (2013). The impact of pretend play on children's development: A review of the evidence. *Psychological Bulletin*, *139*(1), 1–34.

14. Bond, B. J., & Calvert, S. L. (2014). A model and measure of US parents' perceptions of young children's parasocial relationships. *Journal of Children and Media*, *8*(3), 286–304.

15. Calvert, S. L., Strong, B. L., Jacobs, E. L., & Conger, E. E. (2007). Interaction and participation for young Hispanic and Caucasian girls' and boys' learning of media content. *Media Psychology*, *9*(2), 431–445; Lauricella, A. R., Gola, A. A. H., & Calvert, S. L. (2011). Toddlers' learning from socially meaningful video characters. *Media Psychology*, *14*(2), 216–232.

16. Gaskins, S. (2013). Pretend play as culturally constructed activity. In M. Taylor (Ed.), *The Oxford handbook of the development of imagination* (pp. 224–247). New York: Oxford University Press.

17. Including both invisible friends and personified objects, prevalence rates among preschool and school-age children range from 23% (Davis et al., 2011) to 65% (Taylor et al., 2004), with most estimates around 50% (Davis et al., 2013) across Western and Eastern cultures (Moriguchi & Todo, 2018). Davis, P. E., Meins, E., & Fernyhough, C. (2011). Self-knowledge in childhood: Relations with children's imaginary companions and understanding of mind. *British Journal of Developmental*

NOTES *(199)*

Psychology, 29(3), 680–686; Davis, P. E., Meins, E., & Fernyhough, C. (2013). Individual differences in children's private speech: The role of imaginary companions. *Journal of Experimental Child Psychology, 116*(3), 561–571; Taylor, M., Carlson, S. M., Maring, B. L., Gerow, L., & Charley, C. M. (2004). The characteristics and correlates of fantasy in school-age children: imaginary companions, impersonation, and social understanding. *Developmental Psychology, 40*(6), 1173–1187; Moriguchi, Y., & Todo, N. (2018). Prevalence of imaginary companions in children: A meta-analysis. *Merrill-Palmer Quarterly, 64*(4), 459–482; Lin, Q., Zhou, N., & Fu, H. (2020). Prevalence of imaginary companions among Chinese children aged 4 to 6 years. *Social Behavior and Personality: An International Journal, 48*(3), 1–11.

18. Taylor, M., & Carlson, S. M. (1997). The relation between individual differences in fantasy and theory of mind. *Child Development, 68*(3), 436–455.

19. Trionfi, G., & Reese, E. (2009). A good story: Children with imaginary companions create richer narratives. *Child Development, 80*(4), 1301–1313.

20. Myftari, E. (2010). *Imaginary companions among Māori tamariki.* Unpublished honors thesis, University of Otago, Psychology Department.

21. Taylor, M. (1999). *Imaginary companions and the children who create them.* New York: Oxford University Press; Trionfi, G., & Reese, E. (2009). A good story: Children with imaginary companions create richer narratives. *Child Development, 80*(4), 1301–1313.

22. Pearson, D., Burrow, A., Fitzgerald, C., Green, K., Lee, G., & Wise, N. (2001). Auditory hallucinations in normal child populations. *Personality and Individual Differences, 31*, 401–407; Carlson, S. M., & Taylor, M. (2005). Imaginary companions and impersonated characters: Sex differences in children's fantasy play. *Merrill-Palmer Quarterly Journal of Developmental Psychology, 51*(1), 93–118; Gleason, T. R., & Hohmann, L. M. (2006). Concepts of real and imaginary friendships in early childhood. *Social Development, 15*(1), 128–144.

23. Davis, P. E., Simon, H., Meins, E., & Robins, D. L. (2018). Imaginary companions in children with autism spectrum disorder. *Journal of Autism and Developmental Disorders, 48*(8), 2790–2799.

24. McAnally, H. M., Forsyth, B. J., Taylor, M., & Reese, E. (2021). Imaginary companions in childhood: What can prospective longitudinal research tell us about their fate by adolescence? *The Journal of Creative Behavior, 55*(1), 276–283.

25. Taylor, M. (1999). *Imaginary companions and the children who create them.* New York: Oxford University Press.

26. Gleason, T. R. (2013). Imaginary relationships. In M. Taylor's (Ed.), *The Oxford handbook of the development of imagination* (pp. 251–271). New York: Oxford University Press.

27. Gimenez-Dasi, M., Pons, F., & Bender, P. (2016). Imaginary companions, theory of mind and emotion understanding in young children. *European Early Childhood Education Research Journal, 24*(2), 186–197; Trionfi, G., & Reese, E. (2009). A good story: Children with imaginary companions create richer narratives. *Child Development, 80*(4), 1301–1313.

28. Hoff, E. V. (2005). Imaginary companions, creativity, and self-image in middle childhood. *Creativity Research Journal, 17*(2–3), 167–180; Roby, A. C., & Kidd, E. (2008). The referential communication skills of children with imaginary companions. *Developmental Science, 11*(4), 531–540; Taylor, M., & Carlson, S. (1997). The relation between individual differences in fantasy and theory of mind. *Child Development, 68*(3), 436–455. But see a failure to replicate: Davis, P.

E., Meins, E., & Fernyhough, C. (2011). Self-knowledge in childhood: Relations with children's imaginary companions and understanding of mind. *British Journal of Developmental Psychology*, *29*(3), 680–686.

29. Davis, P. E., Meins, E., & Fernyhough, C. (2014). Children with imaginary companions focus on mental characteristics when describing their real-life friends. *Infant and Child Development*, *23*(6), 622–633.

30. Gleason, T. R. (2013). Imaginary relationships. In M. Taylor's (Ed.), *The Oxford handbook of the development of imagination* (pp. 251–271). New York: Oxford University Press; Taylor, M., Hulette, A. C., & Dishion, T. (2010). Longitudinal outcomes of young high-risk adolescents with imaginary companions. *Developmental Psychology*, *46*(6), 1632–1636.

31. Taylor, M. (1999). *Imaginary companions and the children who create them.* New York: Oxford University Press; Aguiar, N. R., Mottweilier, C. M., Taylor, M., & Fisher, P. A. (2017). The imaginary companions created by children who have lived in foster care. *Imagination, Cognition and Personality*, *36*(4), 340–355.

32. Root-Bernstein, M. (2014). *Inventing imaginary worlds: From childhood play to adult creativity across the arts and sciences.* Lanham, MD: Rowman & Littlefield; Gleason, T. R. (2013). Imaginary relationships. In M. Taylor's (Ed.), *The Oxford handbook of the development of imagination* (pp. 251–271). New York: Oxford University Press.

33. Gleason, T. R., Theran, S. A., & Newberg, E. M. (2017). Parasocial interactions and relationships in early adolescence. *Frontiers in Psychology*, *8*, Article 255; Gleason, T. R., Theran, S. A., & Newberg, E. M. (2020). Connections between adolescents' parasocial interactions and recollections of childhood imaginative activities. *Imagination, Cognition and Personality*, *39*(3), 241–260. Note, however, that Gleason et al. (2020) argues that parasocial relationships primarily play a social function and are not related to earlier imaginative play. Tolbert, A. N., & Drogos, K. L. (2019). Tweens' wishful identification and parasocial relationships with YouTubers. *Frontiers in Psychology*, *10*, Article 2781.

34. Dubourg, E., & Baumard, N. (2022). Why imaginary worlds? The psychological foundations and cultural evolution of fictions with imaginary worlds. *Behavioral and Brain Sciences*, *45*, e276; Beck, S. R., & Harris, P. L. (2022). The development of the imagination and imaginary worlds. *Behavioral and Brain Sciences*, *45*, e278.

35. Seiffge-Krenke, I. (1997). Imaginary companions in adolescence: Sign of a deficient or positive development? *Journal of Adolescence*, *20*(2), 137–154.

36. Root-Bernstein, M. (2014). *Inventing imaginary worlds: From childhood play to adult creativity across the arts and sciences.* Lanham, MD: Rowman & Littlefield; Taylor, M., Mottweiler, C. M., Aguiar, N. R., Naylor, E. R., & Levernier, J. G. (2020). Paracosms: The imaginary worlds of middle childhood. *Child Development*, *91*(1), e164–e178.

37. Root-Bernstein, M. (2014). *Inventing imaginary worlds: From childhood play to adult creativity across the arts and sciences.* Lanham, MD: Rowman & Littlefield.

38. Taylor, M., Mottweiler, C. M., Aguiar, N. R., Naylor, E. R., & Levernier, J. G. (2020). Paracosms: The imaginary worlds of middle childhood. *Child Development*, *91*(1), e164–e178. The prevalence of children with paracosms was 17% in two samples.

39. M. Taylor, personal communication via telephone, April 28, 2020.

40. Taylor, M., Mottweiler, C. M., Naylor, E. R., & Levernier, J. G. (2015). Imaginary worlds in middle childhood: A qualitative study of two pairs of coordinated paracosms. *Creativity Research Journal*, *27*(2), 167–174.

41. Gleason, T. R., Theran, S. A., & Newberg, E. M. (2020). Connections between adolescents' parasocial interactions and recollections of childhood

imaginative activities. *Imagination, Cognition and Personality*, *39*(3), 241–260; Taylor, M., Mottweiler, C. M., Aguiar, N. R., Naylor, E. R., & Levernier, J. G. (2020). Paracosms: The imaginary worlds of middle childhood. *Child Development*, *91*(1), e164–e178.

42. Root-Bernstein, M., & Root-Bernstein, R. (2006). Imaginary worldplay in childhood and maturity and its impact on adult creativity. *Creativity Research Journal*, *18*(4), 405–425.

43. Taylor, M., Mottweiler, C. M., Aguiar, N. R., Naylor, E. R., & Levernier, J. G. (2020). Paracosms: The imaginary worlds of middle childhood. *Child Development*, *91*(1), e164–e178.

44. Seiffge-Krenke, I. (1997). Imaginary companions in adolescence: Sign of a deficient or positive development? *Journal of Adolescence*, *20*(2), 137–154.

45. Gleason, T. R., Theran, S. A., & Newberg, E. M. (2020). Connections between adolescents' parasocial interactions and recollections of childhood imaginative activities. *Imagination, Cognition and Personality*, *39*(3), 241–260; Derrick, J. L., Gabriel, S., & Tippin, B. (2008). Parasocial relationships and self-discrepancies: Faux relationships have benefits for low self-esteem individuals. *Personal Relationships*, *15*(2), 261–280.

46. Root-Bernstein, M. (2014). *Inventing imaginary worlds: From childhood play to adult creativity across the arts and sciences*. Lanham, MD: Rowman and Littlefield.

47. Barnes, J. L. (2015, March 3). Imaginary friends and real-world consequences: Parasocial relationships. *YouTube.com*. Retrieved on November 29, 2023, from https://www.youtube.com/watch?v=22yoaiLYb7M&t=122s

48. Derrick, J. L., Gabriel, S., & Tippin, B. (2008). Parasocial relationships and self-discrepancies: Faux relationships have benefits for low self-esteem individuals. *Personal Relationships*, *15*(2), 261–280; Derrick, J. L., Keefer, L. A., & Troisi, J. D. (2019). Who needs friends? Personality as a predictor of social surrogate use. *Personality and Individual Differences*, *138*, 349–354.

49. deGroot, J. M., & Leith, A. P. (2018). RIP Kutner: Parasocial grief following the death of a television character. *OMEGA-Journal of Death and Dying*, *77*(3), 199–216.

50. Cole, T., & Leets, L. (1999). Attachment styles and intimate television viewing: Insecurely forming relationships in a parasocial way. *Journal of Social and Personal Relationships*, *16*, 495–511.

51. Cohen, E. L., & Hoffner, C. (2016). Finding meaning in a celebrity's death: The relationship between parasocial attachment, grief, and sharing educational health information related to Robin Williams on social network sites. *Computers in Human Behavior*, *65*, 643–650.

52. Taylor, L. D. (2015). Investigating fans of fictional texts: Fan identity salience, empathy, and transportation. *Psychology of Popular Media Culture*, *4*(2), 172–187.

53. See Taylor, L. D., & Gil-Lopez, T. (2020). Personality traits and fans' motives for attention to fictional narratives. In R. A. Dunn (Ed.), *Multidisciplinary perspectives on media fandom* (pp. 20–36). Hershey, PA: IGI Global.

54. Kornhaber, S. (2018, December 27). The disturbing truth about Kevin Spacey's "Let Me Be Frank" video. *TheAtlantic.com*. Retrieved on November 29, 2023, from https://www.theatlantic.com/entertainment/archive/2018/12/kevin-spaceys-let-me-be-frank-video-meaning/579034/

55. Zacks, J. M. (2015). *Flicker: Your brain on movies*. New York: Oxford University Press.

56. Taylor, M., Hodges, S. D., & Kohányi, A. (2003). The illusion of independent agency: Do adult fiction writers experience their characters as having minds of their own? *Imagination, Cognition and Personality, 22*(4), 361–380.

57. Rehm, D. (2016, December 29). J. K. Rowling. *DianeRehm.org*. Retrieved on November 29, 2023, from https://dianerehm.org/shows/2016-12-29/j-k-rowling-rebroadcast

58. Root-Bernstein, M., & Root-Bernstein, R. (2006). Imaginary worldplay in childhood and maturity and its impact on adult creativity. *Creativity Research Journal, 18*(4), 405–425.

59. Dubourg, E., & Baumard, N. (2022). Why imaginary worlds? The psychological foundations and cultural evolution of fictions with imaginary worlds. *Behavioral and Brain Sciences, 45*, e276.

60. Routledge, C., Wildschut, T., Sedikides, C., & Juhl, J. (2013). Nostalgia as a resource for psychological health and well-being. *Social and Personality Psychology Compass, 7*(11), 808–818; Kelley, N. J., Davis, W. E., Dang, J., Liu, L., Wildschut, T., & Sedikides, C. (2022). Nostalgia confers psychological wellbeing by increasing authenticity. *Journal of Experimental Social Psychology, 102*, 104379.

61. Stein, N. (2011, November 1). Are rereadings better readings? *TheNewYorker. com*. Retrieved on November 29, 2023, from https://www.newyorker.com/books/page-turner/are-rereadings-better-readings

62. Wendell, S. (2020, May 20). For a lot of book lovers, rereading old favorites is the only reading they can manage at the moment. *WashingtonPost.com*. Retrieved on November 29, 2023, from https://www.washingtonpost.com/entertainment/books/for-a-lot-of-book-lovers-rereading-old-favorites-is-the-only-reading-they-can-manage-at-the-moment/2020/05/01/19c3cd4c-8bbe-11ea-ac8a-fe9b8088e101_story.html

63. Root-Bernstein, M. (2014). *Inventing imaginary worlds: From childhood play to adult creativity across the arts and sciences*. Lanham, MD: Rowman and Littlefield.

64. M. Taylor, personal communication by telephone, April 28, 2020.

65. Anderson, D. R., & Davidson, M. C. (2019). Receptive versus interactive video screens: A role for the brain's default mode network in learning from media. *Computers in Human Behavior, 99*, 168–180.

66. Boyd, B. (2010). *On the origin of stories: Evolution, cognition, and fiction* (p. 350). Cambridge, MA: Harvard University Press.

67. Davis, P. E., Webster, L. A., Fernyhough, C., Ralston, K., Kola-Palmer, S., & Stain, H. J. (2019). Adult report of childhood imaginary companions and adversity relates to concurrent prodromal psychosis symptoms. *Psychiatry Research, 271*, 150–152. See also Merckelbach, H., Otgaar, H., & Lynn, S. J. (2022). Empirical research on fantasy proneness and its correlates 2000–2018: A meta-analysis. *Psychology of Consciousness: Theory, Research, and Practice, 9*(1), 2.

68. Linscott, R. J., & Van Os, J. (2013). An updated and conservative systematic review and meta-analysis of epidemiological evidence on psychotic experiences in children and adults: On the pathway from proneness to persistence to dimensional expression across mental disorders. *Psychological Medicine, 43*(6), 1133–1149.

69. C. Fernyhough, personal communication via email, May 15, 2020.

70. Root-Bernstein, M. (2014). *Inventing imaginary worlds: From childhood play to adult creativity across the arts and sciences*. Lanham, MD: Rowman and Littlefield.

71. The risk for prodromal symptoms turning into psychosis is 4–5 times greater for those who find the voices distressing (Hanssen et al., 2003): Hanssen, M. S., Bijl, R. V., Vollebergh, W., & van Os, J. (2003). Self-reported psychotic experiences in the

NOTES *(203)*

general population: A valid screening tool for DSM-III-R psychotic disorders? *Acta Psychiatrica Scandinavica*, *107*(5), 369–377; see also Alderson-Day, B., Mitrenga, K., Wilkinson, S., McCarthy-Jones, S., & Fernyhough, C. (2018). The varieties of inner speech questionnaire–revised (VISQ-R): replicating and refining links between inner speech and psychopathology. *Consciousness and Cognition*, *65*, 48–58.

72. Alderson-Day, B., Bernini, M., & Fernyhough, C. (2017). Uncharted features and dynamics of reading: Voices, characters, and crossing of experiences. *Consciousness and Cognition*, *49*, 98–109.

73. A related phenomenon called "bleed" in table-top and computerized role-playing games is a weakening of emotional boundaries between the self and the character one is role-playing (Waern, 2015). Waern, A. (2015). I'm in love with someone that doesn't exist! Bleed in the context of a computer game. In J. Enevold & E. MacCallum-Stewart (Eds.), *Game love: Essays on play and affection*, (pp. 25–45). Jefferson, NC: McFarland Books.

74. Fullwood, C., James, B. M., & Chen-Wilson, C. H. (2016). Self-concept clarity and online self-presentation in adolescents. *Cyberpsychology, Behavior, and Social Networking*, *19*(12), 716–720; Fullwood, C., Wesson, C., Chen-Wilson, J., Keep, M., Asbury, T., & Wilson, L. (2020). If the mask fits: Psychological correlates with online self-presentation experimentation in adults. *Cyberpsychology, Behavior, and Social Networking*, *23*(11), 737–742.

75. de Vaate, N. A. B., Veldhuis, J., & Konijn, E. A. (2020). How online self-presentation affects well-being and body image: A systematic review. *Telematics and Informatics*, *47*, 101316.

76. Zimmerman, C. A., & Walker, W. R. (2022). Positivity biases. In R. F. Puhl (Ed.), *Cognitive illusions: Intriguing phenomena in thinking, judgment, and memory* (pp. 341–356). Abingdon, Oxfordshire UK: Routledge.

77. Hayne, H., Gross, J., McNamee, S., Fitzgibbon, O., & Tustin, K. (2011). Episodic memory and episodic foresight in 3-and 5-year-old children. *Cognitive Development*, *26*(4), 343–355.

78. Thomsen, D. K., Lind, M., & Pillemer, D. B. (2017). Examining relations between aging, life story chapters, and well-being. *Applied Cognitive Psychology*, *31*(2), 207–215.

79. Hazan, H., Reese, E. J., & Linscott, R. J. (2019). Narrative self and high risk for schizophrenia: remembering the past and imagining the future. *Memory*, *27*(9), 1214–1223. However, the students with schizotypy did tell stories of past turning points featuring less agency compared to those without schizotypy, indicating that they felt they had less control over life events.

80. Chandler, M., & Proulx, T. (2006). Changing selves in changing worlds: Youth suicide on the fault-lines of colliding cultures. *Archives of Suicide Research*, *10*(2), 125–140.

81. Jing, H. G., Madore, K. P., & Schacter, D. L. (2016). Worrying about the future: An episodic specificity induction impacts problem solving, reappraisal, and well-being. *Journal of Experimental Psychology: General*, *145*(4), 402–418. Madore, K. P., Szpunar, K. K., Addis, D. R., & Schacter, D. L. (2016). Episodic specificity induction impacts activity in a core brain network during construction of imagined future experiences. *Proceedings of the National Academy of Sciences*, *113*(38), 10696–10701.

82. Byrne, R. M. (2016). Counterfactual thought. *Annual Review of Psychology*, *67*(1), 135–157.

83. Van Hoeck, N., Watson, P. D., & Barbey, A. K. (2015). Cognitive neuroscience of human counterfactual reasoning. *Frontiers in Human Neuroscience*, *9*, Article 420.

84. Harris, P. L. (2000). *The work of the imagination*. Oxford: Blackwell. For another view, see Weisberg, D. S., & Gopnik, A. (2013). Pretense, counterfactuals, and Bayesian causal models: Why what is not real really matters. *Cognitive Science*, *37*(7), 1368–1381.

85. Beck, S. R., & Riggs, K. J. (2013). Counterfactuals and reality. In M. Taylor's (Ed.), *The Oxford handbook of the development of imagination* (pp. 325–341). New York: Oxford University Press.

86. Rafetseder, E., Schwitalla, M., & Perner, J. (2013). Counterfactual reasoning: From childhood to adulthood. *Journal of Experimental Child Psychology*, *114*(3), 389–404; Rafetseder, E., & Perner, J. (2014). Counterfactual reasoning: Sharpening conceptual distinctions in developmental studies. *Child Development Perspectives*, *8*(1), 54–58; Beck, S. R., & Riggs, K. J. (2014). Developing thoughts about what might have been. *Child Development Perspectives*, *8*(3), 175–179.

87. Nyhout, A., & Ganea, P. A. (2019). The development of the counterfactual imagination. *Child Development Perspectives*, *13*(4), 254–259; Payir, A., Heiphetz, L., Harris, P. L., & Corriveau, K. H. (2022). What could have been done? Counterfactual alternatives to negative outcomes generated by religious and secular children. *Developmental Psychology*, *58*, 364–391.

88. Maitner, A. T., & Summerville, A. (2022). "What was meant to be" versus "what might have been": Effects of culture and control on counterfactual thinking. *Journal of Personality and Social Psychology*, *123*(1), 1–27; Payir, A., Heiphetz, L., Harris, P. L., & Corriveau, K. H. (2022). What could have been done? Counterfactual alternatives to negative outcomes generated by religious and secular children. *Developmental Psychology*, *58*, 364–391.

89. Byrne, R. M. (2017). Counterfactual thinking: From logic to morality. *Current Directions in Psychological Science*, *26*(4), 314–322.

90. Rye, M. S., Cahoon, M. B., Ali, R. S., & Daftary, T. (2008). Development and validation of the counterfactual thinking for negative events scale. *Journal of Personality Assessment*, *90*(3), 261–269; Bacon, A. M., Walsh, C. R., & Martin, L. (2013). Fantasy proneness and counterfactual thinking. *Personality and Individual Differences*, *54*(4), 469–473.

91. Kasimatis, M., & Wells, G. L. (2014). Individual differences in counterfactual thinking. In N. J. Roese & J. M. Olson (Eds.), *What might have been: The social psychology of counterfactual thinking* (pp. 93–114). London: Psychology Press.

92. Begeer, S., De Rosnay, M., Lunenburg, P., Stegge, H., & Terwogt, M. M. (2014). Understanding of emotions based on counterfactual reasoning in children with autism spectrum disorders. *Autism*, *18*(3), 301–310.

93. Kasimatis, M., & Wells, G. L. (2014). Individual differences in counterfactual thinking. In N. J. Roese & J. M. Olson (Eds.), *What might have been: The social psychology of counterfactual thinking* (pp. 93–114). London: Psychology Press. Note that there are also weak links between counterfactual thinking and rumination, but in part because some of the items in these scales explicitly tap rumination, such as *I cannot stop thinking about how I wish things would have turned out*.

94. Rye, M. S., Cahoon, M. B., Ali, R. S., & Daftary, T. (2008). Development and validation of the counterfactual thinking for negative events scale. *Journal of Personality Assessment*, *90*(3), 261–269.

95. Reese, E., & Robertson, S. J. (2023). *Individual differences in the development of counterfactual thinking*. Manuscript in preparation.

NOTES *(205)*

96. Van Hoeck, N., Watson, P. D., & Barbey, A. K. (2015). Cognitive neuroscience of human counterfactual reasoning. *Frontiers in Human Neuroscience*, *9*, Article 420.
97. Koo, M., Algoe, S. B., Wilson, T. D., & Gilbert, D. T. (2008). It's a wonderful life: Mentally subtracting positive events improves people's affective states, contrary to their affective forecasts. *Journal of Personality and Social Psychology*, *95*(5), 1217.
98. Heintzelman, S. J., Christopher, J., Trent, J., & King, L. A. (2013). Counterfactual thinking about one's birth enhances well-being judgments. *The Journal of Positive Psychology*, *8*(1), 44–49.
99. Pearson, J., Naselaris, T., Holmes, E. A., & Kosslyn, S. M. (2015). Mental imagery: Functional mechanisms and clinical applications. *Trends in Cognitive Sciences*, *19*(10), 590–602; Gamble, B., Tippett, L. J., Moreau, D., & Addis, D. R. (2021). The futures we want: How goal-directed imagination relates to mental health. *Clinical Psychological Science*, *9*(4), 732–751.

CHAPTER 8

1. The following list is by no means exhaustive, but it offers highlights from literary, media, and psychological scholarship on the way different media can affect us in similar or different ways: Bruner, J. S. (1986). *Actual minds, possible worlds*. Cambridge, MA: Harvard University Press; Green, M. C., Kass, S., Carrey, J., Herzig, B., Feeney, R., & Sabini, J. (2008). Transportation across media: Repeated exposure to print and film. *Media Psychology*, *11*(4), 512–539; Hakemulder, J. (2000). The moral laboratory: Experiments examining the effects of reading literature on social perception and moral self-concept. Philadelphia, PA: John Benjamins; McLuhan, M. (1964). *Understanding media*. London: Routledge and Kegan Paul; Mar, R. A. (2018). Evaluating whether stories can promote social cognition: Introducing the Social Processes and Content Entrained by Narrative (SPaCEN) framework. *Discourse Processes*, *55*(5–6), 454–479; Gerrig, R. J., & Prentice, D. A. (1996). Notes on audience response. In D. Bordwell & N. Carroll (Eds.), *Post-theory: Reconstructing film studies* (pp. 388–403). Madison: The University of Wisconsin Press; Oatley, K. (2016). Fiction: Simulation of social worlds. *Trends in Cognitive Sciences*, *20*(8), 618–628; Thoss, J., Ensslin, A., & Ciccoricco, D. (2018). Narrative media: The impossibilities of digital storytelling. *Poetics Today*, *39*(3), 623–643; Valkenburg, P. M., Peter, J., & Walther, J. B. (2016). Media effects: Theory and research. *Annual Review of Psychology*, *67*, 315–338; Spacks, P. M. (2011). *On rereading*. Cambridge, MA: The Belknap Press of Harvard University Press.
2. Furedi, F. (2015). *Power of reading: From Socrates to Twitter*. London: Bloomsbury.
3. Si'ilata, R. K., Jacobs, M. M., Gaffney, J. S., Aseta, M., & Hansell, K. (2023). Making space for young children's embodied cultural literacies and heritage languages with dual language books. *The Reading Teacher*, *77*(1), 24–36.
4. Oatley, K. (2016). Fiction: Simulation of social worlds. *Trends in Cognitive Sciences*, *20*(8), 618–628. But see Mar (2018) and Black and Barnes (2018) that it is the social content and processes of story that matter most: Barnes, J. L. (2018). Imaginary engagement, real-world effects: Fiction, emotion, and social cognition. *Review of General Psychology*, *22*(2), 125–134; Mar, R. A. (2018). Evaluating whether stories can promote social cognition: Introducing the Social Processes and Content Entrained by Narrative (SPaCEN) framework. *Discourse Processes*, *55*(5–6), 454–479.

5. Hakemulder, J. (2000). *The moral laboratory: Experiments examining the effects of reading literature on social perception and moral self-concept*. Philadelphia, PA: John Benjamins; Willems, R. M., & Jacobs, A. M. (2016). Caring about Dostoyevsky: The untapped potential of studying literature. *Trends in Cognitive Sciences, 20*(4), 243–245l Oatley, K. (2016). Fiction: Simulation of social worlds. *Trends in Cognitive Sciences, 20*(8), 618–628.

6. Yeshurun, Y., Nguyen, M., & Hasson, U. (2021). The default mode network: Where the idiosyncratic self meets the shared social world. *Nature Reviews Neuroscience, 22*(3), 181–192.

7. Anderson, D. R., & Davidson, M. C. (2019). Receptive versus interactive video screens: A role for the brain's default mode network in learning from media. *Computers in Human Behavior, 99*, 168–180.

8. Yeshurun et al. (2021, p. 181) proposed that the default network is "an active and dynamic 'sense-making' network that integrates incoming extrinsic information with prior intrinsic information over long timescales to form rich, context-dependent, idiosyncratic models of the situation as it unfolds over time." Yeshurun, Y., Nguyen, M., & Hasson, U. (2021). The default mode network: where the idiosyncratic self meets the shared social world. *Nature Reviews Neuroscience, 22*(3), 181–192.

9. Hutton, J. S., Phelan, K., Horowitz-Kraus, T., et al. (2017). Shared reading quality and brain activation during story listening in preschool-age children. *The Journal of Pediatrics, 191*, 204–211; Hutton, J. S., Dudley, J., Horowitz-Kraus, T., DeWitt, T., & Holland, S. K. (2019). Functional connectivity of attention, visual, and language networks during audio, illustrated, and animated stories in preschool-age children. *Brain Connectivity, 9*(7), 580–592; Hutton, J. S., Dudley, J., Horowitz-Kraus, T., DeWitt, T., & Holland, S. K. (2020). Differences in functional brain network connectivity during stories presented in audio, illustrated, and animated format in preschool-age children. *Brain Imaging and Behavior, 14*, 130–141.

10. Li, H., Liu, T., Woolley, J. D., & Zhang, P. (2019). Reality status judgments of real and fantastical events in children's prefrontal cortex: An fNIRS study. *Frontiers in Human Neuroscience, 13*, 444.

11. Goldstein, T. R., & Alperson, K. (2020). Dancing bears and talking toasters: A content analysis of supernatural elements in children's media. *Psychology of Popular Media, 9*(2), 214–223.

12. Hutton, J. S., Dudley, J., Horowitz-Kraus, T., DeWitt, T., & Holland, S. K. (2020). Differences in functional brain network connectivity during stories presented in audio, illustrated, and animated format in preschool-age children. *Brain Imaging and Behavior, 14*, 130–141.

13. Mar, R. A., Tackett, J. L., & Moore, C. (2010). Exposure to media and theory-of-mind development in preschoolers. *Cognitive Development, 25*(1), 69–78.

14. Turner, R., & Felisberti, F. M. (2018). Relationships between fiction media, genre, and empathic abilities. *Scientific Study of Literature, 8*(2), 261–292; Pigden, A., McCall, E., & Reese, E. (2023). *The pen is mightier than the sword: The role of fiction reading versus watching for empathy and aggression*. Manuscript under review.

15. Actors themselves are more skilled at theory of mind (Goldstein et al., 2009) and can report higher levels of empathy (Nettle, 2006) compared to matched controls. Goldstein, T., Wu, K., and Winner, E. (2009). Actors are skilled in theory of mind but not empathy. *Imagination, Cognition and Personality, 29*, 115–133; Nettle, D. (2006). Psychological profiles of professional actors. *Personality and Individual Differences, 40*(2), 375–383.

16. Orkibi, H., Keisari, S., Sajnani, N. L., & de Witte, M. (2023). Effectiveness of drama-based therapies on mental health outcomes: A systematic review and meta-analysis of controlled studies. *Psychology of Aesthetics, Creativity, and the Arts*. Advance online publication. https://dx.doi.org/10.1037/aca0000582

17. Thomas, M. (2022, January 19). Easy wins: Better than a warm cup of milk—Read for 6 minutes before bed for good sleep. *The Guardian.com*. Retrieved on November 30, 2023, from https://www.theguardian.com/lifeandstyle/2022/jan/20/easy-wins-better-than-a-warm-cup-of-milk-read-for-six-minutes-before-bed-for-good-sleep

18. D. Smith, personal communication by email, June 20, 2020.

19. Macrae, C. N., & Johnston, L. (1998). Help, I need somebody: Automatic action and inaction. *Social Cognition*, *16*, 400–417.

20. Pigden, A. (2021). *Is the pen mightier than the sword? Testing the effects of fiction on empathy and aggression, and introducing a hybrid model of media effects*. Unpublished PhD thesis, University of Otago, Dunedin, New Zealand. In a follow-up, experimenters were blind to the participant's media condition when they performed the pen-drop task. We were unable to replicate the main effect of media condition, but we did find that those undergraduates who had more aggressive tendencies at the outset became less helpful after either viewing or reading the violent passage, compared to those who didn't consume any violent media.

21. Pianzola, F. (2021). *Digital social reading*. Cambridge, MA: MIT Press.

22. Kuzmicova, A. (2016). Audiobooks and print narrative: Similarities in text experience. In J. Mildorf & T. Kinzel (Eds.), *Audionarratology: Interfaces of sound and narrative* (Vol. 52, pp. 217–236). Berlin: Walter de Gruyter.

23. Curcic, D. (2023, June 7). Audiobook statistics. *Wordsrated.com*. Retrieved on November 30, 2023, from https://wordsrated.com/audiobook-statistics/#:~:text=Audiobook%20revenue%20accounted%20for%20around,10%25%20for%20the%20first%20time.

24. National Endowment for the Arts. (2020). *How do we read? Let's count the ways: Comparing digital, audio, and print-only readers*. Washington, DC: National Endowment for the Arts.

25. Eftimova, S., Damianova, I., Atanasov, H., Mincheva, K., & Nikolova, B. (2022). The therapeutic function of reading: Audiobooks and children in a global pandemic. *Proceedings of the 16th International Technology, Education, and Development Conference* (pp. 2416–2021). Seville, Spain: INTED Conference.

26. Kozlowski, M. (2017, June 7). *Audiobooks continues double-digit growth*. Goodereader.com. Retrieved on November 30, 2023, from https://goodereader.com/blog/audiobooks/audiobooks-continues-double-digit-growth

27. Kuzmicova, A. (2016). Audiobooks and print narrative: Similarities in text experience. In J. Mildorf & T. Kinzel (Eds.), *Audionarratology: Interfaces of sound and narrative* (Vol. 52; pp. 217–236). Berlin: Walter de Gruyter.

28. Esteves, K. J., & Whitten, E. (2011). Assisted reading with digital audiobooks for students with reading disabilities. *Reading Horizons*: A *Journal* of *Literacy* and *Language Arts*, *51* (1), 20–40; Milani, A., Lorusso, M. L., & Molteni, M. (2010). The effects of audiobooks on the psychosocial adjustment of pre-adolescents and adolescents with dyslexia. *Dyslexia*, *16*(1), 87–97.

29. Whittingham, J., Huffman, S., Christensen, R., & McAllister, T. (2013). Use of audiobooks in a school library and positive effects of struggling readers' participation in a library-sponsored audiobook club. *School Library Research*, *16*, 1–18 (pp. 13, 15).

30. Moore, J., & Cahill, M. (2016). Audiobooks: Legitimate "reading" material for adolescents? *School Library Research*, *19*, 1–17; Wolfson, G. (2008). Using audiobooks to meet the needs of adolescent readers. *American Secondary Education*, *36*(20), 105–114.

31. Alsamadani, H. A. (2017). The effect of talking story books on Saudi young EFL learners' reading comprehension. *English Language Teaching*, *10*(5), 204–213; Kartal, G., & Simsek, H. (2017). The effects of audiobooks on EFL students' listening comprehension. *The Reading Matrix: An International Online Journal*, *17*(1), 112–123.

32. Poerio, G. L., & Totterdell, P. (2020). The effect of fiction on the well-being of older adults: A longitudinal RCT intervention study using audiobooks. *Psychosocial Intervention*, *29*(1), 29–38.

33. Varao Sousa, T. L., Carriere, J. S., & Smilek, D. (2013). The way we encounter reading material influences how frequently we mind wander. *Frontiers in Psychology*, *4*, 892.

34. Granados, J., Hopper, M., & He, J. (2018, September). A usability and safety study of bone-conduction headphones during driving while listening to audiobooks. In *Proceedings of the Human Factors and Ergonomics Society Annual Meeting* (Vol. 62, No. 1, pp. 1373–1377). Los Angeles, CA: Sage. Caution: This study used a simulated driving task that was not challenging (following a car on a country road), so it's possible that audiobooks do affect drivers' performance in more difficult situations and in real life.

35. Varao Sousa, T. L., Carriere, J. S., & Smilek, D. (2013). The way we encounter reading material influences how frequently we mind wander. *Frontiers in Psychology*, *4*, 892.

36. Deniz, F., Nunez-Elizalde, A. O., Huth, A. G., & Gallant, J. L. (2019). The representation of semantic information across human cerebral cortex during listening versus reading is invariant to stimulus modality. *Journal of Neuroscience*, *39*(39), 7722–7736.

37. Brayley, C., & Montrose, V. T. (2016). The effects of audiobooks on the behaviour of dogs at a rehoming kennels. *Applied Animal Behaviour Science*, *174*, 111–115.

38. Green, M. C., Kass, S., Carrey, J., Herzig, B., Feeney, R., & Sabini, J. (2008). Transportation across media: Repeated exposure to print and film. *Media Psychology*, *11*(4), 512–539.

39. Spacks, P. M. (2011). *On rereading*. Cambridge, MA: The Belknap Press of Harvard University Press.

40. C. Humphreys, personal communication by email, April 24, 2023.

41. Reuters (2007, November 10). Harry Potter most reread book in Britain: Survey. *Reuters.com*. Retrieved on November 30, 2023, from https://www.reuters.com/article/us-britain-books-idUSL0936765020071109/

42. Spacks, P. M. (2011). *On rereading* (p. 53). Cambridge, MA: The Belknap Press of Harvard University Press.

43. Spacks, P. M. (2011). *On rereading* (p. 70). Cambridge, MA: The Belknap Press of Harvard University Press.

44. Oatley, K. (2016). Imagination, inference, intimacy: The psychology of *Pride and Prejudice*. *Review of General Psychology*, *20*(3), 236–244.

45. Breen, A. V., McLean, K. C., Cairney, K., & McAdams, D. P. (2017). Movies, books, and identity: Exploring the narrative ecology of the self. *Qualitative Psychology*, *4*(3), 243.

NOTES *(209)*

46. Spacks, P. M. (2011). *On rereading* (p. 9). Cambridge, MA: The Belknap Press of Harvard University Press.
47. Mares, M. L. (1998). Children's use of VCRs. *The Annals of the American Academy of Political and Social Science*, *557*(1), 120–131.
48. Anderson, D. R., Bryant, J., Wilder, A., Santomero, A., Williams, M., & Crawley, A. M. (2000). Researching Blue's Clues: Viewing behavior and impact. *Media Psychology*, *2*(2), 179–194.
49. Flack, Z. M., Field, A. P., & Horst, J. S. (2018). The effects of shared storybook reading on word learning: A meta-analysis. *Developmental Psychology*, *54*(7), 1334.
50. Fletcher, K. L., & Reese, E. (2005). Picture book reading with young children: A conceptual framework. *Developmental Review*, *25*(1), 64–103; Reese, E. (2019). Learning language from books. In J. S. Horst & J. von Koss Torkildsen (Eds.), *International handbook of language acquisition* (pp. 462–484). New York: Routledge/Taylor & Francis Group.
51. Crawley, A. M., Anderson, D. R., Wilder, A., Williams, M., & Santomero, A. (1999). Effects of repeated exposures to a single episode of the television program Blue's Clues on the viewing behaviors and comprehension of preschool children. *Journal of Educational Psychology*, *91*(4), 630–637; Anderson, D. R., Bryant, J., Wilder, A., Santomero, A., Williams, M., & Crawley, A. M. (2000). Researching Blue's Clues: Viewing behavior and impact. *Media Psychology*, *2*(2), 179–194.
52. Mares, M. L. (1998). Children's use of VCRs. *The Annals of the American Academy of Political and Social Science*, *557*(1), 120–131.
53. Faust, M. A., & Glenzer, N. (2000). "I could read those parts over and over": Eighth graders rereading to enhance enjoyment and learning with literature. *Journal of Adolescent & Adult Literacy*, *44*(3), 234–239; Mares, M. L. (2006). Repetition increases children's comprehension of television content—Up to a point. *Communication Monographs*, *73*(2), 216–241.
54. Crowder, R. G. (1976/2015). *Principles of learning and memory*. New York: Psychology Press.
55. Hill, K. (2022, December 10). Prof Catherine Fowler: The greatest film you've never seen. *Rnz.co.nz*. Retrieved on November 30, 2023, from https://www.rnz.co.nz/national/programmes/saturday/audio/2018870677/prof-catherine-fow ler-the-greatest-film-you-ve-never-seen
56. Ministero, L. M., Green, M. C., Gabriel, S., & Valenti, J. (2022). Back where I belong: Rereading as a risk-free pathway to social connection. *Psychology of Aesthetics, Creativity, and the Arts*, *16*(1), 97–109.
57. Milk, C. (2015, March). How virtual reality can create the ultimate empathy machine. *Ted.com*. Retrieved on November 30, 2023, from https://www.ted.com/talks/chris_milk_how_virtual_reality_can_create_the_ultimate_empathy_mach ine/discussion
58. Herrera, F., Bailenson, J., Weisz, E., Ogle, E., & Zaki, J. (2018). Building long-term empathy: A large-scale comparison of traditional and virtual reality perspective-taking. *PloS One*, *13*(10), e0204494.
59. Pianzola, F., Bálint, K., & Weller, J. (2019). Virtual reality as a tool for promoting reading via enhanced narrative absorption and empathy. *Scientific Study of Literature*, *9*(2), 163–194.
60. Isberner, M. B., Richter, T., Schreiner, C., Eisenbach, Y., Sommer, C., & Appel, M. (2019). Empowering stories: Transportation into narratives with strong protagonists increases self-related control beliefs. *Discourse Processes*, *56*(8), 575–598.

61. This experiment used the self-report scale Vividness of Visual Imagery Questionnaire (VVIQ), but see Suggate and Lenhard (2022) for a critical view of these self-report tests in comparison to more objective measures of visual imagery, such as their Imagery Comparison Test (ICT). Suggate, S., & Lenhard, W. (2022). Mental imagery skill predicts adults' reading performance. *Learning and Instruction*, *80*, 101633.
62. Green, M. C., & Brock, T. C. (2003). In the mind's eye: Transportation-imagery model of narrative persuasion. In M. C. Green, J. J. Strange, & T. C. Brock (Eds.), *Narrative impact: Social and cognitive foundations* (pp. 315–341). New York: Psychology Press.
63. Launay, J., Pearce, E., Wlodarski, R., van Duijn, M., Carney, J., & Dunbar, R. I. (2015). Higher-order mentalising and executive functioning. *Personality and Individual Differences*, *86*, 6–14.
64. Zeman, A., Milton, F., Della Sala, S., et al. (2020). Phantasia—the psychological significance of lifelong visual imagery vividness extremes. *Cortex*, *130*, 426–440. This study relied on a large volunteer sample of 2,000 participants from around the world in response to Zeman et al.'s (2015) paper that coined the term "aphantasia," so it may have suffered from a self-selection bias of those with extreme mental imagery. Research now needs to be conducted with more representative samples.
65. Zeman, A., Dewar, M., & Della Sala, S. (2015). Lives without imagery—Congenital aphantasia. *Cortex*, *73*, 378–380.
66. Dance, C. J., Jaquiery, M., Eagleman, D. M., Porteous, D., Zeman, A., & Simner, J. (2021). What is the relationship between aphantasia, synaesthesia and autism? *Consciousness and Cognition*, *89*, 103087; Milton, F., Fulford, J., Dance, C., et al. (2021). Behavioral and neural signatures of visual imagery vividness extremes: Aphantasia versus hyperphantasia. *Cerebral Cortex Communications*, *2*(2), 1–15.
67. Pearson, J. (2019). The human imagination: The cognitive neuroscience of visual mental imagery. *Nature Reviews Neuroscience*, *20*(10), 624–634.
68. Rademaker, R. L., & Pearson, J. (2012). Training visual imagery: Improvements of metacognition, but not imagery strength. *Frontiers in Psychology*, *3*, 224; Pianzola, F., Bálint, K., & Weller, J. (2019). Virtual reality as a tool for promoting reading via enhanced narrative absorption and empathy. *Scientific Study of Literature*, *9*(2), 163–194.
69. Suggate, S. P., & Martzog, P. (2020). Screen-time influences children's mental imagery performance. *Developmental Science*, *23*(6), e12978; Suggate, S. P., & Martzog, P. (2022). Preschool screen-media usage predicts mental imagery two years later. *Early Child Development and Care*, *192*(10), 1659–1672.
70. See also Suggate, P. S. (in press). Does it kill the imagination dead? The effect of film versus reading on mental imagery. *Psychology of Aesthetics, Creativity, and the Arts*, advance online publication.
71. Isberner et al. (2019) proposed the other direction of effect—that training children's mental imagery skills via more direct means could help their enjoyment of reading. Most likely, these effects are bidirectional, such that any means of enhancing mental imagery will serve to make reading more enjoyable, which then leads to more reading to further strengthen mental imagery skills. Isberner, M. B., Richter, T., Schreiner, C., Eisenbach, Y., Sommer, C., & Appel, M. (2019). Empowering stories: Transportation into narratives with strong protagonists increases self-related control beliefs. *Discourse Processes*, *56*(8), 575–598.

NOTES *(211)*

72. Girls and women tend to score higher on object imagery tasks in which they are asked to visualize the form, color, or brightness of an image, whereas boys and men score higher on spatial imagery tasks involving mental rotation. But many studies do not find gender differences in mental imagery skills—no doubt because of the huge individual differences. Blazhenkova, O., Becker, M., & Kozhevnikov, M. (2011). Object–spatial imagery and verbal cognitive styles in children and adolescents: Developmental trajectories in relation to ability. *Learning and Individual Differences, 21*(3), 281–287. Zeman, A., Milton, F., Della Sala, S., et al. (2020). Phantasia–the psychological significance of lifelong visual imagery vividness extremes. *Cortex, 130*, 426–440; Campos, A. (2014). Gender differences in imagery. *Personality and Individual Differences, 59*, 107–111.

73. Palermo, L., Piccardi, L., Nori, R., Giusberti, F., & Guariglia, C. (2016). The impact of ageing and gender on visual mental imagery processes: A study of performance on tasks from the Complete Visual Mental Imagery Battery (CVMIB). *Journal of Clinical and Experimental Neuropsychology, 38*(7), 752–763.

74. Addis, D. R., Wong, A. T., & Schacter, D. L. (2008). Age-related changes in the episodic simulation of future events. *Psychological Science, 19*(1), 33–41.

75. Grady, C. L., Protzner, A. B., Kovacevic, N., et al. (2010). A multivariate analysis of age-related differences in default mode and task-positive networks across multiple cognitive domains. *Cerebral Cortex, 20*(6), 1432–1447; Huang, C. C., Hsieh, W. J., Lee, P. L., et al. (2015). Age-related changes in resting-state networks of a large sample size of healthy elderly. *CNS Neuroscience & Therapeutics, 21*(10), 817–825.

76. Verhaeghen, P. (2003). Aging and vocabulary score: A meta-analysis. *Psychology and Aging, 18*(2), 332–339.

77. McCabe, A., Hillier, A., Dasilva, C., Queenan, A., & Tauras, M. (2017). Parental mediation in the improvement of narrative skills of high-functioning individuals with autism spectrum disorder. *Communication Disorders Quarterly, 38*(2), 112–118; Hutchins, T. L., Brien, A. R., & Prelock, P. A. (2023). *Supporting social learning in autism: An autobiographical memory program to promote communication and connection.* Baltimore: Brookes.

78. Pearson, J., Naselaris, T., Holmes, E. A., & Kosslyn, S. M. (2015). Mental imagery: Functional mechanisms and clinical applications. *Trends in Cognitive Sciences, 19*(10), 590–602; Pearson, J. (2019). The human imagination: The cognitive neuroscience of visual mental imagery. *Nature Reviews Neuroscience, 20*(10), 624–634.

79. Manninen, S., Tuominen, L., Dunbar, R. I., et al. (2017). Social laughter triggers endogenous opioid release in humans. *Journal of Neuroscience, 37*(25), 6125–6131; Dunbar, R. I., Teasdale, B., Thompson, J., et al. (2016). Emotional arousal when watching drama increases pain threshold and social bonding. *Royal Society Open Science, 3*(9), 160288.

80. In the REPRINTS study, participants were not randomly assigned to intervention versus control; from a larger pool of elderly volunteers, a subset self-selected into the intervention group. This quasi-experimental design limits strong causal conclusions. Murayama, Y., Ohba, H., Yasunaga, M., et al.(2015). The effect of intergenerational programs on the mental health of elderly adults. *Aging & Mental Health, 19*(4), 306–314; Sakurai, R., Yasunaga, M., Murayama, Y., et al. (2016). Long-term effects of an intergenerational program on functional capacity in older adults: Results from a seven-year follow-up of the REPRINTS study. *Archives of Gerontology and Geriatrics, 64*, 13–20.

81. Cammisuli, D. M., Cipriani, G., Giusti, E. M., & Castelnuovo, G. (2022). Effects of reminiscence therapy on cognition, depression and quality of life in elderly people with Alzheimer's disease: A systematic review of randomized controlled trials. *Journal of Clinical Medicine*, *11*(19), 5752; Harris, C. B., Van Bergen, P., Strutt, P. A., et al. (2022). Teaching elaborative reminiscing to support autobiographical memory and relationships in residential and community aged care services. *Brain Sciences*, *12*(3), 374.

82. Thanks to video artist David Green for finding this quote.

83. Valkenburg, P. M., Peter, J., & Walther, J. B. (2016). Media effects: Theory and research. *Annual Review of Psychology*, *67*, 315–338.

84. Poerio, G. L., & Totterdell, P. (2020). The effect of fiction on the well-being of older adults: A longitudinal RCT intervention study using audiobooks. *Psychosocial Intervention*, *29*(1), 29–38.

85. Csikszentmihalyi, M. (2008). *Flow: The psychology of optimal experience.* New York: Harper Perennial.

EPILOGUE

1. Hill, K. (2019, January 26). Barbara Kingsolver—Unsheltered. *Rnz.co.nz.* Retrieved on November 30, 2023, from https://www.rnz.co.nz/national/program mes/saturday/audio/2018679841/barbara-kingsolver-unsheltered

2. Schneider-Mayerson, M., Gustafson, A., Leiserowitz, A., Goldberg, M. H., Rosenthal, S. A., & Ballew, M. (2023). Environmental literature as persuasion: an experimental test of the effects of reading climate fiction. *Environmental Communication, 17*(1), 35–50.

3. Regenbrecht, H., Park, N., Duncan, S., et al. (2022). Ātea presence—enabling virtual storytelling, presence, and tele-co-presence in an indigenous setting. *IEEE Technology and Society Magazine, 41*(1), 32–42.

4. Adobe (2019, August 3). Explore immersive storytelling with AR artists. *YouTube. com.* Retrieved on November 30, 2023, https://www.youtube.com/watch?v=gi7r x_r9niU

5. Perales, F. J., & Aróstegui, J. L. (2024). The STEAM approach: Implementation and educational, social and economic consequences. *Arts Education Policy Review, 125*(2), 59–67. Incorporating the humanities into medical education is also critical, with a growing body of evidence documenting the benefits for both health professionals and their patients alike (Kaptein et al., 2018). Kaptein, A. A., Hughes, B. M., Murray, M., & Smyth, J. M. (2018). Start making sense: Art informing health psychology. *Health Psychology Open, 5*(1), 2055102918760042. doi:10.1177/2055102918760042.

6. Jeong, S., Kim, H., & Tippins, D. J. (2020). From conceptualization to implementation: STEAM education in Korea. In A. J. Stewart, M. P. Mueller, & D. J. Tippins (Eds.), *Converting STEM into STEAM programs: Methods and examples from and for education* (pp. 241–258). Cham, Switzerland: Springer Nature.

7. Cohen-Mansfield, J., & Golander, H. (2022). Responses and interventions to delusions experienced by community-dwelling older persons with dementia. *Journal of Geriatric Psychiatry and Neurology, 35*(4), 627–635.

8. A longitudinal study of 1,651 older adults (age 55+) found that both early-life and late-life cognitive activity (including reading books, visiting the library, and writing letters) together protected against cognitive decline by 14%, even after

NOTES *(213)*

accounting for other crucial factors like education and neuropathology (Wilson et al., 2013). Wilson, R. S., Boyle, P. A., Yu, L., Barnes, L. L., Schneider, J. A., & Bennett, D. A. (2013). Life-span cognitive activity, neuropathologic burden, and cognitive aging. *Neurology, 81*(4), 314–321.

9. Bluck, S., & Mroz, E. L. (2018). The end: Death as part of the life story. *The International Journal of Reminiscence and Life Review, 5*(1), 6–14.

INDEX

For the benefit of digital users, indexed terms that span two pages (e.g., 52–53) may, on occasion, appear on only one of those pages.

Addis, Donna Rose, 165–66n.18, 167n.33, 167n.35
ADHD. *See* attention-deficit/ hyperactivity disorder
Adler, Jon, 94
adult children, stories in connections with parents of, 145–46
Against the Wall, 10
AI. *See* artificial intelligence
Alcott, Louisa May, 22, 145–46
Alderson-Day, Ben, 118
Altmann, Ulrike, 5–6
American Psychiatric Association, 84
Anderson, Craig, 74–75, 80
Anderson, Daniel, 69, 130
Anderson, L. V., 31–32
anthropomorphism, in children's books, 71–72
aphantasia, 138, 210n.64
Arahanga-Doyle, Hitaua, 15–16
Ardern, Jacinda, 105
Aristotle, 138
artificial intelligence (AI), 144
attention-deficit/hyperactivity disorder (ADHD), 48, 84
audiobooks, 59–60, 130–32
Austen, Jane, 51, 53, 68, 115, 134
Auster, Paul, 121–22
Author Recognition test, 2, 18, 165n.15
autism, 31, 35–36, 38, 110, 122, 144, 170n.21
autofiction, 119

babies and toddlers
default networks of, 38, 40, 47, 107

joint attention of, 35–36, 37
language and brain development, 38–39, 40–42, 46–48
nature and nurture of stories for, 33–37
reading to, 34–35, 36–37, 41–46, 48
real-life stories and, 38–39, 43, 44–45, 67
rereading and rewatching, 134–35
social attention of, 35–36
speech development, 37
story memories of, 33–34
story play, 107–8
TV for, 46–48, 77
visual stories and, 46–48, 77
Baker, Michael, 41
Bandura, Albert, 74
Barnes, Jennifer Lynn, 8, 10, 114
Baron-Cohen, Simon, 2, 31, 35, 99, 158n.6, 164n.3
Baumard, Nicolas, 116
Bavelier, Daphne, 83–84
Beall, Sandra, 13
Beaty, Andrea, 70
Becoming (Obama), 130–31
Bergen, Penny van, 43
Berntsen, Dorthe, 95–96
Black, Jessica, 10
Bluck, Susan, 145–46
Blue's Clues, 134, 135
"Bobo doll" experiments, 74
book clubs, 20–24, 31–32, 41–42, 61, 141
Book Discussion Scheme, 20–21, 22
"Bookworms Versus Nerds" (Mar and Oatley), 2–3

Index

Boorman, Daniel, 10
Boyd, Brian, 117
brain
    development, 38–39, 40–42, 46–48
    neuroscience and, 16–17, 59–60, 81–
        82, 97, 121, 127
    social media and, 100
    stories and, 16–17, 23–24, 30
    teens, 62–64, 65, 100
    video game violence and, 81–82
    visual stories, 76–77
    See also default network
Brock, T. C., 138
Brönte, Branwell, 112, 113–16, 117
Brönte, Charlotte, 112, 113–16
Brooks, Geraldine, 72
Brown, Barbara, 20, 22
Bush Hager, Jenna, 22, 41–42
Bushman, Bradley, 74–75, 80
Butler, Andrew, 79
Byrnes, Will, 23

Call of Duty, 58–59, 80, 81–82, 84
Carlson, Stephanie, 109
Carroll, Jane, 44
Carroll, Lewis, 33
Cat in the Hat, The (Seuss), 33–34
CBT. *See* cognitive behavioral therapy
Chall, Jeanne, 52
Chancer, John, 130–31
Chandler, Michael, 120
Chen, Yan, 65
Choice, The (Eger), 94, 99
Clifford, Amanda, 44
climate fiction, 143–44
cognitive behavioral therapy (CBT), 16
Common Sense Media, 43, 51–52, 73,
        75, 100
Connellan, Jennifer, 35
contamination narratives, 93–94
cosplay, 116
counterfactual thinking, 121–24
COVID-19 pandemic, 15–16, 23, 54–55,
        77, 144–45, 146
Cox Gurdon, Meghan, 129

Daniel Tiger's Neighborhood, 46–47
Das, Shika, 44
Davis, Paige, 117
Davis scale, 29

DeCasper, Anthony, 33–34
default network, 5–6, 206n.8
    autism and, 31, 170n.21
    of babies and toddlers, 38, 40, 47, 107
    counterfactual thinking and, 121
    empathy and theory of mind and, 5–6,
        9, 29–30, 31, 40
    fiction reading and, 5–6, 8, 9, 16–17,
        23–24, 118
    gender and, 23–24, 29–30
    memory and, 16–17, 92
    mental imagery skills and, 138, 139
    PTSD and, 97
    of teens, 63–64
    visual media and, 126
DeLillo, Don, 4
depression, 56, 94–95, 100, 101, 102,
        103, 114–15, 119, 123, 192n.35
Derrick, Jaye, 114
Dillard, Annie, 18
Displaced, The, 136
diversity, in children's books, 70–71
Doctor Seuss, 33–34, 70
DSM-5, 84
Dubourg, Edgar, 116
Dunbar, Robin, 10
Duncan, Lynne, 55
Dunlop, Will, 12
Dunn, Judy, 36
Dutro, Elizabeth, 48
Dynasty Warriors 5, 82
dyslexia, 48, 49, 55, 131

e-books, 54, 55, 59
Edwards, Greg, 61
Eger, Edith, 94, 99
embodied literacies, 125
EMDR. *See* eye movement
        desensitization and reprocessing
        therapy
empathy and theory of mind
    audiobooks and, 132
    from books *versus* TV, 127
    default network and, 5–6, 9, 29–
        30, 31, 40
    defining, 158n.6
    fiction reading and, 2–9, 25–26, 143
    gender in, 29–32
    movies and, 46
    rereading and, 134, 135–36

video games and, 144
visual fiction and, 9–11
VR and, 136
episodic memory, 91–93
Es, Bart van, 98–99
Evaristo, Bernardine, 71
Evil Dead, 83
expressive writing, 11, 13–16, 30–31,
67–68, 98
eye movement desensitization and
reprocessing therapy (EMDR), 16

Facebook, 101–4, 105, 114–15
false memories, 89–91, 93, 97, 104
family stories, 64–67, 98–99
fan fiction, 115
fantasy. *See* imagination and fantasy
Farrant, Brad, 36
Feiler, Bruce, 11–12
Ferguson, Chris, 80
Ferguson's Night Fright, 42
Fernyhough, Charles, 117–18
fictional films, 10–11
fictional stories, dangers of, 69
from books, 70–73
screen time, excessive, 84–87
visual, 73–79, 80–84
fiction reading
by boys, 41
default network and, 5–6, 8, 9, 16–17,
23–24, 118
in empathy and theory of mind, 2–9,
25–26, 143
gender and, 18–20, 22, 23–24, 25–
26, 30
genres, 3–4, 8, 25–26
hallucination and, 118
by men, 18–19, 23–24, 31–32
misinformation from, 72–73,
79, 91, 92
nonfiction reading *versus*, 2–3, 5–
6, 143–44
real-life stories and, 141
stress reduction and, 128–29
by women, 18–20, 25, 30–31
Fivush, Robyn, 43, 98–99
Flanagan, Richard, 125
fMRI. *See* functional magnetic resonance
imaging
Fowler, Catherine, 135

Frattaroli, Joanne, 30–31
Frenda, Steven, 93
functional magnetic resonance imaging
(fMRI), 30, 38–39, 47, 81–82

Galdone, Paul, 44
GAM. *See* General Aggression model
Game of Thrones, 114, 115–16, 129
Ganea, Patricia, 71–72
Garry, Maryanne, 90
Gecko Press, 49
gender, 28, 59–62, 166–67n.29
in book reading for tweens and
teens, 57
in book reading with boys and girls,
41–42, 48–50
default network and, 23–24, 29–30
in empathy and theory of mind, 29–32
fiction reading and, 18–20, 22, 23–24,
25–26, 30
in mental imagery, 139, 211n.72
nonfiction reading and, 18–19, 22
paracosms and, 113
school age children, stories and, 48–49
sex and, 164n.3
social media use and, 101
stereotypes, 70–71, 78, 83–84
in toddler language
development, 40–42
video game violence and, 83
visualization of stories and, 26–29
visual stories and, 24–26
General Aggression model (GAM),
74–75
George, Nina, 1
Gibson, Mel, 115–16
Gilmore Girls, 78–79, 86
Girl, Woman, Other (Evaristo), 71
Gone Home, 10, 141
Goodman, Gail, 91
Goodreads, 23
Gottschall, Jonathan, 24
Grand Theft Auto, 83, 186–87n.66
Green, M. C., 132–33, 138
Green, Shawn, 83–84
Greitemeyer, Tobias, 10, 58, 80, 81, 103
Grose, Jessica, 60
Growing Memories study, 67
Growing Up in New Zealand study,
34–35, 40, 45

Index

Grysman, Azriel, 28

Habermas, Tilmann, 63–64
Haidt, Jonathan, 100
Hall, G. Stanley, 54
hallucinations, 117–18, 119, 140
Hanford, Emily, 52
Hari, Johann, 100
Harry Potter book and film series, 55–56, 111, 114, 116, 133–34
Hazan, Hadar, 119
Headey, Lena, 115–16
Heavenly Creatures, 116
Heintzelman, Samantha, 123
Heller, Nathan, 20, 21
Hello Sunshine, 21–22, 25
Herrera, Fernanda, 136
Herzog, Werner, 141
High School Musical, 78–79
Hirsh-Pasek, Kathy, 108
historical fiction, 72, 119
House, 114
Hudson, Judith, 28
Humphreys, Clive, 133
Hutton, John, 47–48, 59–60, 77, 127
hyperphantasia, 138, 139

IGD. *See* Internet gaming disorder
imaginary friends, 109–11, 113–17
imaginary worlds and paracosms, 111–14, 115, 116
imagination and fantasy
  in counterfactual thinking, 121–24
  downsides of, 117–18
  fictional genre, 111
  functions of, 107
  parasocial friendships, 108–9, 111, 113–16, 130–31
  reality, real-life stories and, 119–21
  story play and, 107–8
  video games and, 117
Innocence Project, 90
Internet gaming disorder (IGD), 84

Jang, Eric, 102
Jeanne Dielman, 23, quai du Commerce, 1080 Bruxelles, 135
joint attention, 35–36, 37
Jones, Brady, 64

Kahneman, Daniel, 104

Kaur, Rupi, 144
Kingsolver, Barbara, 143–44

language development, 38–39, 40–42, 46–48, 52–53, 108
Lark, Caroline, 133
Larrick, Nancy, 70
learning disabilities, 48, 49
Lecce, Serena, 52–53
Lemmings, 58–59, 82–83
Lewis, C. S., 106, 132
life stories, 11–16, 17. *See also* real-life stories
Lillard, Angeline, 76
Linscott, Richard, 119
Lion, The Witch, and the Wardrobe, The, 132
literary fiction, popular fiction and, 5, 6, 7–9
Little Engine That Could, The, 47–48
Little Raccoon Learns to Share, 71
Little Women (Alcott), 22, 145–46
Loftus, Elizabeth, 89, 91
Longitudinal Study of Australian Children, 36
Lost in the Mall study, 89–90
Lowry, Lois, 60

Macron, Emmanuel, 105
Man Book Club, 22
Mar, Raymond, 2–3, 9, 23–24, 46
Markey, Patrick, 80
Marsh, Elizabeth, 72
Marshall, Sean, 15–16, 67
Martzog, Phillipp, 138–39
McAdams, Dan, 11, 15–16, 25–26, 64, 93, 119
McCall Smith, Alexander, 6, 7–8, 115
McLean, Kate, 64
McLuhan, Marshall, 130
memories
  default network and, 16–17, 92
  false, 89–91, 93, 97, 104
  misinformation and, 89, 91, 92–93
  for real-life stories, 88–98
  rereading, rewatching and, 135
  semantic and episodic, 91–93
  trauma, PTSD and, 95–98
men
  in book clubs, 22, 23, 31–32

INDEX *(219)*

fiction reading by, 18–19, 23–24, 31–32

visual stories and, 24–26

mental imagery, 137–40, 210–11nn.71–72

children developing skill, 138–39

mental simulation (mental time travel), 23–24, 165–66n.18

Merga, Margaret, 41, 59, 61–62

Milk, Chris, 136

Millan, Cesar, 132

Millenium Cohort Study, 55–56

Miller, Jennifer, 22

Milligan, Kevin, 41

Mind in the Eyes test, 3, 4, 9–10, 29, 129, 138

MindLab, 128

misinformation

from fiction reading, 72–73, 79, 91, 92

memory and, 89, 91, 92–93

from movies, 79, 91, 92

on social media, 104–5

Mitchell, Claire, 67

Monitoring the Future survey, 53, 54, 56

movies, 46, 73–75, 126, 141

misinformation from, 79, 91, 92

versions of books, 132–33

Mrs. Dalloway (Woolf), 6–7

Mügge, Dirk, 81

Murakami, Haruki, 51–52, 130–31

Murphy, Sheila, 10–11, 20

Nabokov, Vladimir, 133

National Endowment for the Arts (NEA), 19

Neha, Tia, 44–45

Netflix effect, 85

neuroticism, 96

Nikolajeva, Maria, 72

Nixon, Richard, 72–73

nonfiction reading

fiction reading *versus*, 2–3, 5–6, 143–44

gender and, 18–19, 22

by girls, 41

Normal People (Rooney), 133

Norwegian Wood (Murakami), 130–31

Number the Stars (Lowry), 60

Nyhout, Angela, 71–72

Oatley, Keith, 2–3, 23–24, 134

Obama, Michelle, 130–31

On Rereading (Spacks), 134

Origins of Memory study, 3

contamination narratives and, 93–94

on counterfactual thinking, 123

on empathy and fiction reading, 25–26

on gender and empathy, 29

on gender and fiction reading, 18–19

on imaginary friends, 109, 110, 111

on language development skills, 39

on movies, 73

on reading comprehension, 52–53

real-life stories and, 12–13, 65–67

on social media, 101

on video games, 80, 84–85

visual fiction and, 10

Our Shared Shelf, 22

Over the Hedge, 78–79

Paley, Vivian, 108

Paolini, Christopher, 113

paracosms, 112–14, 115, 116–17

parasocial friendships and relationships, 108–9, 111, 113–16, 130–31

Pennebaker, James, 13–16, 67, 98

Perry, Anne, 116

Peterson, Jordan, 23–24

Pianzola, Federico, 59

Pigden, Abigail, 129

Pink, Daniel, 122

PISA. *See* Programme for International Student Assessment

Plato, 125

Plomin, Robert, 36

Polaschek, Devon, 90

popular fiction, literary fiction and, 5, 6, 7–9

posttraumatic stress disorder (PTSD), 95–96, 97–98, 99, 140, 193n.42

Poulin, Michael, 94

Pride and Prejudice (Austen), 134

Programme for International Student Assessment (PISA), 57, 58

PTSD. *See* posttraumatic stress disorder

Rainmaker, The, 132–33

Raizy Nathan, Judith, 79

Read with Jenna, 22

real-life stories

benefits of, 11–16, 17, 140

fantasy, imagination and, 119–21

real-life stories (*cont.*)
    fiction reading and, 141
    as fully embodied, 126
    teens and, 62–67
    toddlers and, 38–39, 43, 44–45, 67
real-life stories, dangers of, 88
    family stories, 98–99
    memory and, 88–98
    on social media, 99–105
redemption theme, in life stories, 12
reminiscence bump, 64–65, 134
Rentfrow, Peter, 25–26
rereading and rewatching, 133–36
Rhodes, Marjorie, 40–41
Right Attitude to Rain, The (McCall
    Smith), 7–8
Riordan, Jessica, 44
romance fiction, 3–4, 8, 9
Romeo, Rachel, 38–39
Romero, Catherine, 15
Rooney, Sally, 133
Root-Bernstein, Michèle, 112, 113–
    14, 116–17
Rowling, J. K., 116
Rubin, David, 95–96
rumination, 97
"Runner, The" (DeLillo), 4

Saglioglou, Christina, 103
Salmon, Karen, 15–16, 43
Salten, Felix, 143
Schacter, Dan, 91, 120–21
Schaughency, Elizabeth, 44
schizotypy, 119–20, 203n.79
Schneier, Matthew, 85
Scholastic Books surveys, 53, 56
science, technology, engineering, the arts,
    and mathematics (STEAM), 145
science fiction, 3–4, 8, 9
screen time, 54, 56, 84–87, 100
Secret Life of Pronouns, The
    (Pennebaker), 14–15
Sedo, DeNel, 22–23
Segal, Keren, 15–16
self-regulation, visual stories and, 76–
    77, 82
semantic memory, 91–92
Sesame Street, 46–47
sexism and gender stereotypes, 70–71,
    78, 83–84

Sibley Hyde, Janet, 166–67n.29
Singer, Dorothy, 108
Singer, Jerome, 108
Singer, Tania, 30
Smith, Duncan, 128
Smyth, Joshua, 14
social media, 54, 56, 62, 68
    misinformation on, 104–5
    real-life stories on, 99–105
    teens on, 54, 56, 62, 68, 100–1, 103,
        119, 195n.74
Socrates, 125
Sound of Things Falling, The
    (Vásquez), 72–73
Spacey, Kevin, 115–16
Spacks, Patricia Meyer, 116, 133, 134
Stanovich, Keith, 2
Star Wars, 115
STEAM. *See* science, technology,
    engineering, the arts, and
    mathematics
story delivery systems, 127–30, 140–42
story play, 107–8
Strouse, Gabrielle, 46, 71–72
Strout, Elizabeth, 88
Stuart, 10
Suggate, Sebastian, 49, 65, 138–39

Tamale Lesson, The, 10–11
Taylor, Marjorie, 109, 110, 112–13, 116
Taylor, Sydney, 112
teens
    audiobooks for, 131
    benefits of books for tweens
        and, 52–56
    book reading decreases among, 53–55
    brains of, stories and, 62–64, 65, 100
    default networks of, 63–64
    diary-keeping, 112
    e-book reading by, 54, 55, 59
    expressive writing by, 67–68, 98
    gender gap in reading, 57, 59–62
    paracosms of, 113–14
    parasocial relationships of, 111, 113–15
    reading comprehension, 55, 57
    real-life stories and, 62–67
    rereading and rewatching, 135
    screen time, 54, 56, 100
    on social media, 54, 56, 62, 68, 100–1,
        103, 119, 195n.74

INDEX *(221)*

trauma and, 96–98
TV for, 78–79
video games and, 58–59, 80–84, 140, 186–87n.66
VR and, 137
well-being and mental health, 56
Tender Shoots program, 44, 47–48, 71
Tetris, 83
Thomas the Tank Engine, 70, 71, 182n.8
Three Billy Goats Gruff, The (Galdone), 44
TikTok, 80, 103–4
Time, 53–54
Tracy, Jessica, 12
Transportation-Imagery theory, 138
trauma, 95–98, 99, 193n.42
Trionfi, Gabriel, 109
TV, 24–25, 73–79
  binge-watching, 85–86, 144–45
  characters, parasocial friends and, 108–9
  child language development and, 46–48
  stories as dual-channel, 126
  stories from books *versus*, 127–28, 129
tweens
  benefits of books for teens and, 52–56
  expressive writing by, 67
  gender gap in reading, 57, 59
  language development skills, 52–53
  parasocial relationships of, 111, 113–14
  parents reading with, 60–61
  reading, 51–52
  real-life stories and, 66–67
  social media and, 103
  TV for, 78–79
Twenge, Jean, 100

UK National Literacy Trust survey, 49, 53, 56, 59–61
Underwater, 79

Vásquez, Juan Gabriel, 72–73
video games, 10, 16–17, 24–25, 143
  empathy and theory of mind and, 144
  IGD and, 84

imaginary play and, 117
teens playing, 58–59, 80–84, 140, 186–87n.66
as three-channel, 126
violence in, 80–84, 140, 186n.63, 186–87n.66
VR and, 140
virtual reality (VR), 136–37, 138, 140
visualization of stories, 26–29
visual stories, 9, 24, 144–45
  action, 80–84
  child language development and, 46–48
  dangers of, 73–79, 80–84
  empathy and theory of mind and, 9–11
  gender and racial stereotypes in, 78
  men and, 24–26
  self-regulation and, 76–77, 82
  stories from books *versus*, 126, 127
  violence in, 73–76
VR. *See* virtual reality

Wang, Qi, 13
Watson, Emma, 22
We Need Diverse Books, 70
Willens, M., 85, 86
Williams, Robin, 114–15
Winfrey, Oprah, 21–22
Witherspoon, Reese, 21–22, 25, 41–42, 133
women
  in book clubs, 20–23
  empathy and theory of mind, 29–32
  fiction reading by, 18–20, 25, 30–31
  gaming, 84
  memories and visualization of stories, 27–29
Woolf, Virginia, 6–8

YouTube, 80

Zacks, Jeffrey, 9
Zigler, Edward, 108
Zubrick, Stephen, 36
Zunshine, Lisa, 5–7